CONCEPT TO REALITY: CONTRIBUTIONS OF THE NASA LANGLEY RESEARCH CENTER TO U.S. CIVIL AIRCRAFT OF THE 1990s

by

Joseph R. Chambers

NASA SP-2003-4529

Library of Congress Cataloging-in-Publication Data

Chambers, Joseph R.
   Concept to Reality : Contributions of the Langley Research Center to U.S. Civil Aircraft
of the 1990s / by Joseph R. Chambers.
      p. cm. -- (NASA history series)
   "SP-2003-4529"
   Includes bibliographical references and index.
   1. Langley Research Center. 2. Private planes—United States—Design and construction.
3. Transport planes--United States—Design and construction. I. Title. II. Series.

TL862.L35 C49 2003
629.133'34'0973--dc21

                                                                    2002026352

ACKNOWLEDGMENTS

I am sincerely indebted to the dozens of current and retired employees of the NASA Langley Research Center who consented to be interviewed and submitted their personal experiences, recollections, and files from which this documentation of Langley contributions was drawn. The following individuals contributed vital information to this effort:

Dennis W. Bartlett	Moses G. Farmer	Donald F. Keller	Jerry C. South, Jr.
Percy "Bud" Bobbitt	Bruce D. Fisher	Holly M. Kenney	Cary R. Spitzer
Roland L. Bowles	Stuart G. Flechner	John C. Lin	James H. Starnes, Jr.
James S. Bowman, Jr.	Neal T. Frink	James M. Luckring	Harry P. Stough III
Richard L. Campbell	George C. Greene	Cornelius J. O'Conner	James L. Thomas
Michael F. Card	Charles E. Harris	Donald B. Owens	Dan D. Vicroy
Huey D. Carden	David A. Hinton	Felix L. Pitts	Richard A. Wahls
Norman L. Crabill	Robert J. Huston	Fred H. Proctor	Raymond D. Whipple
Robert H. Daugherty	Peter F. Jacobs	Edward J. Ray	Richard T. Whitcomb
John G. Davis, Jr.	Joseph L. Johnson, Jr.	Wilmer H. Reed III	Thomas J. Yager
H. Benson Dexter	Lisa E. Jones	Dan M. Somers	Long P. Yip
Robert V. Doggett, Jr.			

The following representatives of the civil aviation sector provided their unique perspectives on the value, timeliness, and significance of the Langley contributions to their respective organizations and to the Nation: Frank T. Lynch (The Boeing Company—retired), Douglas N. Ball (Boeing), Robert J. Mills (Gulfstream Aerospace Corporation), and Jay D. Hardin (Cessna Aircraft Company).

The majority of photographs in this document are taken from NASA files. However, I am indebted to The Boeing Company, Cessna Aircraft Company, Gulfstream Aerospace Corporation, Raytheon Aircraft Company, Cirrus Design Corporation, and Lancair Company for permission to use their photographs. In addition, Chris Coduto of ChrisAir Commercial Airline Photography, William Bunting of the National Weather Service, and Robert Stoyles of Cathay Airlines (retired) contributed unique photographs that added greatly to the quality of this publication.

Special thanks to Jerry N. Hefner and Patricia A. West, who provided their superb technical editing and proofreading skills to the project. Also, I would like to express my special gratitude to Noel A. Talcott and Darrel R. Tenney, who provided the inspiration and mechanism to undertake this activity.

Thanks also to Percival J. Tesoro for the cover design, Leanna D. Bullock for assistance with the figures, Peggy S. Overbey for desktop publishing services, Christine R. Williams for printing coordination, the late Eloise L. Johnson and Denise M. Stefula for editing, Mary Edwards for proofreading, and Gail S. Langevin for document production coordination.

Ultimately, however, the greatest thanks go to the thousands of current and retired researchers, technicians, administrators, and support personnel of the NASA Langley Research Center who provided the personal dedication, expertise, and innovation that enabled the legendary contributions covered in this work.

Joseph R. Chambers
Yorktown, VA
December 15, 2002

CONTENTS

PREFACE

The Langley Memorial Aeronautical Laboratory was established in 1917 as the Nation's first civil aeronautics research laboratory under the charter of the National Advisory Committee for Aeronautics (NACA). With a primary mission to identify and solve the problems of flight, the highly productive laboratory utilized an extensive array of wind tunnels, laboratory equipment, and flight research aircraft to conceive and mature new aeronautical concepts and provide databases and design methodology for critical technical disciplines in aircraft design. Prior to World War II (WWII), research at Langley on such diverse topics as airfoils, aircraft structures, engine cowlings and cooling, gust alleviation, and flying qualities was widely disseminated within the civil aviation community, and well-known applications of the technology to civil aircraft were commonplace. During WWII, however, the facilities and personnel of Langley were necessarily focused on support of the Nation's military efforts. Following WWII, aeronautical research at Langley was stimulated by the challenges of high-speed flight and the associated problems that were exhibited by high-speed aircraft configurations operating at relatively low speeds, such as those used for takeoff and landing. Much of Langley's research during that time would ultimately be useful to both the civil and military aviation industries. With the emergence of the new National Aeronautics and Space Administration (NASA) in 1958, Langley retained its vital role in aeronautical research and assumed a leading position as NASA Langley Research Center, along with Ames Research Center, Lewis Research Center (now Glenn Research Center), and Dryden Flight Research Center.

Langley's legacy of critical contributions to the civil aviation industry includes a wide variety of activities ranging from fundamental physics to applied engineering disciplines. Through the mechanisms of NASA technical reports, technical symposia, meetings with industry, and cooperative projects, the staff of Langley Research Center has maintained an awareness of the unique problems and challenges facing the U.S. civil aviation industry. With a sensitivity toward these unique requirements, Langley researchers have conceived and conducted extremely relevant research that has been applied directly to civil aircraft. These applications have resulted in increased mission performance, enhanced safety, and improved competitiveness.

This document is intended to be a companion to NASA SP-2000-4519, *Partners in Freedom: Contributions of the Langley Research Center to U.S. Military Aircraft of the 1990s.* Material included in the combined set of volumes provides informative and significant examples of the impact of Langley's research on U.S. civil and military aircraft of the 1990s. As worldwide advances in aeronautics and aviation continue at a breathtaking pace, documenting the significant activities, individuals, and events that have shaped the destinies of U.S. civil and military aviation has become increasingly important. In the research and development communities, many instances have occurred where fundamental, groundbreaking efforts have been forgotten or confused because of turnover of staffs, loss of technical records, and lack of documentation.

This volume, *Concept to Reality: Contributions of the NASA Langley Research Center to U.S. Civil Aircraft of the 1990s*, highlights significant Langley contributions to safety, cruise performance, takeoff and landing capabilities, structural integrity, crashworthiness, flight deck technologies, pilot-vehicle interfaces, flight characteristics, stall and spin behavior, computational design methods, and other challenging technical areas for civil aviation. The contents of this volume include descriptions of some of the more important applications of Langley research to current civil fixed-wing aircraft (rotary-wing aircraft are not included), including commercial airliners, business aircraft, and small personal-owner aircraft. In addition to discussions of specific aircraft applications, the document also covers contributions of Langley research to the operation of civil aircraft, which includes operating problems. NASA's role in the dissemination of research information and partnerships with the civil aircraft industry differs considerably from its relationship with the military. Competitive pressures in the marketplace, the sensitivity of proprietary information, and even international trade agreements can constrain NASA's interactive role for civil aircraft research and development. These constraints become especially visible during the startup and development of commercial aircraft involving huge industry investments and sensitivities. Nonetheless, the extremely valuable technologies provided by NASA's fundamental generic research, general guidelines for advanced design, unique facilities, and specialized expertise have been valued and applied by industry to a large number of current civil aircraft.

This document is organized according to disciplinary technologies, for example, aerodynamics, structures, materials, and flight systems. Within each discussion, examples are cited where industry applied Langley·technologies to specific aircraft that were in operational service during the 1990s and the early years of the new millennium. This document is intended to serve as a key reference for national policy makers, internal NASA policy makers, Congressional committees, the media, and the general public. Therefore, it has been written for a broad general audience and does not presume any significant technical expertise. An extensive bibliography is provided for technical specialists and others who desire a more in-depth discussion of the contributions.

INTRODUCTION

*"To supervise and direct the scientific study of the
problems of flight with a view to their practical solution."*

The foregoing statement was included in the charter of the National Advisory Committee for Aeronautics (NACA) upon its creation by Congress in 1915. The Langley Memorial Aeronautical Laboratory in Hampton, Virginia, was the first—and until 1941 the only—NACA research center. Langley became one of the brilliant jewels in the crown of U.S. government research establishments, and its contributions to the Nation's military and civil aircraft are legendary. After it was incorporated into the National Aeronautics and Space Administration (NASA) as the Langley Research Center in 1958, it continued to play a key role in aeronautical research and development. NASA Langley has historically excelled in maintaining a leading position in many critical aircraft design and development disciplines, such as aerodynamics, structures and materials, flight deck technology, flight dynamics, and instrumentation and measurement research. The development and operation of world-class aeronautical testing facilities and research aircraft is a priority of the Center, as well as maintaining a close working relationship with the civil aviation sector.

Within its charter, NASA conducts cooperative research with U.S. industry, other government agencies, and educational institutions if appropriate common interests and cooperative funding are provided. The breadth of these critical organizational interfaces includes the airframe and engine industries, airport and airline operators, and government agencies such as the Federal Aviation Administration (FAA). Under cooperative study guidelines, considerable benefits occur for both parties. For example, NASA researchers benefit from participating in projects that extrapolate, challenge, and validate their individual disciplinary concepts, while industry benefits from the expertise and unique facilities of the NASA Centers. A high priority is placed by NASA on the rapid, timely dissemination of information to appropriate U.S. organizations, while being extremely sensitive to proprietary interests and the protection of technology and critical intellectual property.

Traditionally, NASA's aeronautical research studies are basic (fundamental, physics-based, or applied science) or focused (specific systems-level goals). NASA formulates, develops, and conducts research programs to meet the requirements for national needs. Such programs can be stimulated by either a rapid acceleration in basic research that leads to progress for certain critical or beneficial technologies (technology push) or critical national requirements for certain technologies (requirements pull).

Numerous NASA focused programs for civil aircraft have emerged and delivered unprecedented opportunities for the maturation of key technologies to the U.S. airframe, propulsion, and avionics and flight controls industries for the design of advanced aircraft. In addition, data provided by these programs have led to significant improvements in the efficiency and safety of the U.S. air transportation system and an improved quality of life for both the flying and nonflying public. Focused programs have touched virtually every aspect of civil aviation, from fuel efficiency to the advancement of personal owner aircraft systems.

Several of these focused programs have stimulated Langley's contributions to civil aircraft of the 1990s. Three of the most important of these programs for civil aeronautics were

- The Aircraft Energy Efficiency (ACEE) Program

- The Advanced Subsonic Technology (AST) Program

- The Advanced General Aviation Transport Experiments (AGATE) Program

The ACEE Program was a national research and development response to the potentially disastrous impact of the fuel crisis of the early 1970s on the air transportation system. From 1973 to 1975, the fuel prices paid by U.S. airlines almost tripled, and fuel costs rose from about 20 percent of a typical airline's direct operating costs in the early 1970s to 60 percent by 1982. In recognition of the potentially devastating impact of the situation on air transportation, the U.S. Senate, in January 1975, requested that NASA develop a program that would provide the structural, engine, aerodynamics, and control technologies required for future air transport industry designs. NASA responded with a program plan for a 10-year, $600 million program that involved industry as a major partner. The ACEE Program was approved and launched in 1976. In 1978, the ACEE Program accounted for almost 70 percent of the funding in NASA's research for advanced civil aircraft. The NASA aeronautical research centers of Langley, Glenn, Ames, and Dryden participated in the ACEE Program. The results of research conducted during ACEE have had a profound and enduring effect on large commercial aircraft of the 1980s and 1990s, and its impact will continue far into the future. The scope of the program included engine component improvements, energy efficient engine technologies, turboprop technologies, energy-efficient transport aerodynamics and controls, laminar flow control, and advanced composites.

The AST Program was initiated in 1992 as a research partnership of NASA, U.S. industry, and the FAA. The vision of the AST Program was a new generation of environmentally compatible and economically viable aircraft. Technical goals were directed at several elements of technology for large commercial transports. Perhaps the most unique aspect of the AST Program was the fact that integrated NASA and industry teams were formed to conduct research in several critical areas. Technical exchanges within disciplinary lines between competitors had been virtually unprecedented prior to the AST Program, yet the technical work of the NASA program permitted the sharing of results and information without concern for proprietary disclosure. Following this pioneering arrangement, the AST Program elements proceeded to make enormous progress in design methods and analysis tools until NASA canceled the program in 1999. Unfortunately, the results of these efforts occurred after the design and operational entry of the latest large U.S. commercial transport, the Boeing 777. Although these technologies did not contribute directly to operational aircraft of the 1990s, the technology and method improvements will certainly be used for derivative and future aircraft in the early twenty-first century.

In the 1980s, the U.S. general aviation industry nearly collapsed. At its peak in 1978, the U.S. general aviation industry delivered 14,398 aircraft. In 1994, the number of aircraft deliveries had fallen to an all-time low of 444. The average age of general aviation aircraft flying at that time was about 30 years. Flight deck technologies in use dated back as late as the 1950s, and piston propulsion technologies had remained unchanged for the past

40 years. Building on its long established relationship with the general aviation industry, Langley took the lead in cooperative planning with industry to create a new future for general aviation. Under the General Aviation Element of the AST Program Office, the AGATE Consortium was formed in 1994. The AGATE alliance included industry, universities, the FAA, and other government agencies. AGATE goals included the development of affordable new technologies, as well as new approaches to meeting industry standards and certification methods for airframe, cockpit, flight training systems, and airspace infrastructure for next-generation single pilot, 4–6 place, all-weather light airplanes. Starting with NASA seed funding of $63 million in 1994, NASA, the FAA, the Small Business Innovation Research Program (SBIR), industry, and universities have pooled nearly $200 million in combined resources among 39 cost-sharing partners. About 30 other partners also joined the effort as non-cost-sharing, supporting members of the AGATE Consortium, for a total of nearly 70 members to revitalize U.S. general aviation through the rapid development and fielding of new technologies for a small aircraft transportation system. In addition to restoring the health of manufacturers that provided aircraft from business jets to personal-owner aircraft, it was projected that the general aviation transportation capability may become a viable answer to the increased demand for air transportation expected in the 2000s.

The cumulative result of AGATE produced a revolution in the research and technology deployment capacity for all sectors of the U.S. general aviation industry. AGATE provided a voice for industry to provide national clarity and action on key technology development, certification, and standards-setting activities. During AGATE, which ended in 2001, the research and technology capacity of the general aviation industry advanced from virtually nonexistent to world-class in avionics, propulsion, airframes, and flight training.

NASA Langley Research Center has made significant contributions to civil aircraft and the operation of the civil aviation system. Langley's critical contributions to the civil aviation industry come from a staff that is experienced in research and highly trained in disciplines that range from fundamental physics to applied engineering. With sensitivity toward the unique problems and challenges facing the U.S. civil aviation industry, Langley researchers have conceived and conducted extremely relevant research that has been applied directly to civil aircraft. These contributions have benefited U.S. citizens through an improved civil aviation system that transports people and goods with greater safety, efficiency, and economy.

SELECTED LANGLEY CONTRIBUTIONS
TO CIVIL AIRCRAFT OF THE 1990s

The following discussions document contributions of the NASA Langley Research Center to the civil aircraft of the United States in the 1990s. The specific examples were selected on the basis of demonstrated applications of Langley's research concepts and the importance of the impact and value to civil aviation and the general public. The contributions to civil aircraft include applications to large commercial transports, business jets, and small personal-owner aircraft. The discussions focus on the conceptual research processes that produced these contributions, the key researchers involved, the technology maturation processes that reduced risk and prepared the technology for industrial applications, and examples of specific industry and government applications of the Langley contributions.

The Langley research culture that produced these contributions is solidly based on team participation and the personal dedication and technical contributions of many individuals. Names of some of the key researchers involved have been included for guidance to those interested in expanding the information and gathering more detailed data regarding the accomplishments. The reader will also observe the extensive interactive and cooperative research activities between Langley; other NASA Centers; and industry, government, and university partners. Such interactions have consistently been major factors in the success of the NASA aeronautics research program. Also evident throughout the material are the key roles played by Langley facilities, including wind tunnels, laboratories, special test facilities, advanced computing and simulation facilities, and research aircraft. These unique national assets have permitted the development of advanced concepts and technology that have removed roadblocks and met significant challenges—and, in so doing, enabled a strong U.S. aviation industry.

Many of the aircraft of the 1990s used technology that was first explored by NASA as long as 30 years prior to its application. This fact serves to emphasize the necessity of the continuous pursuit of research concepts through technical barriers into maturity, so that technology can be transferred when the Nation requires it. It is also appropriate to point out that the development and the introduction of new, large commercial transport aircraft have occurred at relatively infrequent intervals in recent years. For example, the first flights of the Boeing 737 and Boeing 747 occurred in 1967 and 1969, respectively. The first flights of the 767 and 757 took place in 1981 and 1982, respectively, and the first 777 flew over a decade later in 1994. No new nonderivative large commercial jets entered the U.S. inventory during the last half of the 1990s. On the other hand, a large number of new business jets and general aviation aircraft have been developed on a more frequent basis, and these configurations have incorporated many of the newest technology advances provided by NASA research.

SUPERCRITICAL WING TECHNOLOGY

Background

The acceleration of airflow over the upper surfaces of wings of conventional subsonic jet transports at high subsonic speeds results in a region of supersonic (supercritical) flow above the upper surface of the lifting airfoil that terminates in a shock wave. The formation of the shock wave causes an increase in drag known as wave drag, which dramatically increases the thrust required to cruise at higher speed conditions. In addition, flow through the shock wave eventually encounters unfavorable conditions that may lead to shock-induced separation of the boundary layer, which typically causes an additional increase in drag, potential aircraft stability and control problems, and buffet. These locally supersonic flow characteristics are experienced by the wings of subsonic jet transports even though the aircraft is flying at subsonic conditions (typically at about Mach 0.80).

The supercritical airfoil, developed at the Langley Research Center, uses a unique geometric shape to control the characteristics of the supersonic flow in a manner to minimize drag and enhance the cruise efficiency of the transport. The curvature of the middle region of the upper surface of the supercritical airfoil is significantly reduced and carefully tailored to result in a more rearward location and substantial decrease in the strength of the shock wave, and drag for a given lift coefficient is reduced. The onset of boundary-layer separation is also substantially delayed to a higher Mach number. The relatively small amount of lift lost by reducing the curvature of the upper surface of the airfoil is regained and substantially augmented by the larger extent of supersonic flow on the upper surface and by incorporating a substantial camber into the rear portion of the airfoil. The leading-edge shape of the supercritical airfoil is also considerably blunter than those of conventional airfoils; this provides improved high-lift performance of the wing at cruise and landing conditions. The supercritical airfoil enables the performance-enhancing options of cruising at higher values of Mach number or cruising at the same Mach number with a substantial increase in wing thickness, which permits wing planform (aspect ratio) and structural design trade-offs to enhance cruise efficiency.

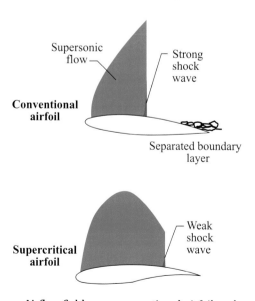

Airflow fields over conventional airfoil and supercritical airfoil at high subsonic speeds.

Langley Research and Development Activities

After the first U.S. swept-wing jet transports became operational in the late 1950s, most of the research community in the United States regarded the design of subsonic jet transports as a mature science, and many began to join the national effort that was emerging to develop a Mach 3 supersonic civil transport. In contrast, the European community continued to develop advanced airfoils for increased high-speed subsonic cruise efficiency. In Britain, H. H. Pearcey of the National Physical Laboratory showed, in 1962, that airfoils whose curvature decreased abruptly downstream from the leading edge could exhibit shock-free recompression and a significantly weaker upper-surface shock at high-speed conditions. With this modification, the critical Mach number (Mach number where drag abruptly increases) could be delayed by about 0.03.

Following his brilliant scientific development of the area rule (to be discussed in a later section), Richard T. Whitcomb of Langley became deeply involved in the NASA research activities of the U.S. Supersonic Transport (SST) Program. Whitcomb had developed a particularly efficient SST design in his research efforts. However, the relatively high fuel and operating costs of the supersonic transport configurations that were evolving in the U.S. program represented formidable barriers to the economic feasibility of these configurations, regardless of aerodynamic efficiency. Recognizing the tremendous penalties of the supersonic transport relative to advanced subsonic transports, Whitcomb terminated his efforts on supersonic transports and searched for more productive research in support of advanced subsonic aircraft.

Initially, Whitcomb explored the potential application of the area rule to the fuselages of conventional subsonic transports. However, the industry saw no cost-effective applications for the concept and did not provide the advocacy required for additional research. (Whitcomb, however, did return to fuselages with area rule in the maturation of supercritical wing technology, as mentioned in a later section.) While Whitcomb searched for new concepts to improve subsonic transports, a milestone event occurred during day-to-day business that resulted in yet another major breakthrough by Whitcomb. As frequently happened, Whitcomb was requested by the Langley Director for Aeronautics, Laurence K. Loftin, Jr., to review wind-tunnel data that had been obtained by the Ling-Temco-Vought (LTV) Company for a radical new vertical takeoff and landing (VTOL) concept known as Air Deflection and Modulation (ADAM). The ADAM concept used a unique configuration that incorporated a slot in the upper wing surface from which engine air was blown for lift augmentation in VTOL flight. Whitcomb noted that at high-speed conditions, air flowing from the slot resulted in a substantial increase in the drag-divergence Mach number. He hypothesized that the increase in Mach number was caused by delayed shock-induced separation, and he immediately envisioned an application to the swept-wing subsonic transport.

Based on this inspiration, Whitcomb and his staff initiated research in 1964 in the Langley 8-Foot Transonic Pressure Tunnel that would ultimately lead to the first NASA supercritical airfoils. Whitcomb's chief assistant and lead researcher for the airfoil studies was Charles D. Harris. Initially, tests were conducted on a two-dimensional airfoil with a self-actuated slot from which high-pressure air was ejected. Research objectives focused on delaying and reducing the shock-induced separation losses. After several iterations of airfoil shapes, and led by Whitcomb's intuitive wisdom, the work focused on a slotted airfoil with a flattened upper surface ahead of the slot, which naturally resulted in large negative camber. A large portion of the lift was carried by a short, positively cambered portion aft of the slot. This innovative airfoil shape showed a substantial increase in drag-rise Mach number. However, concern arose over the feasibility of scaling, fabricating, and maintaining the geometric tolerances of the slot, as well as operational problems and costs. Thus, Whitcomb and his staff conducted additional research that enabled the slot to be eliminated with only a small penalty in the onset of drag rise and with considerable simplification in the potential fabrication and application to three-dimensional wings. This so-called integral airfoil was first tested in 1966. Later, in recognition of the structural problems that might arise with the thin trailing edge of the integral airfoil, a thickened trailing edge was developed and underwent subsequent modifications through 1974.

At the time of Whitcomb's unique, experimental development of supercritical sections, no computer-based theories were available to guide his work, and the development work at Langley was entirely experimental. In 1969, Loftin recognized that the development and application of this technology would be severely impeded if industry applications demanded unique experimental facilities and the methodical experimentally based development process employed by Whitcomb and his staff. Loftin pushed for the development of an analytical design method, and with the recommendations of Clinton Brown of NASA Headquarters, Paul R. Garabedian of the Applied Mathematical Department of New York University was chosen to develop a practical theoretical program that could be used by designers as a routine airfoil design tool. Jerry C. South, Jr. served as Langley's manager for the grant, with I. Edward Garrick also monitoring this breakthrough activity. Garabedian, along with other pioneering individuals (including Anthony Jameson and Earll Murman) developed and validated the theory. Garabedian led this breakthrough in computational research for the supercritical airfoil in 1971, and Jameson led the way in computational wing design in 1977. Both Garabedian and Jameson later received major NASA awards in recognition of their brilliant contributions. Although this pioneering theory has now been superseded by more sophisticated analysis methods, it served as a critical historical building block in the development of transonic aerodynamic analyses now used by industry.

As the supercritical wing technology continued to mature, Whitcomb and his team provided critical design information on the integration of supercritical airfoils into three-dimensional wings and the effects of advanced propulsion systems on supercritical wing performance. Key Langley team members for studies of supercritical applications included Thomas C. Kelly, Dennis W. Bartlett, Charles D. Harris, and James A. Blackwell. In addition, Stuart G. Flechner, James C. Patterson, Jr., and Paul G. Fournier conducted extensive tests on advanced, energy-efficient subsonic transport models in the Langley 8-Foot Transonic Pressure Tunnel to add to the rapidly growing national database on the effects of engine nacelle and pylon cant angle and engine longitudinal and vertical position on cruise performance, including the effects of powered nacelles. The substantial database and design

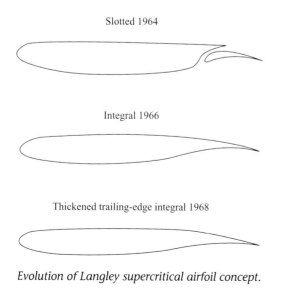

Slotted 1964

Integral 1966

Thickened trailing-edge integral 1968

Evolution of Langley supercritical airfoil concept.

guidelines supplied by the staff of the 8-Foot Transonic Pressure Tunnel provided extremely valuable information to both the airframe and engine industries.

Another key member of Whitcomb's staff, Theodore G. Ayers, led studies on the potential applications of supercritical airfoil technologies to military aircraft, including fighter-bombers (F-111), transports (YC-15), fighters (F-14), and bombers (B-1). Ayers later transferred to NASA Dryden Flight Research Center where he played a key leadership role in the highly successful flight tests of a modified F-8 aircraft in a joint Langley-Dryden program, as well as other flight programs on supercritical wings and advanced airfoils.

Flight Evaluations

The first flight demonstration project of supercritical wing technology was initiated in 1969, when the Navy and NASA cosponsored a joint project to demonstrate the ability of the supercritical wing to accommodate increased wing thickness with no reduction in cruise Mach number. The benefits realized from an increase in thickness included improved structural efficiency (and reduced wing weight) and increased internal wing volume. For example, if a supercritical wing of 17-percent thickness could be designed to have the cruise efficiency of a 12-percent-thick conventional wing, the internal fuel volume could be increased by about 40 percent and the amount of wing volume devoted to fuel could be increased by over 50 percent. Initial wind-tunnel tests by North American Rockwell, Columbus Division, of wings with this range of thickness values indicated that the drag-divergence Mach number of a 17-percent-thick supercritical airfoil shape was equal to that for a conventional 12-percent-thick airfoil, that the buffet onset was considerably higher, and that the low-speed maximum lift was increased considerably. With these promising results in hand, the interest turned to flight verification of the wind-tunnel results.

The test aircraft for the project was a T-2C Buckeye trainer aircraft on loan from the Navy. With Whitcomb and his staff serving as technical consultants, Rockwell International designed, developed, and manufactured a modified 17-percent-thick supercritical wing. A standard production T-2C wing was modified by the addition of balsa wood and fiberglass to obtain the desired thickness and configuration. A 0.09-scale model of the modified T-2C was tested in the Langley 8-Foot Transonic Pressure Tunnel for correlation with flight. First flight of the modified T-2C occurred in 1970, and the results indicated that for the Mach number of interest (about 0.60), the 17-percent-thick supercritical wing provided the same performance as the conventional 12-percent-thick wing.

In fulfilling his responsibilities as Director for Aeronautics, Loftin recognized that the new supercritical technology would have to be tested, matured, and demonstrated during actual flight tests of full-scale aircraft before the technology would be considered mature enough for applications to future aircraft. In 1967, he strongly advocated for a flight demonstration program to be conducted at the NASA Dryden Flight Research Center with an F-8 Crusader aircraft obtained from the Navy. The F-8 was an ideal test bed for the supercritical wing demonstration. It could achieve the speed of sound at high altitudes, and its unique variable incidence wing could be replaced with a modified wing by simply lifting the original wing off the aircraft. A joint Langley-Dryden program was approved in early 1968. The wing investigated in this test program was designed and developed in the 8-Foot Transonic Pressure

Basic T-2 (left) and modified T-2 with 17-percent-thick supercritical wing (right).

Tunnel by Whitcomb and his staff for a cruise Mach number of about 0.98. This particular wing was not intended for retrofitting to the F-8 but was representative of wings that might potentially be used on a near-sonic transport with an area-ruled fuselage. The leading-edge sweep of the baseline F-8 was increased to about 42° and the wing aspect ratio was increased to 6.8. The gradual increase in cross-sectional area required by the area rule for near-sonic conditions required a modified fuselage as well as a graceful extension of the inboard leading edge of the wing.

Preliminary wind-tunnel tests on the modified F-8 configuration indicated that the new high-aspect-ratio wing with more sweepback exhibited severe longitudinal instability (pitch up) at transonic, high-lift conditions. The problem was caused by spanwise flow toward the wingtips on the wing upper surface. Charles D. Harris and Dennis W. Bartlett conducted wind-tunnel tests that ultimately developed small vertical vortex generator surfaces on the lower outboard part of each wing panel that created vortices on the upper surface which acted as aerodynamic "fences" to block the spanwise flow and eliminated the problem.

In 1969, Rockwell International, North American Aircraft Division, received a contract to fabricate the supercritical wing for the F-8, which was delivered to NASA in December 1969. Thomas C. Kelly was the Langley project engineer for the program, whereas John McTigue served as Dryden's Supercritical Wing (SCW) program manager.

Project pilot Tom McMurtry flew the first F-8 SCW flight on March 9, 1971; the last flight of the aircraft was piloted by Ron Gerdes on May 23, 1973, ending an 86-flight program. Results of the flight tests vividly demonstrated the significant improvements afforded by the

Richard T. Whitcomb with model of F-8 supercritical wing configuration in Langley 8-Foot Transonic Pressure Tunnel.

F-8 supercritical wing test-bed aircraft in flight with an area-ruled fuselage and underwing leading-edge vortex generators.

F-8 on static display at Dryden.

supercritical wing. The concept had improved the transonic efficiency of the F-8 by as much as 15 percent, and the projected benefits to transport aircraft were very significant.

Today, the F-8 SCW is on permanent display at Dryden. A plaque mounted at the aircraft site reads as follows:

> *This research aircraft was the first airplane to demonstrate the transonic performance capabilities of a supercritical wing. This airplane demonstrated a drag-rise Mach number of 0.96 at cruise lifting conditions. The resulting technology base permitted an increase in cruise Mach number for transport aircraft from approximately 0.82 to above 0.9.*

On February 29, 1972, NASA reported to industry and the Department of Defense (DOD) on the progress of the F-8 and T-2C flight programs at a classified conference held at the NASA Dryden Flight Research Center.

Intense interest over the results coming from the F-8 Supercritical Wing Program spurred NASA and the Air Force to modify an F-111A to explore the application of supercritical wing technology to maneuverable military aircraft. The joint Transonic Aircraft Technology (TACT) Program was approved in 1969. By 1971, NASA and General Dynamics Corporation had over 1,600 hours of wind-tunnel time on perfecting a suitable wing. Whitcomb and his staff determined its shape, twist, and airfoil coordinates. General Dynamics built the wing, and the Air Force Flight Dynamics Laboratory provided the funding for the aircraft modification and flight tests. The first flight of the F-111 TACT aircraft occurred in 1973. The supercritical wing substantially improved the performance of the aircraft. The wing delayed the drag rise at transonic speeds, delayed the onset of buffet, and produced substantially more lift than the conventional wing.

Applications

The aerodynamic performance improvements provided by the supercritical airfoil technology are extremely significant. The drag-rise Mach number can be significantly delayed, the onset of buffet is also delayed, and high-lift performance is improved. However, most applications of the supercritical airfoil have utilized the concept and its performance-enhancing characteristics to permit the use of thicker wings and lower sweep (enabling higher wing aspect ratio), rather than to increase the drag-rise Mach number. Thicker wings can be structurally lighter; thereby, larger payload fractions and improved operational economics are provided. The use of higher aspect-ratio wings contribute directly to increased performance and economic benefits.

Ironically, the application of this innovative concept has involved uses (more efficient flight at existing speeds) that were not envisioned during the initial development process (flight at near-sonic speeds). Thus, the experience of the supercritical wing once again underscores the fact that it is often impossible to identify in advance all the real-world applications and justification for a research activity.

In recognition of his outstanding accomplishment in supercritical wing technology, Whitcomb was awarded the maximum $25,000 prize by NASA for the invention in 1974, and that same year he also won the Wright Brothers Memorial Trophy of the National Aeronautic Association for his enduring contributions to aeronautics.

The revolutionary gains provided by the supercritical wing were initially directed at increasing the cruise speed of subsonic transport configurations. In mid-1970, NASA initiated a new focused research program known as the Advanced Technology Transport (ATT) Program to provide technology for a superior subsonic long-haul aircraft that could cruise just below the speed of sound. Langley's initial manager for the program was William J. Alford, Jr. In the ATT Program, NASA initiated several studies of the near-sonic transports that utilized the benefits of the supercritical wing to drive the cruise speed up to the point where area ruling of the fuselage became necessary. Industry studies of candidate near-sonic transports by The Boeing Company, McDonnell Douglas Corporation, and General Dynamics were undertaken by using aerodynamic data obtained for a representative transport configuration in the 8-Foot Transonic Pressure Tunnel. Results of the industry studies indicated that a new aircraft of this design would have operating costs similar to those of aircraft at that time, but the new aircraft would have an increase in speed of about 20 percent and be capable of cruising at a Mach number of about 0.98. As a matter of interest, during this time frame Boeing was actually involved in preliminary design of the Boeing 767 transport, and one of the initial 767 configurations employed the trademark area-rule shaping to its fuselage and wings—far different than its eventual production shape.

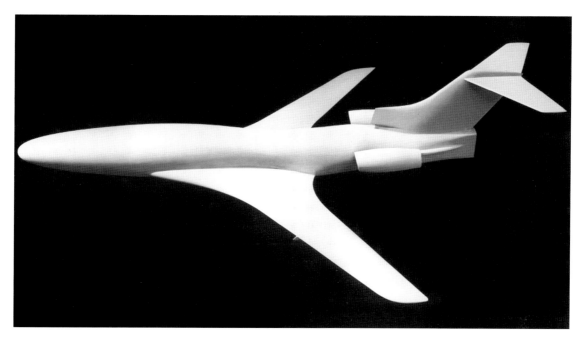

Near-sonic transport wind-tunnel model with area ruling and advanced supercritical wing.

Unfortunately, about 2 months after the industry studies were completed, the Organization of Petroleum Exporting Countries (OPEC) tripled the price of crude oil and the airlines were no longer interested in flying faster. Rather, the industry wanted technology that would reduce fuel consumption. Whitcomb and his team justifiably terminated the work under way on near-sonic transports and redirected their efforts to using the trades provided by supercritical technology to obtain more aerodynamic efficiency. At that time, the program was also renamed the Advanced Transport Technology Program.

The industry-wide design approach to using supercritical wing technology was to increase the thickness ratio of the wing airfoil, reduce the wing sweep to reduce the structural weight, and increase the aspect ratio of the wing to reduce the drag due to lift. This design approach resulted in significant increases in fuel efficiency and has basically been the major application of supercritical technology used by designers of today's new subsonic transports.

As mentioned in an earlier section, the NASA Aircraft Energy Efficiency (ACEE) Program initiated a number of technology thrusts to increase the fuel efficiency of subsonic transports. Within this program, an element known as the Energy Efficient Transport (EET) Program addressed the improvements promised by advances in aerodynamic technologies that included supercritical wings, winglets, advanced high-lift systems, and active load alleviation. The EET Program was the stimulus for extensive Langley activities in advanced transport aerodynamics—especially the supercritical wing.

As previously mentioned, the supercritical airfoils developed by Whitcomb embodied three primary geometrical factors: a relatively uncambered upper surface, an increased leading-edge radius, and a cambered trailing edge. Industry applications of the technology have included specific configurations that include all three features. Other applications include only the upper-surface and leading-edge principles because of concerns over pitching moments resulting in increased trim drag and trailing-edge flap actuator implementation caused by the reflexed trailing-edge shape.

The design and analysis of advanced airfoils and wing performance within industry is conducted with extensive proprietary computer codes and sophisticated methods. Many computational methods developed by Langley researchers have been embedded in industry design tools. The flexibility provided by the codes significantly reduces the scope of design variables and reduces the number of potential wing designs to be studied in new aircraft programs.

The evolution of supercritical airfoil technology embodied in current jet transport aircraft is depicted in the accompanying sketch of typical airfoil shapes and camber distributions used by industry for conventional, intermediate, and aft-loaded airfoils. As discussed earlier, virtually all subsonic transports exhibit a region of supersonic flow on the upper surface of the wing in cruise flight; therefore, the use of the word "supercritical" has somewhat confused the layman's understanding of the aerodynamic design of aircraft of the 1990s. As depicted in the sketch, the conventional airfoil (A), which is typical of aircraft such as the older DC-10, is characterized by forward and mid-camber distribution. The intermediate airfoil (B), which is typical of aircraft such as the Boeing 767, utilizes a relatively mild degree of aft camber to provide a limited amount of the performance benefits provided by the more aggressive supercritical airfoils. A typical aft-loaded supercritical airfoil (C) is characterized by its blunt nose, virtually no leading-edge camber, and a relatively high level of trailing-edge camber (about 2 percent). This type of airfoil is employed by the more modern Boeing 777.

Following the dissemination of flight results for the F-8 and T-2C to industry in 1972, initial applications of the supercritical wing technology to U.S. civil aircraft occurred within the business jet aircraft community. The first application of supercritical technology in the U.S. to a production civil transport aircraft was by Cessna Aircraft Company for the Citation III in 1981. The supercritical wing design process for the Citation III was a joint effort between Cessna, McDonnell Douglas, and NASA. Working with Boeing, Cessna subsequently developed the supercritical wing design of the Citation X. This advanced business jet incorporates a highly swept, second-generation supercritical wing and is capable of Mach 0.92 and a maximum altitude of 51,000 feet.

Other U.S. business jet applications include the Sabreliner 65 and

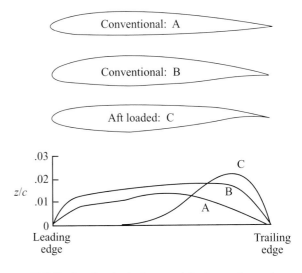

Airfoils showing typical geometric shapes (upper) and distribution of camber along airfoils (lower).

Cessna Citation III was the first application of supercritical technology to production aircraft in the U.S.

Cessna Citation X.

the Gulfstream V, which uses certain principles of supercritical technology (leading-edge radius and upper-surface contouring) to obtain exceptional speed and efficiency. The winglets of the Gulfstream V also utilize supercritical technology. During 1997, the Gulfstream V aircraft demonstrated its capabilities by setting 46 world and national records consisting of 21 speed records and 25 performance records. The Gulfstream V was named the winner of the 1997 Collier Trophy for "the most significant aeronautical achievement in the United States." Other U.S. business jets using supercritical technology include the Hawker Horizon, which is designed, built, and marketed by the Raytheon Aircraft Company.

Boeing 777 with supercritical wing technology.

*In-flight photograph of Boeing 777 shows lower wing
trailing-edge curvature associated with supercritical airfoils.*

Applications of supercritical wing technology to larger transport aircraft in the United States began with prototype military transports in 1976—Boeing's application to the YC-14 and McDonnell Douglas' application to the YC-15. The first application of aggressive supercritical wing technology to a large production transport in the United States was by McDonnell Douglas (now Boeing) for the military C-17 Globemaster III. The McDonnell Douglas technology and design expertise for this application was built on Langley's pioneering efforts in developing supercritical airfoils, McDonnell Douglas design activities sponsored by the ACEE Program, and the YC-15 design experience. McDonnell Douglas was awarded the Collier Trophy for 1994 in recognition of the superior design of the C-17.

The application of supercritical wing technology to large U.S. commercial transport aircraft has been more conservative. Several factors are responsible for this situation, including extremely important cost/benefit considerations that trade off increased aerodynamic performance with production costs and other variables. The wings of the Boeing 757, Boeing 767, and McDonnell Douglas MD-11 employ certain principles of supercritical technology such as an increased aft loading, although these applications are not the more aggressive supercritical technology design features identified by earlier NASA research. The most recent U.S. large transport to incorporate a more aggressive supercritical wing is the Boeing 777, which entered commercial service in May 1995. Supercritical technology principles and proprietary supercritical airfoils used by Boeing in the design of the 777 are much more advanced than those used by earlier Boeing transports and provide exceptional structural and aerodynamic efficiency. In recognition of its superior efforts in the design of the 777, Boeing was awarded the Collier Trophy for 1995.

LOW-SPEED, MEDIUM-SPEED, AND NATURAL LAMINAR FLOW AIRFOILS

Background

The breakthroughs in supercritical airfoil applications further stimulated Langley's efforts to develop improved airfoils for broad classes of general aviation, commercial, and military aircraft. By 1973, Langley's efforts in airfoil research had expanded and become formalized as a focused research program. Efforts were under way in experimental and theoretical investigations for a wide scope of airfoil applications: low-speed general aviation, low-speed natural laminar flow; medium speed; supercritical transport type, large cargo supercritical, laminar-flow control, rotorcraft, fighter, remotely piloted vehicles (RPVs), and propellers. The passing of the era of the NACA airfoil catalogue, ushered in during the 1940s by Ira H. Abbott and Albert E. von Doenhoff, was at hand. This new era offered lower cost and more rapid means to design the desired airfoil properties for lift, drag, and pitching moment. The results were envisioned to reduce aircraft fuel consumption, increase speed and range, reduce landing speeds, and improve safety at slow speeds.

In 1975, the resurgence of interest in airfoils resulted in a NASA and Industry Airfoil Workshop held at NASA Headquarters. Recommendations and guidelines from industry were solicited, and NASA's plans and activities were critiqued by enthusiastic industry representatives. NASA-wide leadership of the evolving airfoil program was provided by Alfred Gessow of NASA Headquarters, and the leaders from Langley included Robert E. Bower (Director for Aeronautics) and Percy J. "Bud" Bobbitt (Chief of the Subsonic-Transonic Aerodynamics Division). Under the administrative direction of P. Kenneth Pierpont, a major NASA conference on Advanced Technology Airfoil Research was held at Langley in March 1978. The high level of national interest in research activities was reflected at this conference by an attendance of over 450 NASA, industry, university, and DOD participants.

The rapid pace of developments in advanced computational methods and the refinement of airfoil analyses changed the general focus of research in the 1980s and 1990s. Even Richard T. Whitcomb—widely recognized for his brilliant experimental approach to research—became a chief advocate for the new computational methods and utilized them extensively in his work. Research efforts became focused on multielement airfoils, optimization, the prediction of maximum lift, and the effects of dynamic phenomena. In the 1990s, research efforts at Langley were directed to three-dimensional wing design and the fundamental understanding and modeling of flow physics and Reynolds number effects exhibited by high-lift systems, including boundary-layer transition and turbulence.

Langley Research and Development Activities

Results of the initial research efforts on supercritical airfoils were quickly disseminated to the U.S. industry in the early 1970s. Wind-tunnel and flight results were analyzed independently by designers within the general aviation industry for potential applications to a wide variety of aircraft, especially high-speed business jets. The benefits of the supercritical wing technology for high-speed cruise were appreciated by the general aviation industry; however, other beneficial effects were also appealing to designers of low- and medium-speed aircraft. In particular, the exceptional high-lift characteristics of the supercritical airfoils were viewed with great interest by the general aviation community.

Following a Langley briefing to industry on the new supercritical airfoil technology, Whitcomb was approached by several general aviation representatives who displayed great enthusiasm over the potential low-speed, high-lift benefits of supercritical-type airfoils. The benefits included higher lift as well as a more docile stall. The improvement in high-lift characteristics was a direct result of the increased bluntness of the leading edge of the supercritical airfoils. At that time, many of the industry designs used the NACA 63- and 64-series airfoils, which had tendencies to stall abruptly at the leading edge. After the intense interest of the general aviation industry in improved high-lift characteristics was known by Whitcomb, he responded with an experimental and analytical research program to provide specialty airfoils for this segment of the U.S. aviation sector. This new airfoil program used a variety of unique Langley facilities and computer codes. The Langley Low-Turbulence Pressure Tunnel was the key experimental facility for wind-tunnel investigations, and a two-dimensional airfoil computer code developed by J. A. Braden, S. H. Goradia, and W. A. Stevens of Lockheed-Georgia, under Langley sponsorship, was a key tool for the development of the new airfoil family.

The goal of Langley's efforts was not the design of a new series of airfoils for various applications; rather, Langley adopted the philosophy of developing and validating theoretical methods that could be used as useful tools for designing airfoils for specific applications. Such an approach was necessitated by the increasing diversity of airfoil applications, which made the NACA "airfoil catalog" approach impractical.

Langley's Low- and Medium-Speed Airfoil Program was led by Whitcomb; key members of his research team included P. Kenneth Pierpont, Robert J. McGhee, and William D. Beasley. Pierpont's responsibilities involved management of the day-to-day challenging wind-tunnel operations, while McGhee and Beasley led the technical investigations.

The Low-Speed Airfoil Program was initiated in 1972 with the development of the GA(W)-1 airfoil, which was analytically developed by Whitcomb with the previously mentioned computer code developed at Lockheed-Georgia under Langley contract. This 17-percent-thick low-speed airfoil exhibited low cruise drag; high climb lift-drag ratios; high maximum lift; and predictable, docile, stall behavior. National interest in this new airfoil rapidly accelerated as the data were disseminated in a NASA report. In fact, a rare second printing of the technical report was required because of the unanticipated demand. An entire series of airfoils with varying thickness ratios was subsequently developed for low-speed applications by Whitcomb's team, including a new GA(W)-2 airfoil. The GA(W)-2 section employed a 13-percent-thick profile and generated considerable interest within the general aviation community. This low-speed family of airfoils also included 9-percent- and 21-percent-thick airfoils that were designed for fully turbulent boundary layers (negligible laminar flow) and Mach numbers below about 0.50. Langley conducted both wind-tunnel and flight research to support the development and application of these airfoils. Wind-tunnel tests were conducted to develop trailing-edge flaps and control surfaces, and flight tests were conducted to evaluate performance, stall characteristics, and handling characteristics.

In the mid-1970s, NASA's first flight tests for verification of the potential performance benefits of the GA(W)-1 airfoil were conducted with a research aircraft known as the Advanced Technology Light Twin-Engine Airplane (ATLIT). The ATLIT was a modified Piper Seneca airplane having a GA(W)-1 wing section, a wing with increased aspect ratio, full-span Fowler flaps, and roll-control spoilers; it also incorporated Langley-developed winglets. The flight tests were conducted at Langley from 1974 to 1976, under the management of Joseph W. Stickle, with a test team that included Bruce J. Holmes (then a graduate student from the University of Kansas). Holmes was later employed by Langley, and he subsequently became an internationally recognized NASA leader in advanced general aviation transportation systems and the revitalization of the industry in the 1990s. Other ATLIT team members included Harold L. Crane, Joseph H. Judd, Robert T. Taylor, and research pilots Robert A. Champine and Philip W. Brown. Following the flight test program in 1976, the airplane was mounted in the Langley 30- by 60-Foot (Full-Scale) Tunnel for performance, stability, and control evaluations, including pressures and boundary-layer flow instrumentation. Lead researchers for the study were James L. Hassell, Jr., and Long P. Yip. The results of the extensive flight and wind-tunnel testing validated the desirable cruise, high-lift, and roll-control performance of a wing designed with the new airfoil, flaps, and spoiler control system.

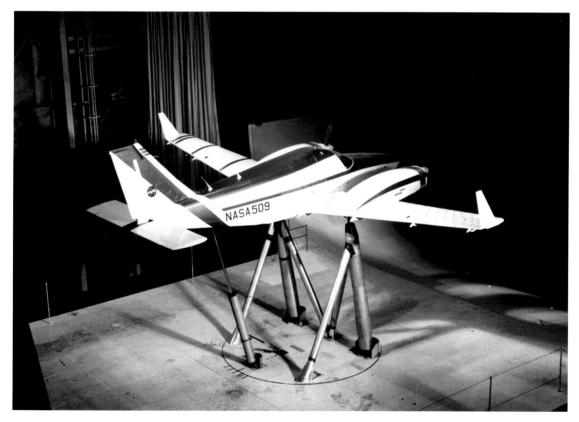

*Advanced Technology Light Twin (ATLIT) mounted for tests
in Langley 30- by 60-Foot (Full-Scale) Tunnel in 1977.*

Aerodynamic research on general aviation aircraft was especially well suited for university involvement, and extensive Langley sponsorship of efforts at Ohio State University (OSU), Wichita State University (WSU), and the University of Kansas (KU), among several others, resulted in a tremendous stimulation and focus on aerodynamic research by academia. Under the direction of Gerald M. Gregorek of OSU, the university managed the Langley-sponsored General Aviation Airfoil Design and Analysis Center created in 1976 to meet the increasing demands of industry for assistance in airfoil design, analysis, and testing services. William H. Wentz of WSU led extensive wind-tunnel tests to develop design databases for trailing-edge flaps and control surfaces for the low-speed series of airfoils. Flight testing to validate the new airfoils, high-lift systems, and spoiler-roll-control systems was also conducted by David L. Kolhman of KU at the university. These flight tests made use of a highly modified Cessna 177 Cardinal airplane, dubbed "Redhawk."

First flight tests to evaluate the characteristics of the GA(W)-2 airfoil were conducted by the OSU, under Langley sponsorship in 1976, with a modified Beech Sundowner aircraft. An OSU team under the direction of Gregorek conducted detailed in-flight measurements of the aerodynamic characteristics of the wing (including pressure distributions at several spanwise stations). The results validated the predicted performance of the airfoil in a highly successful flight test program.

In 1976, a requirement emerged from the business jet community for airfoils with higher cruise Mach numbers than the foregoing low-speed airfoils, while retaining good high-lift, low-speed characteristics. Thus, two medium-speed airfoils (13- and 17-percent thick) were developed to fill the gap between the low-speed airfoils and the high-speed supercritical airfoils. These new airfoils were specifically designed for applications to light executive-type aircraft having cruise Mach numbers on the order of 0.70.

With the expansion of the airfoil family from the low-speed to the medium-speed airfoils, a new airfoil designation system was put into effect by Langley in 1977. The airfoil designations were changed to the form LS(1)-xxxx for the low-speed series. LS(1) indicated the first series of low-speed airfoils, the next two digits designated the airfoil design lift coefficient in tenths, and the final two digits gave the airfoil thickness in percent chord. Thus, the GA(W)-1 airfoil became LS(1)-0417 and the GA(W)-2 airfoil became LS(1)-0413. A similar designation system was developed for the medium-speed airfoils of the form MS(1)-xxxx.

Langley's progress in technology relative to low- and medium-speed airfoils was summarized at the Advanced Technology Airfoil Research Conference held at Langley in March 1978. Together with the directed distribution of technical reports and close communications with the general aviation industry, the dissemination of information led to widespread applications of advanced airfoil technology and computer design tools.

Applications

Early applications of the Langley low-speed airfoils included a wide variety of personal-owner and sport aircraft. Within the mainstream general aviation industry, the GAW(1) airfoil saw applications in 1977 by Beechcraft to the 77 Skipper trainer and by Piper Aircraft to their new trainer, the PA-38 Tomahawk. The airfoil was also applied by several independent

Beechcraft Model 77 Skipper was one of the first applications of GAW(1) airfoil in 1977.

designers within their own start-up configurations including the Bede 5, the American Hustler, and the Rutan Vari-Eze (main wing and winglets). More recently, applications have included the Stoddard-Hamilton Glassair III (LS(1)-0413) and the Saab 340 regional transport (MS(1)-0316).

Natural Laminar Flow Airfoils

The initial emphasis in the Langley Advanced Airfoil Research Program for low-speed and medium-speed airfoils was to develop a series of airfoils that could achieve higher maximum lift coefficients than those produced by airfoils used on general aviation airplanes at that time. The assumption was that the flow over the entire airfoil would be turbulent because of the riveted sheet metal construction techniques used by the industry. Although the new low-speed airfoils did achieve higher maximum lift, the cruise drag was no lower than the earlier NACA airfoils used by the industry. The emphasis in the Langley program therefore shifted toward natural laminar flow (NLF) airfoils in an attempt to obtain lower cruise drag while retaining the maximum lift of the low-speed airfoils.

Research on natural laminar flow airfoils at Langley dates back to the 1930s when a team under Eastman N. Jacobs conducted its famous research for the NACA, which culminated in the development of the 6-series airfoils that were applied to many of the famous U.S. military aircraft of World War II, including the P-51 Mustang. The 6-series airfoils were not as operationally successful as low-drag airfoils because the riveted construction techniques employed at the time introduced physical disturbances that disrupted laminar flow.

In the mid-1970s, the emergence of smooth, composite structures led to a resurgence in interest in NLF research. For decades, the NLF interest resided in the sailplane community, but the advent of relatively lightweight composite structures for powered general aviation aircraft such as the Bellanca Skyrocket II, Elbert "Burt" Rutan's family of aircraft, and the Windecker Eagle stimulated aerodynamicists to reexamine the feasibility of NLF airfoils. The Langley research efforts were pursued with airfoil research as well as substantiating flight test evaluation and validation.

The Skyrocket II had demonstrated exceptional performance in flight tests by Bellanca and had achieved an exceptionally low level of cruise drag that suggested some amount of laminar flow was being achieved by the wing. The aircraft had been designed to use an NACA 6-series airfoil similar to those developed by Jacobs in the NACA program. Under a cooperative program stimulated by Langley's Joseph Stickle, special flight tests of the all-composite Skyrocket were conducted at Langley, under the direction of Bruce Holmes, to determine the extent of laminar flow on the aircraft.

The disappointment that had been experienced in the application of natural laminar flow airfoils in World War II carried over into the 1970s, and many critics in the engineering community doubted that the Skyrocket would exhibit any significant laminar flow—even

Sublimating chemicals on right wing of Bellanca Skyrocket indicating large extent of natural laminar flow during Langley flight tests.

with the smooth composite wing structure. Holmes and his assistant, Clifford J. Obara, utilized a spray-on sublimating chemical technique to visually identify the presence of laminar flow on the Skyrocket at cruise conditions. In flight, a gray-white area (aft of the front spar) covered by the sublimating chemical would indicate laminar flow; the presence of high surface shear turbulent flow would cause the gray-white sublimating coating to disappear. The results of the Skyrocket flight test vividly demonstrated the presence of laminar flow on the wing to the point of maximum wing thickness. This research activity represented a significant milestone because aerodynamic wing design for future low- and medium-speed general aviation composite aircraft could now consider laminar flow as an achievable goal.

Holmes and Obara subsequently conducted similar laminar flow visualization investigations of other composite aircraft, including the Vari-Eze, Long-EZ, and Laser Biplane Racer designed by Burt Rutan. These researchers also investigated the limits of the stability of NLF at higher speeds on a Learjet and Cessna Citation Jet aircraft. In virtually every case, extensive laminar flow was detected for the aircraft involved.

Concurrent with the flight testing, Langley initiated a research program to develop NLF airfoils that would combine the high maximum lift capability of the NASA low-speed airfoils with the low-drag characteristics of the NACA 6-series airfoils. Langley's lead researcher in this effort was Dan M. Somers. Using a computational design code developed by Richard Eppler of the University of Stuttgart, Somers designed and tested a new NLF airfoil in the Langley Low-Turbulence Pressure Tunnel. Results obtained for the new NLF(1)-0416 airfoil were compared with maximum lift and drag data for the low-speed GA(W)-1 airfoil as well as 6-series airfoils. An overriding goal in the research for the NLF airfoil was that the maximum lift would not be significantly affected with transition fixed near the leading edge. This condition represented the worst-case scenario in which laminar flow was lost and turbulent flow existed over the airfoil surface.

The results showed that the new NLF airfoil, even with transition fixed near the leading edge, achieved the same maximum lift as the NASA low-speed airfoils. At the same time, the NLF airfoil, with transition fixed, exhibited no higher cruise drag than comparable turbulent-flow airfoils. Thus, if the new NLF airfoil was used on an aircraft where laminar flow was not achieved (due to bug residue and other factors), nothing was lost relative to the performance of the NASA low-speed airfoils. If laminar flow was achieved, however, a very substantial drag reduction would result.

Because of the very successful collaboration that occurred between Eppler and Somers, the Eppler Airfoil Design and Analysis Code has become one of the most widely used airfoil codes in the world.

In the mid-1980s, Cessna and Langley conducted exploratory flight and wind-tunnel tests of a modified high-wing Cessna T-210 Centurion to determine the aerodynamic and flight characteristics of a new NLF wing for the Centurion. The new wing incorporated a smooth composite upper surface and had an NLF(1)-0414 airfoil. At Langley, the aircraft was subjected to the sublimating chemical laminar flow visualization technique during flight tests; extensive laminar flow was detected over most of the upper wing surface. Following the flight test program, the aircraft was mounted in the Langley 30- by 60-Foot Tunnel where

Chemical sublimation patterns on wing of modified Cessna Centurion showing large areas of laminar flow at 125 knots in NASA-Cessna flight tests. Note wedges in pattern caused by intentional trips.

aerodynamic forces and moments, performance, and controllability were measured by a Langley and Cessna team led by Daniel G. Murri and Frank L. Jordan, Jr. Sublimating chemicals were again used for correlation with flight results. The detection of large amounts of natural laminar flow and the correlation of design tools with flight results resulted in considerable excitement within the research community at Langley and Cessna.

The double-pronged approach of complementary ground-based airfoil research and flight demonstrations by Langley was extremely valuable. Almost certainly, neither approach would have been as successful alone. Together, they had convinced the industry that the design process could be used to develop NLF airfoils that could sustain laminar flow in flight.

One of the first applications of the new natural laminar flow airfoils to business jets was by Cessna for the Citation II-S2. Cessna later incorporated an NLF(1)-0414 (modified) airfoil in its Citation Jet series, which was announced at the National Business Aircraft Association (NBAA) convention in 1989. These aircraft types both exhibited about a 10- to 20-percent improved range as a result of NLF. Other applications of the natural laminar flow technology included the Swearingen SX 300 (NLF(1)-0416); the Lancair 320/360 (NLF(1)-0215F); the Prescott Pusher (NLF(1)-0215F); and the Mooney 301 (NLF(1)-0315).

Postflight inspection of Centurion still displays extent of laminar flow exhibited in-flight at test condition.

Following highly successful flight test program, Centurion was tested in Langley 30- by 60-Foot Tunnel in 1985.

Cessna Citation Jet with natural laminar flow airfoil.

Although NLF airfoils have become widely used in the homebuilt and certified personal aircraft segments, the primary roadblock in their adaptation to the higher speed end of the general aviation spectrum was their incompatibility with current deice systems, which permit ice to build on the leading edge before breaking it free with inflatable boots (typically used by the propeller-driven aircraft family), or anti-ice systems, which prevent the formation of ice with heated leading edges (typically used by jet aircraft). Achieving laminar flow across the junction aft of a leading-edge deice device currently requires an enormous amount of postproduction work. Because this junction is typically at 5- to 15-percent chord, achieving laminar flow beyond this point was extremely difficult in production. Thus, extensive use of laminar flow technology for higher speed aircraft is hindered by airframe ice protection technology. This NASA research on NLF airfoils provided tolerance data for surface imperfections for the mating of a deicing leading edge to a production-painted metal or composite wing surface. The challenge of laminar-compatible ice protection systems for future aircraft was largely solved by the AGATE design database developed in wind-tunnel testing at WSU and Glenn Research Center in the late 1990s. These data provide laminar flow tolerance information for installing smooth pneumatic boots as well as their alternatives (electroexpulsive or heated leading edges).

Wing sweep represents an additional physics challenge for NLF. On straight (unswept) wings, the stability of laminar flow is relatively greater than on wings with more than modest amounts of sweep. The Langley NLF research produced a clearer understanding of these limitations.

Large nose-down pitching moments and the associated high-magnitude control-surface hinge moments, in addition to trim drag, are another concern for NLF-type airfoils. Similar to supercritical airfoils, as previously mentioned, a large amount of aft camber is required to achieve high maximum lift on airfoils with extensive laminar flow. Some industry teams believe that new NLF airfoils should have little or no trailing-edge reflex. In their opinions, future NLF airfoils will have to exhibit much lower pitching moments, and the required maximum lift will have to come from advanced, yet simple, high-lift systems. The advent of the latest knowledge and computer design tools provides the means for designers to tailor the desired pitching-moment characteristics to meet their unique requirements.

The Fall and Resurgence of General Aviation

In 1978, piston aircraft manufacturers in the United States had a record year, with shipments of 14,398 airplanes. It had been the best year for general aviation in the history of the business, and few had anticipated the dramatic downturn in the light aircraft industry during the 1980s. Troubled by product liability lawsuits, poor management decisions (especially regarding technology readiness), and a stale economy, the general aviation industry suddenly experienced a free-fall drop in sales. By 1986, Cessna stopped making single-engine personal-owner planes altogether, and Piper filed for Chapter 11 bankruptcy. In 1990, the industry only shipped 608 airplanes and it appeared that the general aviation industry would disappear from the domestic scene. The demise of the general aviation industry curtailed any interest in advanced technology, and applications of the emerging NASA low- and medium-speed airfoil technology in the 1980s and early 1990s were few and far between.

In the early 1990s, an upswing in the business jet sector brought some relief to the legacy industry members such as Beechcraft (now Raytheon Aircraft) and Cessna. At the same time, however, two factors began to reshape the national interest in technology for light personal-owner aircraft. The first important factor was the emergence of a new breed of small, enthusiastic companies that offered the interested private pilot a range of relatively low-cost, advanced aircraft in the form of kits or fabricated designs. Advanced technologies, such as composite construction and advanced aerodynamics, became strong selling points and led to numerous evaluations of new wing and airfoil designs. The second major factor that stimulated technology insertion in the 1990s was the implementation of the NASA Advanced General Aviation Transport Experiment (AGATE) Program, which recognized the potential of the general aviation aircraft industry to relieve the impending saturation of the major air carrier

Cirrus SR20.

NASA's Columbia 300 research aircraft showing shape of natural laminar flow airfoil used by the wing.

transportation system. This revolutionary program rapidly accelerated the transfer and implementation of NASA-developed and NASA-sponsored research and technology.

Because of these two stimuli, advanced airfoil technology has again become of widespread interest, and the emerging stable of new aircraft incorporates many of the airfoils and design tools produced by the Langley program of the 1970s. Typical of these advanced aircraft are the Stoddard-Hamilton Glassair III kit, which uses the LS(1)-0413 airfoil; the Lancair Columbia 300, which uses a natural laminar flow airfoil; and the Cirrus SR22, which also utilizes a natural laminar flow section. Each of these applications has demonstrated performance gains because of laminar flow. In January 2001, the Langley Research Center acquired production versions of the Lancair Columbia and the Cirrus SR22 for research studies in its follow-on program to AGATE, known as the Small Aircraft Transportation System (SATS) Program.

WINGLETS

Background

As early as the 1800s, it was widely recognized that the aerodynamic efficiency and drag of aircraft wing shapes were dependent on not only profile drag (largely a two-dimensional effect) but also the induced drag or drag due to lift. The induced drag is produced by the generation of three-dimensional airflow characteristics near the tips of aircraft wings. As the flow encounters the wingtip shape, it rolls up over the tip side edge resulting in the well-known trailing vortices displayed by lifting wings. The energy expended in this phenomenon is directly responsible for the induced drag, which can be extremely large for certain aircraft wing configurations—particularly under high-lift, low-speed flight conditions. Induced drag also represents a significant decrement in aircraft efficiency for subsonic transports operating at high subsonic speeds and accounts for as much as 50 percent of total drag.

Early studies by Frederick W. Lanchester and others in England indicated that vertical surfaces located at the wingtips could significantly reduce the three-dimensional effects and thereby reduce induced drag. On the basis of theoretical studies, experimental investigations of vertical endplates were undertaken and the results showed significant reductions in drag at high-lift conditions (Lanchester patented the endplate concept in 1897). Unfortunately, near cruise conditions, these configurations exhibited large areas of local flow separation; this resulted in large viscous drag increments in profile drag, which essentially negated the benefits to induced drag. Thus, although the potential drag-reducing effects of endplates on induced drag had been identified, the net effect of simple endplates was regarded as inconsequential because of the increase in profile drag.

Following his intensive studies that led to the development and application of supercritical airfoils, Langley's Richard T. Whitcomb continued his quest to reduce cruise drag for high subsonic speeds. Inspired by an article in *Science Magazine* on the flight characteristics of soaring birds and their use of tip feathers to control flight characteristics, Whitcomb zeroed in on the wingtip flow phenomena associated with induced drag. Although many scientists had proposed wingtip configurations that mimicked birds (numerous wingtip feathers) for the reduction of induced drag, Whitcomb's guiding principle was to analyze the detailed aerodynamics involved in the flow at the wingtip and develop a more practical wingtip configuration.

Whitcomb's analysis of flow phenomena at the tip showed that the airflow about the wingtip of the typical aircraft in flight is characterized by flow that is directed inward above the wingtip and flow that is directed outward below the wingtip. Whitcomb hypothesized that a vertical, properly cambered and angled

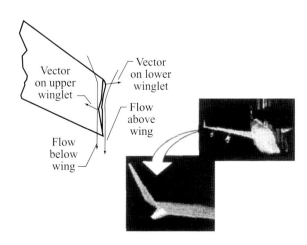

Aerodynamic flow mechanisms of winglet concept.

surface above or below the tip could utilize this crossflow tendency to reduce the strength of the trailing vortex and, thereby, reduce the induced drag. The drag reduction mechanism is achieved by a forward vectoring of the side force generated by the winglets. The aerodynamic effect of the winglet is very similar to that of a sailboat tacking upwind. The resulting reduction in aircraft drag for a properly designed winglet configuration can be extremely significant in terms of fuel consumption and range.

In essence, Whitcomb and his team provided the fundamental knowledge and design approach required for an extremely attractive option to improve the aerodynamic efficiency of civil and military aircraft. Throughout these development efforts, he emphasized to the technical community that the design of winglets requires considerable care and attention to airfoil aerodynamic characteristics. To emphasize this point, Whitcomb called the wingtip surfaces winglets to stress the fact that the design process required efforts similar in sophistication to those required for wing design.

Langley Research and Development Activities

Whitcomb's initial studies of winglets followed his time-proven experimental approach in the Langley 8-Foot Transonic Pressure Tunnel in the early 1970s. Leading a team of researchers that included Stuart G. Flechner and Peter F. Jacobs, he launched an extensive research program that included theoretical calculations, physical flow considerations, and extensive exploratory wind-tunnel experiments. These studies recognized that the acceptability of the winglet concept would depend on the impact of the winglets on structural weight and the high-lift off-design performance of the wing, as well as the magnitude of drag reduction at design conditions. Many of his technical peers pointed out to Whitcomb that the improvement in induced drag could also be achieved by simply increasing the span of the wing. However, an increase in span also increases the bending moments in the wing structures; thus, the required increase in the wing structure to accommodate these additional loads produces an increment in aircraft weight that is larger than for winglets for the same aerodynamic improvement. In fact, in most applications the reduction in drag at the cruise condition for winglets is about twice that for a simple tip extension with the same increase in wing-root bending moment. An additional, very significant advantage of using winglets rather than wing extensions is that the configuration has a smaller wingspan. Therefore, winglets provide special benefits for configurations whose wings are structurally constrained or span constrained by airport ramp dimensions or runway length.

Early experiments on the winglet concept began in the 8-Foot Transonic Pressure Tunnel in 1974. Whitcomb's team initially evaluated and developed winglet configurations that consisted of both upper and lower wingtip surfaces, with each surface designed for the local flow conditions. The upper winglet, which was the primary component of the winglet, was placed rearward on the wingtip to minimize adverse interference effects at the intersection of the wing and winglet. The experimental results showed that the leading edge of the root of the winglet should not be significantly ahead of the upper-surface crest of the wingtip section, and that the greatest winglet effectiveness was achieved with the trailing edge of the winglet near the trailing edge of the wing. In addition, the winglet airfoil should be shaped so that the desired inward force is obtained for the aircraft design flight condition,

Semispan model of KC-135 with winglets in Langley 8-Foot Transonic Pressure Tunnel.

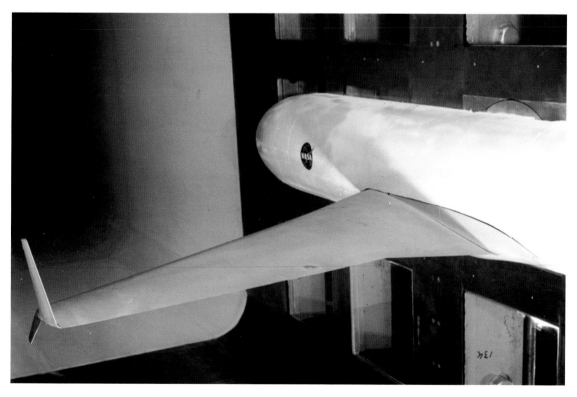

DC-10 model during winglet studies in 8-Foot Transonic Pressure Tunnel in 1974.

particularly for high subsonic supercritical conditions. In achieving this side-force requirement, designers can make use of Whitcomb's supercritical airfoil technology for the cross-
sectional shape of the winglet airfoil. The winglets must also be designed to avoid flow separation both on the winglet surface and the winglet-wing juncture at low-speed, high-lift conditions as well as cruise conditions.

The winglet concept was evaluated and tested extensively in the 8-Foot Transonic Pressure Tunnel from 1974 to 1976. In July 1976, Whitcomb published a general design
approach that summarized the aerodynamic technology involved in winglet design. At that
time, the tunnel tests indicated that, for typical subsonic transport aircraft configurations,
the induced drag could be reduced by about 20 percent and the aircraft lift-drag ratio could
be increased by about 9 percent. The improvement in lift-drag ratio was more than twice as
great as that achieved by a wingtip extension producing the same wing-root bending
moment. Because the lower winglet could adversely impact the ground-handling equipment
for low-wing aircraft configurations, the lower winglets were subsequently eliminated from
some low-wing applications, such as the Boeing 747-400.

The impressive results of the winglet studies were quickly disseminated to the U.S. civil
and military communities. Flechner presented a summary of Langley wind-tunnel results
obtained for winglet technology applied to four configurations (KC-135, Lockheed L-1011,
McDonnell Douglas DC-10, and a generic high-aspect-ratio model) to an extremely large
audience at a meeting on transport technologies at Langley in early 1978. Widespread interest and application studies for large commercial transports, business jets, and personal-
owner aircraft rapidly grew on a nationwide basis.

As part of the NASA ACEE Program, Boeing, Douglas, and Lockheed studied the impact
of winglets on near-term derivative aircraft. Boeing's initial wind-tunnel and design evaluations for the Boeing 747 configuration in May 1977 indicated that the winglet would not provide adequate economic return to the airlines for the cost of fabrication. Despite this early
negative assessment, Boeing later adapted winglets to the 747-400, as is discussed in a subsequent section. Lockheed's studies indicated that extending the wingtips of the L-1011,
together with the use of active controls to relieve loads, was a more favorable approach than
the use of winglets. Douglas, however, was impressed with the potential benefits of winglets
to structurally or span-constrained configurations, and the company proceeded to modify a
DC-10 for flight tests.

Flight Evaluations

As NASA searched for a potential aircraft for in-flight evaluations and demonstrations of
winglet technology, Langley carefully examined the impact for candidate configurations.
The early jet transports featured an elliptical-type span loading with relatively high loads on
the outer wing panels. The KC-135 exemplified this family of aircraft, as did its civilian
derivative, the Boeing 707. The application of winglets was known to be more effective for
configurations with highly loaded wingtips. In contrast, second-generation subsonic transports such as the DC-10 and L-1011 used nonelliptic loading to avoid pitch-up characteristics
at postbuffet conditions; thereby the wing bending moments and structural requirements
were reduced. Whitcomb and his staff emphasized the importance of wingtip loading as a

KC-135 winglet flight tests at Dryden Flight Research Center.

beneficial factor in winglet performance, and preferred the KC-135 as a test vehicle because of its advantageous wingtip loading. In addition, the Air Force had expressed a keen interest in a potential winglet retrofit to the KC-135 fleet for improved fuel efficiency following a series of industry studies. The mutual NASA and Air Force interests quickly resulted in proposals for a flight program.

The aerodynamic winglet design for the KC-135 was completed by Whitcomb and his staff at Langley, and the structural design and fabrication were accomplished by Boeing, Wichita Division. Joint NASA-Air Force flight tests of the modified KC-135 military tanker aircraft were conducted at the Dryden Flight Research Center in 1979 and 1980. The results of the KC-135 flight tests verified the wind-tunnel results obtained in the Langley 8-Foot Transonic Pressure Tunnel. A 7-percent gain in lift-drag ratio and a 20-percent reduction in drag due to lift were achieved at the cruise condition. Despite these impressive benefits, Air Force priorities and limited budget options resulted in a decision to retrofit the KC-135 fleet with new engines, rather than winglets, as a more efficient fleet modification.

Under sponsorship of the NASA ACEE Program, Douglas proceeded with its flight evaluation of winglets on a modified DC-10 Series 10 aircraft in 1981 following a series of tunnel tests including performance tests of a 4.7-percent semispan model in the 8-Foot Transonic Pressure Tunnel. The 16-month flight test program involved leasing a test aircraft from Continental Airlines in April 1981, conducting 61 total flights with and without winglets,

Modified DC-10 during Douglas winglet flight tests in 1981.

Full-span KC-135 model testing in Langley 8-Foot Transonic Pressure Tunnel preceding flight tests in 1977.

and returning the aircraft in November. Douglas conducted the configuration aerodynamic and structural designs and fabrication (two winglet spans were flown). The flights were made at the Douglas Long Beach facility at Edwards Air Force Base and the Douglas facility at Yuma, Arizona.

During the DC-10 tests, a buffet problem was experienced in low-speed flight due to aerodynamic flow separation at the winglet-wingtip intersection; leading-edge shape modifications on the upper and lower winglets were found to eliminate the problem. Douglas also found that the greatest drag reduction was obtained with both upper and lower winglets used and that the use of aileron droop improved the drag reduction.

From flight test results the estimation was that the application of a reduced-span winglet and aileron droop to a DC-10 Series 10 aircraft would yield a 3-percent reduction in fuel burned at the range for capacity loads. Although not retrofitted to the DC-10 because of unacceptable recertification costs, the improved performance provided by the winglets favorably impressed the Douglas organization, and winglets were later designed and implemented for the McDonnell Douglas MD-11 transport.

Applications

Arguably, the most aggressive initial U.S. applications of winglet technology came from within the general aviation and business jet community. The first aircraft to fly with winglets was the propeller-driven Vari-Eze light homebuilt aircraft, designed in 1974 by Burt Rutan, designer and builder of the Voyager aircraft, which made the first nonstop, nonrefueled around-the-world flight in December 1986. Rutan incorporated control surfaces on the winglets for rudder control. He designed the Vari-Eze to prove that the canard (wing stabilizer near the nose of the aircraft) configuration could be more efficient and safer than conventional designs. He demonstrated that efficiency by setting a world record in the under-500 kg (1100 lb) class in 1975. Advanced design features which helped the Vari-Eze achieve this world record performance included low-weight composite materials, a lightweight engine, innovative aerodynamic configuration, high-aspect-ratio wings, and winglets. Other propeller aircraft that utilize winglets include the Beech 1900D regional transport and Beech King Air 350 corporate turboprop.

In 1977, Learjet displayed an exciting new test-bed aircraft designated the Learjet Model 28 at the National Business Aircraft Association convention. The Model 28 had been involved in high priority developmental testing of a new wing for a major new Learjet project to be known as the Model 55. The Model 28 prototype employed the first winglets ever used on a jet and a production aircraft, either civilian or military. Learjet developed the winglet design without NASA assistance, and referred to the new wing as the Longhorn, which coupled the new NASA winglet technology with a wing that had higher aspect ratio. Although the Model 28 was intended to be a prototype experimental aircraft, the performance of the new aircraft was extremely impressive and resulted in a production commitment from Learjet. Flight tests made with and without winglets showed that the winglets increased range by about 6.5 percent and also improved directional stability.

Learjet Model 28/29, first production jet aircraft to utilize winglets.

Record-setting Gulfstream V with supercritical airfoil sections for its winglet design.

Following the highly successful application of winglets, one of the Learjet prototype aircraft used in the winglet development program (aircraft 25-064) was acquired by the Langley Research Center for flight tests of new NASA research concepts in October 1984. Joseph Stickle was instrumental in the acquisition of the aircraft. Flying as NASA 566, the aircraft was used extensively by Langley researchers Cynthia C. Lee, Bruce J. Holmes, Clifford J. Obara, and Bruce D. Fisher in flight tests of natural laminar flow airfoils (1984 to1989) and studies of lightning phenomena (1990 to 1993).

Learjet's application of winglets to production aircraft continued through the Model 28 to subsequent current applications including the Model 55, Model 31, Model 60, and Model 45.

Gulfstream had also been aggressively studying applications of winglets in the late 1970s (contemporary with the Lear activities) and incorporated winglets in its line of business jet

Boeing 737-800 with winglets.

Boeing B747-400, first large U.S. commercial transport to incorporate winglets.

transports including the Gulfstream III, Gulfstream IV, and Gulfstream V. The performance of the Gulfstream V has been spectacular. Its operational range of 6,500 nmi at a cruise Mach number of 0.80, and cruise speed capability up to Mach 0.89, permits routine nonstop business travel for routes such as New York–Tokyo. The Gulfstream V also holds over 70 world and national flight records.

In October 1985, Boeing announced a new version of the 747, known as the 747-400, with extended range and capacity. With this particular model, Boeing introduced winglets for enhanced performance. The winglets increase the 747-400 range by about 3 percent. In addition to the 747 application, Boeing offers its winglet designs as customer options in its 737 business jet and its 737-800 aircraft. Building on the foundation acquired in its Energy Efficient Transport (EET) studies for the DC-10, McDonnell Douglas included the winglet concept in its design for the MD-11, which entered service in December 1990.

As frequently happens with the introduction of new technology, widespread interest quickly grew in the potential application of winglets as a retrofit to existing aircraft. Within the U.S. industry, a number of small consulting organizations have attempted to meet this interest with retrofit capabilities. For example, winglets have been retrofitted to the Boeing 727 configuration. The retrofit process involves a number of Federal Aviation Administration (FAA) regulatory constraints that must be complied with to permit such modifications. For example, the 727 modification was accomplished by removing part of the outboard wing before the winglet was added so as to maintain the same root-bending moments for the wing.

Worldwide applications of winglets have extended far beyond transport aircraft and business jets. For example, personal-owner aircraft have been modified and several competition gliders (15-m class) have been modified or designed with winglets. In this somewhat surprising application (the performance of high-aspect-ratio gliders would not be expected to benefit greatly from winglets), the winglets considerably improved the roll response of the aircraft. Other interesting applications have included the use of winglets to control the flow fields and wake turbulence behind an aircraft for aerial applications. By modifying the trailing wake and moving the tip vortex up from the wingtip to the winglet tip, Langley researchers were able to beneficially affect the dispersal characteristics of particles and sprays for aircraft used in agricultural or forestry missions.

Perhaps no single NASA concept has seen such widespread use on an international level as Whitcomb's winglets. The multitude of applications is clearly visible across the spectrum of civil aircraft, even to the most casual air traveler.

McDonnell Douglas built on development experience gained
in NASA ACEE Program to design winglets for the MD-11.

AREA RULE

Background

With the frantic development of advanced aircraft in World War II, the speed of sound became an operational barrier characterized by severe aerodynamic problems, including substantial increases in aerodynamic drag and buffet, rapid increases in structural loadings, and potentially catastrophic loss of controllability. During the war and immediately thereafter, the Langley Research Center conducted extensive wind-tunnel and flight investigations to provide a fundamental understanding of and solutions to the physical phenomena causing these problems.

A breakthrough occurred in 1950, when Langley modified the operational Langley 8-Foot Transonic Pressure Tunnel with an innovative slotted throat transonic test section to permit valid aerodynamic testing in the complex transonic regime. Using this unique facility, Richard T. Whitcomb and others conducted experimental studies of flow fields about aircraft at transonic conditions to understand the problems that had first been experienced during the war and to improve aerodynamic efficiency by reducing or delaying the transonic drag rise. A particularly informative source of data was photographs of the extensive shock waves observed about aircraft models during the tests in the 8-Foot Transonic Pressure Tunnel. Instead of individual shock waves for the wing and the fuselage, as had been expected by many researchers, a single strong shock wave was observed nearly normal to the flow direction, crossing the flow field near the tip of the wing. This observed shock wave was very similar to that exhibited by a body of revolution without wings. Given this important clue, researchers turned their attention to defining the equivalent body of revolution to minimize the increased drag caused by the shock wave at transonic conditions.

Inspired by a presentation on transonic flows made at Langley by Adolph Busemann, a world famous German aerodynamicist who had come to Langley following World War II, Whitcomb realized that the transonic disturbances and shock waves produced by aircraft were a function of the longitudinal variation of cross-sectional area. As a result of this phenomenon, the drag near the speed of sound for a wing-body combination was the same as that of a body of revolution with the same longitudinal distribution of cross-sectional area.

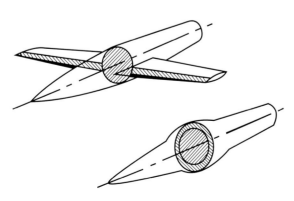

Cross-sectional area for wing-body configuration and for equivalent of revolution. Note bump in cross-sectional area of body of revolution caused by addition of wing area.

For most airplane configurations, adding the cross-sectional area of the wing to that of the fuselage results in an abrupt increase, or bump, in the overall longitudinal area distribution. Thus, to obtain the minimum shock wave drag, the overall distribution should be that of a smooth body with minimum drag. Whitcomb theorized that the most obvious way to achieve this distribution was to remove the equivalent wing cross-sectional area from that of the fuselage cross-sectional area

Richard T. Whitcomb with area-ruled F-106 aircraft (NASA 816) at the retirement of NASA 816
(used for flight research at NASA Glenn and NASA Langley) at Langley in 1991.

in the region of the wing; thereby the abrupt bump was avoided in area distribution. This approach resulted in a pronounced "wasp-waist" or "Coke-bottle" fuselage shape. The cross-sectional areas of other aircraft components (nacelles, etc.) are also included for analysis of typical aircraft configurations, and the total area distribution is examined for compliance with the area rule.

Whitcomb's discovery was initially highly classified, but the aircraft industry was immediately notified and briefed on the results of wind-tunnel tests that verified his hypothesis. Whitcomb was subsequently awarded the coveted Collier Trophy for his discovery and the development of the area rule, and history has recorded numerous applications to military aircraft beginning with the U.S. Navy's F11F Tiger, which almost flew faster than speed of sound without an afterburner in August 1954. Perhaps the most dramatic application of the area rule was for the U.S. Air Force's delta-winged F-102 aircraft. After a contract was awarded for the advanced interceptor, wind-tunnel tests in the Langley 8-Foot Transonic Pressure Tunnel in 1953 revealed that the transonic drag was much higher than predicted, and that the aircraft would not be able to penetrate the speed of sound. Subsequent flight tests in August of that same year verified the wind-tunnel predictions when the YF-102 could not exceed the speed of sound in level flight. On December 21, 1954, the F-102 with a modified, area-ruled fuselage (known as the YF-102A) flew through the speed of sound while still climbing. Whitcomb's area rule had saved a critical national military program and had proven to be the major breakthrough for routine supersonic flight. Following this famous application, other famous military aircraft, such as the F-105, F-106, F-4, B-58, and B-1, were designed with the area rule as a guiding principle.

Today, the operational flight envelopes of high-performance supersonic military aircraft still require consideration of the principles of the area rule. In the early 1970s, an interest in higher cruise speeds for commercial transports resulted in extensive NASA and industry studies of near-sonic transports that incorporated the area rule. Today, however, the more limited subsonic flight speeds used by civil aircraft have not resulted in any significant use of the area rule for fuselage shaping of large transports. On the other hand, as the speed and altitude capabilities of today's business jet aircraft continue to increase, the area rule has entered the design process.

Langley Research and Development Activities

At the time of Whitcomb's discovery of the area rule, the dominant theme of the user community for both military and civil aircraft was "higher, faster, and farther." Therefore, having successfully applied the area rule to military aircraft in the 1950s and 1960s, Whitcomb turned his efforts to potential applications for subsonic civil transports. Unfortunately, the relatively low cruise speeds at the time precluded the application of the concept.

When the supercritical airfoil permitted serious consideration of higher cruise speeds, Whitcomb and his staff explored the advantages of area ruling for advanced transport aircraft. Several generic models were tested in the 8-Foot Transonic Pressure Tunnel, and the results indicated that the concept of area ruling, together with supercritical wing technology, might permit near-sonic cruise capability. The integrated principles of area ruling resulted in configurations with geometries that provided vivid visual evidence of the careful tailoring of the cross-sectional area distribution of the total aircraft. These exciting results and data were quickly disseminated to the U.S. airframe industry. Meanwhile, the growing national interest in faster cruise speeds for commercial transports maintained Langley's interest in the area.

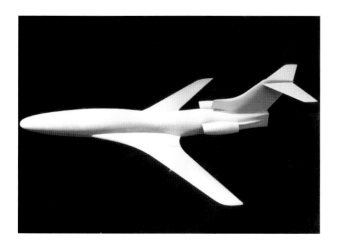

Near-sonic transport wind-tunnel model with area ruling and advanced supercritical wing.

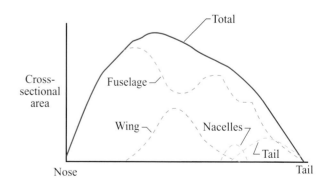

Area distribution for near-sonic transport design. Note variations in fuselage area required to provide relatively smooth area variation for total aircraft.

Boeing configuration in ATT studies included area-ruled fuselage.

A series of industry studies by Boeing, Lockheed, and General Dynamics in the NASA-sponsored Advanced Technology Transport (ATT) Program resulted in candidate near-sonic cruise configurations that employed all of the geometric principles dictated by the area rule. Each individual industry design incorporated the graceful, curved fuselage and shaping characteristics of area-ruled aircraft.

Langley research on advanced area-ruled subsonic transports continued until the fuel crisis of the 1970s virtually eliminated worldwide interest in near-sonic transport development. Langley then turned its research emphasis to improving aerodynamic efficiency at lower cruise speeds by using the beneficial characteristics of the supercritical wing. The principles of the area rule, however, continued to be employed by designers for solutions to configuration integration issues.

Applications to Civil Aircraft

None of the current U.S. large commercial aircraft operate at cruise speeds high enough to require the radical area-ruled fuselage shapes necessary for a near-sonic transport. However, designers of large commercial transports have used the principles of area ruling to solve "local" flow problems and interference effects—especially nacelle integration issues for wing- or fuselage-mounted engines. Following the early development of the area rule, Whitcomb continued his remarkably intuitive approach to transonic aerodynamics in efforts that showed how the principles involved in the area rule could be used to enhance the overall performance of transport aircraft, without the radical reshaping of the entire aircraft required for the near-sonic transport configurations. For example, in 1958 he developed a special fuselage addition on the forward part of the upper fuselage that significantly reduced the shock-induced separation noted on the inboard upper-wing surface for representative transport configurations. The fuselage addition resembled the upper forward fuselage fairing that was later incorporated into the Boeing 747 transport. Whitcomb also used area-rule principles in studies of the beneficial impact of "antishock" wing-mounted bodies on raising the drag-divergence Mach number for representative fuselage-wing configurations. In a series of wind-tunnel studies, he validated the potential beneficial effects of semiconical bodies located at several spanwise and chordwise wing locations. The bodies reduced the local curvature of the upper surface, a characteristic that favored the potential for supercritical flow—a concept that Whitcomb would later explore in the development of the supercritical airfoil. Fundamentally, the beneficial effects of these bodies included a deceleration of the supersonic flow ahead of the shock wave above the wing, and a decrease in the strength of the shock and the associated flow separation. Furthermore, the local pressure fields produced by the bodies greatly reduced the adverse outward flow of the separated boundary layer on

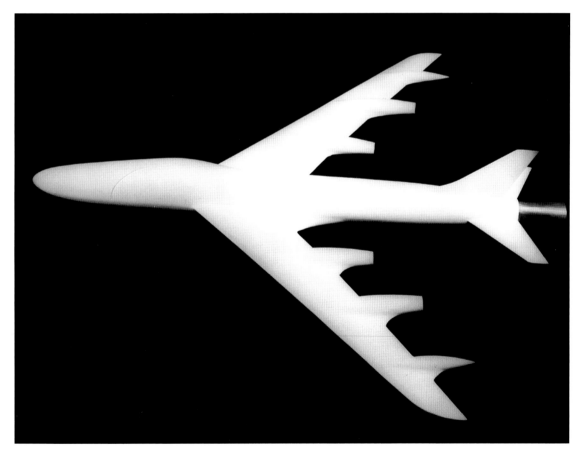

Wind-tunnel research model in Langley 8-Foot Transonic Pressure Tunnel showing upper forward fuselage fairing and antishock bodies on wing.

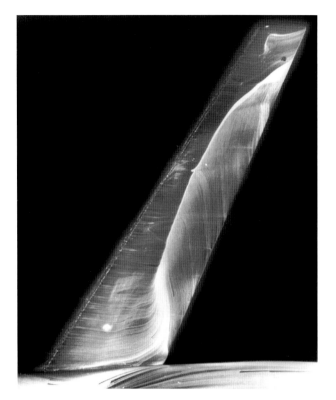

*Oil flow visualization of model wing with 35° sweepback at Mach number of 0.90 and angle of attack of 4°
(flow is left to right). A significant amount of unacceptable flow separation is evident for basic wing (left)
on rearward part of wing; the addition of antishock bodies (right) greatly reduces separation.*

swept-back wings. Experiments in the Langley 8-Foot Transonic Pressure Tunnel were conducted for Mach numbers from 0.60 to 1.00 for several configurations. The shapes of the auxiliary bodies were carefully designed by Whitcomb in adherence to a special extension of the area rule. In this application, he carefully chose specific areas of the wing to be considered in the development of cross-sectional area distributions. For example, he omitted the cross-sectional areas of the bodies downstream of the wing trailing edge because the aerodynamic effects of those sections were relatively complex and unknown; however, these effects were probably secondary to those of the sections of the bodies above the wing surface. The semiconical forward and upper surfaces of the bodies were accompanied by a flat lower surface aft of the wing trailing edge.

The results of wind-tunnel tests verified Whitcomb's intuitive local application of area-rule principles. For a representative lift coefficient, the drag-rise Mach number was increased by approximately 0.05 (from Mach 0.85 to 0.90). A very significant additional benefit of the bodies was that they eliminated an unacceptable pitch-up instability exhibited by the high-aspect-ratio swept-wing models for Mach numbers of 0.80 and greater. In fact, the configuration with added bodies experienced significant pitch-down at several of the test Mach numbers. The pitch-up of the basic swept wing was expected and caused by severe separation on the outboard region of the wing, which resulted in a greater loss of lift on the outer sections. This favorable effect of the bodies was attributed to reducing the separation on the outboard

NASA's Convair 990 aircraft in 1992. Note antishock bodies on wing.

View from beneath Convair 990 showing flattened lower surface of semiconical antishock bodies.

region, which resulted from the lessening of the strength of the local shock and the retardation of the outflow of the boundary layer into the outer region.

Design trade-offs for applications of the body concept include an assessment of the additional parasite drag (including interference effects) caused by the additional bodies. Data on this novel antishock body concept were quickly disseminated to the U.S. industry, and Whitcomb was subsequently awarded a patent for the antishock body concept.

One of the more significant examples of the application of the area rule for local flow problems involved the four-engine Convair 990 jet transport. The 990 was an attempt by the Convair Corporation to compete with Boeing and Douglas in the highly competitive jet transport marketplace of the late 1950s. Unfortunately for Convair, Boeing and Douglas had captured the early market with sales of the 707 and DC-8, respectively, whereas Convair's initial attempt to enter the rapidly growing industry was marred by massive losses of over $425 million on its Convair 880 transport. When Boeing marketed their new 720 transport it threatened to eliminate Convair from the competition; Convair responded with a new design designated the Convair 990, which would be marketed on speed and luxury. The aircraft would differ from the earlier 880 in having a stretched fuselage for increased capacity, a larger wing, and the first turbofans ever used by a civil transport. The new turbofans were supplied by the General Electric Company.

During briefings with Convair engineers, Whitcomb advised them to incorporate his concept of concial wing-mounted antishock bodies for local area ruling of the wing and enhanced high-speed performance. Impressed with the potential of the antishock body concept, Convair designed the 990 with the wing-mounted bodies. The first flight of the new aircraft occurred on January 24, 1961, and even with the beneficial effects of the bodies, high-speed drag problems were immediately noted during the flight tests. The top speed was limited to 580 mph (40 mph less than the guarantee) and a serious range deficit was also noted that would prevent coast-to-coast operations. An extensive drag reduction program was initiated that led to modifications that resulted in the achievement of cruise performance in excess of the original guarantees. The modifications included a sharper, less-drooped wing leading edge; a nacelle afterbody extension; a wing-fuselage fillet redesign; and the addition of engine nacelle and pylon fairings.

During the drag reduction program, General Electric representatives requested the assistance of Whitcomb in minimizing an extremely large nacelle-wing-pylon interference drag problem that had been identified in flight tests. Pressure measurements made around the nacelle afterbody, pylon, and wing indicated the presence of a strong shock wave with significant wave drag for aircraft Mach numbers from 0.80 to 0.90. In addition, shock-induced separation contributed to the drag problem. The new turbofan engines had the fan located toward the rear of the engine; this location resulted in a sudden increase in area distribution near the wing trailing edge. Essentially, flow encountering the convergent-divergent channel between the nacelle, pylon, and lower wing surface was being accelerated to supersonic conditions, which resulted in a standing shock. The

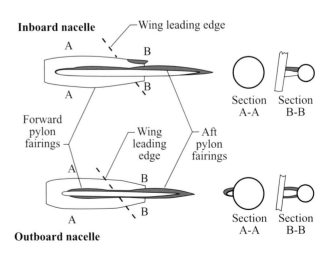

Sketch of 990 pylon and nacelle fairings used for production aircraft. Cross-sectional views at right are looking forward.

The Douglas DC-8 Super 62 aircraft with long nacelles.

level of drag rise for the entire aircraft with increasing Mach number above 0.80 was approximately equal to the nacelle afterbody pressure drag. Whitcomb analyzed the problem using the principles of his area rule on a local basis. In particular, the area contained by the nacelle upper surface, pylon side surface, and wing lower surface was analyzed for each nacelle in terms of smoothness of the area distribution and found to have abrupt changes in area distribution (due to the pylon and fan location) along the length ranging from the nacelle intake to the trailing edge of the wing for both the inboard and outboard nacelles. Any fixes for the problem could not change the wing or the nacelle basic lines, but auxiliary fairings could be added to the pylons and nacelles. Following applications of the local area rule, several pylon, nacelle, and wing fairings were proposed to smooth out the area distribution, and the most effective configurations, consisting of forward and aft pylon fairings, were adopted for production aircraft. This configuration resulted in a significant increase in the drag-rise Mach number for the aircraft, from about 0.80 for the basic configuration to about 0.89 for the modified aircraft. NASA later acquired a Convair 990 aircraft for use in its research programs at the Dryden Flight and Ames Research Centers for activities ranging from evaluating new landing gear and brake designs for the space shuttle to direct lift control and medium-altitude research missions.

Another successful example of the use of the area rule for local interference drag analysis occurred in the Douglas DC-8 transport program. During a prototype flight investigation of a new long duct nacelle for the DC-8, flight results obtained with a proposed new nacelle afterbody resulted in a much greater interference drag than had been indicated by wind-tunnel tests. In fact, the penalty measured in flight was double the wind-tunnel value for

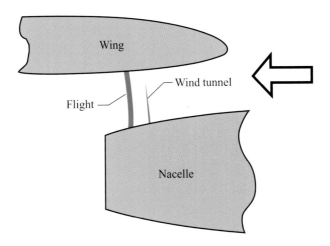

Illustration of wing-pylon-nacelle interference drag flow phenomenon for DC-8 indicating difference in shock wave locations and relative strengths for wind tunnel and flight.

Cessna Citation X with local area-ruled features incorporated in its lower and aft-fuselage shapes.

representative cruise conditions. Examination of pressure distributions on the nacelle in the channel between the wing and nacelle indicated that the shock in the channel was significantly stronger and farther aft in flight than in the wind tunnel; this caused very high levels of drag. The difference between the tunnel and flight results was attributed to the differences in boundary-layer growth because of corresponding differences in Reynolds number. Applications of Whitcomb's local area-rule methodology resulted in fairing candidates that eliminated the problem. The successful application of the area-rule process and the elimination of what would have been a major performance penalty for the long duct nacelle configuration provided Douglas with the confidence and enabling technology to proceed with the new versions of the DC-8, the highly successful "Super Sixties" (DC-8-62 and DC-8-63).

Another example of the use of local area ruling was the successful design of the centerline engine installation on the DC-10. Application of the area-rule concept by McDonnell Douglas provided the guidance needed to properly locate the various components (i.e., the inlet cowling relative to the support strut, strut shaping versus horizontal tail location). This approach significantly contributed to the aircraft meeting its nominal (not just guarantee) performance levels. Yet another, more recent, application of this principle by McDonnell Douglas was for the engine pylon design for the MD-90.

Aircraft designers quickly absorbed the lessons learned through application of the principles of the area rule for local flow interference solutions, and the approach became a general design technique that has been used for the analysis and improvement of high-speed aerodynamics for pylon-mounted engines on wings, pylon-mounted engines on fuselages, and externally mounted stores.

In recent years, competing elements within the business jet community have pushed the cruise speed and altitude capabilities of advanced business jet aircraft to near-sonic conditions, requiring the incorporation of Whitcomb's principles for efficient cruise. A current application of area ruling within the civil community is the advanced Cessna Citation X business jet aircraft, which nominally cruises at a Mach number of about 0.92 at altitudes of about 30,000 ft. Careful tailoring of the fuselage, wing, engine pylon, and engine nacelle geometries according to the general and local principles of the area rule, along with the implementation of other innovations such as the supercritical wing, has resulted in the fastest civil aircraft in the world (excluding the supersonic Concorde). In recognition of the outstanding performance and design of the aircraft, Cessna was awarded the Collier Trophy for 1996 for the most significant aeronautical achievement in the United States. The SX-30, Raytheon Premier I and Hawker Horizon, and Dassault Falcon 50, 900, and 2000 aircraft all exhibit significant contouring in the aft-fuselage area to minimize nacelle interference drag at transonic speeds.

COMPUTATIONAL FLUID DYNAMICS

Background

The single technology area that had the most significant impact within the discipline of aerodynamics for civil aircraft of the 1990s was the explosive growth and versatility of advanced computer-based methods in computational fluid dynamics. Following years of pioneering efforts within NASA, industry, DOD, other agencies, and universities, the powerful computational capabilities of rapidly evolving modern computers and computational fluid dynamics (CFD) methodologies have provided civil aircraft designers with unprecedented flexibility to assess the impact of configuration variables and conduct fundamental studies of fluid phenomena.

The utilization of CFD methods within the civil sector has permitted detailed studies that have dramatically changed the aircraft design process. In addition to providing relatively rapid and detailed understanding of aerodynamic characteristics, CFD has also provided guidance that has significantly reduced the number of experimental tests, wind-tunnel hours, and models required to develop modern aircraft. Virtually every aspect of aircraft design now includes analyses using CFD to evaluate and assess both viscous and inviscid aerodynamic effects on airfoil and wing design, high-lift performance, component interference, propulsion-airframe integration, and cruise performance.

Major challenges that have been, and continue to be, faced by researchers in the CFD community revolve around accurate modeling of critical flow physics, rapid and effective modeling of the aircraft components under study, solutions to nonlinear equations with millions of degrees of freedom in a timely and cost-effective manner, and establishing the validity and feasibility of the computational approaches. In this area, NASA aerodynamicists at Langley, Ames, Glenn, and Dryden work closely with their peers in other organizations to mutually provide this Nation with leading-edge design and analysis tools. Many aircraft in the current civil fleet have been impacted by these capabilities.

Langley Research and Development Activities

Langley and the other NASA aeronautics Centers (Ames, Glenn, and Dryden) have been at the forefront of research and development for CFD codes and the maturation and validation of integrated computational methodology. The relationship of the NASA Centers with the civil aircraft industry has been especially significant because NASA researchers have been able to supply computational codes and technology used as building blocks within the industry for further development of proprietary codes and design tools. At Langley, significant CFD contributions to aircraft of the 1990s resulted directly from a Center management commitment to computational excellence and the innovation and world-class expertise of its staff.

In the 1960s and 1970s, management at Langley became increasingly aware of the significant value of CFD to the analysis and design of future aircraft. They observed emerging computational efforts in areas ranging from relatively simple nonviscous codes such as "panel" methods to tremendously complex approaches required to provide viscous flow solutions to the Navier-Stokes equations for fluid flow and made a decision that Langley should be a leader in developing and disseminating CFD codes to industry for the analysis of aircraft characteristics across the speed range from subsonic to supersonic flight.

Langley's Director for Aeronautics, Robert E. Bower, made a major commitment to establish and nurture a major new CFD organization in the 1970s. It was during this time that lead researchers such as Percy J. "Bud" Bobbitt, Jerry C. South, Jr., Richard W. Barnwell, Ajay Kumar, Douglas L. Dwoyer, and others established the vision, hiring policies, investments, and organizational dedication that permitted Langley's emerging CFD organizations to flourish. Investments in leading-edge computers and other hardware provided the staff with the tools required to advance the state of the art. A key leadership action came from Roy Harris, who collocated the CFD researchers together in a common work area so that they could communicate their methods, progress, and ideas. Thus, Langley avoided a splintered and disparate activity and rapidly nurtured a world-class capability.

Even a modest discussion of the key individuals, technical advances in CFD, and broad contributions of Langley's historical CFD program is far beyond the scope and intent of this document. Thus, the reader is referred to the extensive NASA literature for more details and a broader perspective on all aspects of the Langley CFD effort.

Applications by the Civil Aircraft Industry

As might be expected, every major civil aircraft manufacturer has an aerodynamics group that is well versed in the latest technology for both experimental and computational approaches to aircraft design and development. Typically, each company develops and utilizes its own highly protected and proprietary methods and codes for the computational design process. Fundamental research conducted by NASA on computational methods is, of course, evaluated by the industry and inserted into proprietary toolboxes if cost-effective or technically required. NASA extensively tests and uses the codes, along with wind tunnels, flight tests, and other analytical approaches, to carry out its own programs. In the interest of achieving effective technology transfer and dissemination of results, NASA contracts with and/or works cooperatively with industry and academia to further accelerate CFD technology.

The civil industry is especially critical of evolving computational methods from the perspective of cost, timeliness, and validity. For example, the development of a computational code that requires excessive computer hardware resources, unacceptable costs, unattainable computational speeds, or excessive program run times is not highly valued by industry. Therefore, the acknowledged utilization of Langley-developed computational methods by the civil industry is an impressive endorsement of the value and critical nature of the technology from the user's perspective. Many companies regard detailed information on aerodynamic design—especially wing design—as the heart of proprietary advantage and are very reluctant to share knowledge regarding specific tools or even the extent of their human and monetary resource commitments in this critical area. Nonetheless, several Langley contributions and key individuals have been cited for particularly valuable contributions to the industry in the design of specific aircraft for the 1990s.

Unstructured grid representation of Boeing 747-400 in USM3D code application.

One of the most important contributions of Langley to CFD technology involves the development of the Direct Iterative Surface Curvature (DISC) code by Richard L. Campbell and Leigh A. Smith of Langley. Known as an inverse design method, DISC is an automated design method that iteratively computes modifications to a wing to meet a specified target pressure distribution. By inputting the target pressure distribution, the designer is able to, in effect, work the problem from the desired aerodynamic characteristics back to the generating geometry. DISC has been incorporated into virtually all design codes used by industry. Examples of the use of the DISC code by industry include applications by Gulfstream during the development of the Gulfstream V advanced business jet and by Cessna in the design of the Citation X.

Other Langley codes used by the civil aircraft industry include advanced methods that provide relatively rapid solutions to the complex equations that govern the physics of fluid flows. Two of the most widely used methods are known as the TLNS3D code and the USM3D code. The TLNS3D code is used to solve the Navier-Stokes equations by using multiple grid blocks to accommodate complex aircraft geometries and a multigrid scheme to accelerate the solution. The code was developed by Veer N. Vatsa and others at Langley for use on vector computers and has been used for sophisticated aerodynamic computations by Boeing in the development of the 777 and the 737, and by Gulfstream in the development of the V jet. This code was the first Navier-Stokes solver to demonstrate improved speed and accuracy over the full potential codes with interacted boundary layers, which was the industry standard. The USM3D code is an innovative, efficient solver of the Euler and Navier-Stokes equations by using an approach known as unstructured gridding. In this approach, developed by Neal T. Frink and others of Langley, tetrahedral cells are used in the representation and solution for flow about the aircraft. Cessna applied USM3D in the design of the Citation X.

Cooperative Studies

At the Paris Air Show in June 1985, McDonnell Douglas announced a follow-on to the wide-body DC-10 transport, to be known as the MD-11. This stretched version of the DC-10 incorporated a number of advanced technologies, including redesigned airfoil sections with more trailing-edge camber, winglets, and an advanced horizontal tail that included an integral trim tank. First flight of the MD-11 occurred on January 10, 1990, and service entry began later that year. Commercial customers for the new aircraft numbered over 200, including Federal Express, which accepted its first all-cargo MD-11F in June 1991.

Initial flight tests of the MD-11 indicated an unacceptable range shortfall of over 400 nmi. McDonnell Douglas initiated a modification program for the MD-11 known as the Performance Improvement Program (PIP), which included focused efforts to improve the

A cooperative Langley and McDonnell Douglas redesign effort helped the MD-11 reach its performance goals.

aircraft's weight, fuel capacity, engine performance, and aerodynamics. Cumulative improvements from modifications identified by the PIP from 1990 to 1995 recovered and subsequently extended the range for the aircraft.

During the PIP activities, McDonnell Douglas representatives approached William P. Henderson and James M. Luckring of Langley for assistance in implementing Langley's advanced CFD methods for analysis of an engine-pylon flow separation problem that had been observed in flight tests. The flow separation region occurred on the outboard side of the juncture between the engine pylon and the lower surface of the wing. The challenges faced by McDonnell Douglas in solving the problem were significant. The opportunity for flight-test evaluations of proposed aircraft modifications was constrained by the availability of the flight test aircraft, and as a result, all analyses, design, and fabrication had to be completed within 3 months. Previous wind-tunnel tests had not identified the problem prior to flight because of scale effects involving laminar, rather than turbulent, separation characteristics. McDonnell Douglas recognized that advanced CFD methods in existence at Langley provided a potential mechanism (perhaps the only one) for pylon redesign efforts within the time constraints.

Langley and McDonnell Douglas subsequently formed an analysis team that conducted a 6-week effort at Langley Research Center using several computational tools to identify the problem, assess the effects of geometric changes to the pylon, and arrive at the new pylon

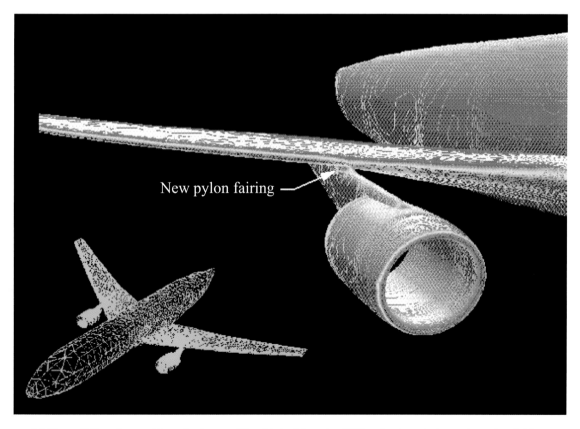

McDonnell Douglas and Langley team utilized latest Langley CFD codes to redesign pylon-wing fairing.

MD-11 pylon fairing retrofitted to MD-11 fleet. Photograph ©Chris Coduto.

design. Working with McDonnell Douglas computational experts on-site at Langley, a team led by Neal T. Frink that included Richard L. Campbell, Leigh A. Smith, Shahyar Z. Pirzadeh, and Paresh C. Parikh provided expertise and analysis during the intensive pylon study. Critical computational tools used in the effort included Langley-developed codes such as the VGRID tetrahedral grid generator (developed by Pirzadeh of ViGYAN, Inc.), the USM3D computational solver for unstructured grids (developed by Frink), a McDonnell Douglas version of Anthony Jameson's computational unstructured flow solver known as AIRPLANE, and the inverse design method known as DISC (developed by Campbell and Smith).

Extensive calculations using the foregoing CFD tools provided insight into the complex flow characteristics occurring in the regions near the intersection of the pylon and wing leading-edge lower surface. After analyzing pressure distributions, suction peaks, and the effects of geometric modifications, the Langley and McDonnell Douglas team identified a candidate redesign for the pylon fairing that significantly reduced adverse pressure peaks and eliminated flow separation at cruise conditions. Thanks to the guidance and analysis provided by the CFD effort, a new pylon fairing was designed, fabricated, and evaluated within the 3-month flight test window. The flight tests of the new pylon fairing validated the performance enhancements predicted by the computational methods. A very significant

Cooperative Langley and Cessna tests of multipoint wing design for Citation X in National Transonic Facility.

drag reduction of about 0.75 percent was achieved. The fairing was installed in an all-new MD-11 aircraft and was retrofitted to existing aircraft. As a final positive result of this classical cooperative venture, McDonnell Douglas engineers became fluent in the use of Langley computational methods, and the methods were subsequently integrated into the McDonnell Douglas design capabilities.

Although less successful than the McDonnell Douglas MD-11 experience, Langley researchers also participated in a cooperative computational-experimental study with Cessna during the development of the Citation X. In that study, the objective was to consider a single wing design that would perform most efficiently at two design points—a high-speed condition and a slower, but more efficient, cruise condition. Under the direction of James M. Luckring and L. Elwood Putnam, Leigh A. Smith and Raymond E. Mineck led the multipoint wing design study that utilized Campbell's DISC code and other methods to arrive at a multipoint wing design for the Citation X. The program proceeded from computational design through testing in the National Transonic Facility, but the study encountered unanticipated delays and had no impact on the production configuration.

Langley's staff also supported industry CFD in other ways. For example, McDonnell Douglas requested that Campbell actively help at the Long Beach, California, site in the transfer of his DISC code. Campbell subsequently spent 3 months at the McDonnell Douglas facility to develop a version of his code with appropriate constraints injected by McDonnell Douglas. He also trained company engineers in the use of his code and participated in the design of the MD-XX transport. Although McDonnell Douglas decided not to proceed with the MD-XX, they commended Campbell's contributions to the project and his personal transfer of critical technology for future utilization.

Close working relationships among the CFD staffs of the Langley Research Center, the Ames Research Center, academia, and industry have resulted in the effective development and dissemination of extremely valuable codes for the civil aircraft industry. Industry has incorporated NASA codes into its design methodology and applied them to its ongoing product lines. An impressive perspective of the impact and value of NASA's building block technology can be obtained with an overview of Boeing's experiences with wing design for recent transport aircraft. Boeing's use of advanced CFD methods has dramatically reduced the number of candidate wing designs required for experimental wind-tunnel testing during development programs.

For example, during the development of the 757 and 767, Boeing conducted wind-tunnel testing of over 40 different wing configurations for each of these aircraft, which represented the 1980 state of the art in wing design. With the flexibility, guidance, and analysis provided by CFD, only 18 different wings were tested in the 777 development program using technology of the 1990s. The reduction in wings tested is even more impressive because the 777 wing is 21 percent thicker than the wings of the 757 and 767 and has a higher cruise speed capability. With even more sophisticated CFD codes now under development, Boeing projects that future aircraft programs may only require as few as 5 wings to be tested in a wind tunnel.

FLOW CONTROL

Background

The discipline of aerodynamics includes three distinct areas of interest: the fundamental understanding of flow physics and basic fluid phenomena, the experimental and computational prediction and analysis of aerodynamic applications, and flow control to enhance the aerodynamic performance of aircraft. The concepts and mechanisms that permit flow control are among the most important products of the modern aerodynamicist, and they will lead to new paradigms in the aerodynamic design of future aircraft. To enable the identification and development of flow control concepts, the researcher will generally have expertise in all three of the foregoing components of aerodynamics. The key to flow control, however, is a thorough understanding of the fundamental physics of three-dimensional, high Reynolds number aerodynamic phenomena including vortical flows, boundary-layer transition and turbulence, and flow separation.

Langley Research and Development Activities

The rich history of Langley research on flow control concepts includes pioneering research for concepts such as boundary-layer control for high-lift, upper surface blowing and the externally blown flap for short takeoff and landing capability, supercritical airfoils, winglets, and laminar flow control and numerous turbulence control concepts (e.g., mass injection, riblets, vortex generators, passive porous surfaces) for skin friction drag reduction and/or separation control. Although tremendous progress has been made in flow control, more effective and versatile concepts are constantly being explored to enhance the aerodynamic performance and reduce the costs of future civil and military aircraft. Currently, research on flow control has been directed at several specific objectives: fundamental studies of the relative efficiency and optimum configuration for passive control devices such as vortex generators, assessments of unconventional advanced passive concepts such as passive porosity, development and evaluation of emerging active flow control concepts including steady and unsteady flow control concepts, and the development of advanced actuators and sensors for active control—especially microelectromechanical systems (MEMS). Unfortunately, many of the more recent advances in flow control concepts have not yet been incorporated in current civil aircraft because of lack of maturity, risks, and concerns over unknowns regarding the costs associated with aircraft component redesign and manufacturing. Cost concerns today require that all new technologies must "buy" a way onto the production aircraft.

One of the most widely applied concepts for flow control is vane-type, passive vortex generators that transfer high-energy fluid outside the boundary layer to the surface region inside the boundary layer. First introduced in 1947, vortex generators consist of a row of small plates or airfoils that project normal to the surface and are set at an angle of incidence to the local flow to produce an array of streamwise trailing vortices. These devices are used to energize the boundary layer such that boundary-layer separation is eliminated or delayed, and this can be used to enhance wing lift, improve control effectiveness, and/or tailor wing buffet characteristics at transonic speeds. Many commercial transports utilize vortex generators to enhance wing aerodynamic performance over an enlarged flight envelope. Air travelers can readily view vortex generators that are normally arranged in a spanwise direction on the upper surface of the wing or the empennage of modern transports; single vortex generators can also be found on the sides of the fore and aft sections of the fuselage and on engine nacelles.

Microvortex Generators

Although aircraft designers have made wide use of relatively large vortex generators (VGs) to solve numerous flow control problems, the relative size of the auxiliary vanes can unfavorably impact the performance of aircraft. Conventional VGs usually produce residual drag through conversion of aircraft forward momentum into unrecoverable turbulence in the aircraft wake. Therefore, the design and implementation of a passive, effective VG configuration that prevents flow separation for critical flight conditions yet imposes little or no drag penalty on the aircraft is a formidable challenge to the aerodynamicist.

Led by John C. Lin, a team of Langley researchers dramatically improved the characteristics of VGs by developing smaller microvortex generators (MVGs) to produce streamwise vortices that more efficiently transfer momentum within the boundary layer. Langley's research on MVGs began as a fundamental investigation of boundary-layer separation control in the early 1990s. Within that fundamental objective, researchers attempted to determine the minimum effective size for vortex generators. Langley organized an aggressive experimental program to obtain detailed information on the mechanism by which vortex generators reenergize the turbulent boundary layer and prevent separation. The resulting optimization to a sub-boundary-layer scale provided a major breakthrough in the fundamental understanding of the nature of vortex generator flow control and potential applications. The initial laboratory experiments were conducted in the Langley 20- by 28-Inch Shear-Flow Control Tunnel.

Following the exploratory tests, Langley discussed the results of the MVG research with the aircraft industry, and this peaked industry's interest in the MVGs quite significantly. A cooperative investigation with McDonnell Douglas in 1991 focused on the impact of MVGs on the high-lift performance of a flapped wing model in the Langley Low-Turbulence Pressure Tunnel (LTPT). The model was a McDonnell Douglas two-dimensional, single-flap, three-element airfoil. The use of MVGs to eliminate flow separation enabled the flap configurations to be more aggressive than conventional design would permit. The results showed that the more aggressive design with MVGs dramatically enhanced aerodynamic performance including a 10-percent increase in lift, a 50-percent decrease in drag, and a 100-percent increase in lift-to-drag ratio. For commercial transport aircraft, these positive aerodynamic effects could lead to improved landing performance with the simpler (more economical) single-flap design and, more importantly in many instances, to reduced approach noise (i.e., less engine power to achieve the same lift). Another practical benefit of using the MVGs for high-lift applications is that they are small enough to be stowed with the flap at cruise and hence do not increase the cruise drag.

In addition to industry interests in applications to commercial transport aircraft, the Langley-developed MVG concept has also been applied by the general aviation industry to enhance performance and high-lift characteristics. In a cooperative investigation with

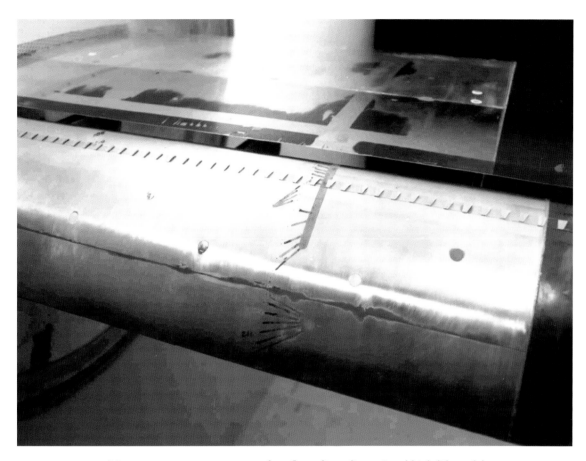

*Microvortex generators mounted on flap of two-dimensional high-lift model
in the Langley Low-Turbulence Pressure Tunnel. View is looking upstream.*

Gulfstream V uses microvortex generators on outer wing for enhanced performance.

Microvortex generators on flap element of Piper Malibu aircraft.

Close-up view of microvortex generators.

Gulfstream Aerospace Corporation, tests were conducted in the LTPT to improve the Gulfstream V high-lift geometry using microvortex generators in 1994 and 1995. In addition, during flight tests conducted in 1996 and 1997 by Gulfstream, the microvortex generators outperformed conventional vortex generators for controlling shock-induced separation. The Gulfstream V now incorporates MVGs on the outboard upper surfaces of its wing for enhanced cruise performance. With the MVGs installed, the Gulfstream V was able to achieve a higher maximum cruise speed, extend its operational range capability, and exhibit better controllability. The enhanced aerodynamic performance provided by MVGs allowed Gulfstream to meet their technical goals and assure a timely and successful product. As previously discussed, the Gulfstream V aircraft has set numerous domestic and world speed and performance records and was named the winner of the 1997 Collier Trophy presented by the National Aeronautic Association.

Another highly successful application of MVG technology involved a transfer of design information to the New Piper Aircraft, Inc., in 1996. New Piper applied the MVG concept to enhance the low-speed, high-lift characteristics of the Malibu Meridian aircraft. MVGs were mounted along the leading edge of the wing trailing-edge flap to enhance flow turning and avoid separation. This technology enabled the Piper Malibu Meridian aircraft to easily pass the FAA certification requirements for stall speed (below 61 knots), which it had previously not met.

COMPOSITES

Background

Weight reduction has been a critical goal since the earliest days of crewed flight. Following initial applications of wood, fabric, and wire for structural components, the aircraft industry made a major transition to aluminum and all-metal aircraft. As a result of this approach to structural design, modern civil aircraft are designed with greatly reduced aircraft operating empty weight to achieve a significant payload to weight fraction that contributes directly to aircraft flight efficiency. In the transition to aluminum components, the industry accepted the significant costs that were required to retool and modify its manufacturing processes.

In the continual quest for reduced weight, aircraft manufacturers began to introduce applications of nonmetallic materials, such as fiberglass-reinforced plastic composites. For example, initial applications of structural fiberglass parts by Boeing on commercial transports started with about 200 square feet on the Boeing 707 for the radome and small closure fairings. By the time the Boeing 747 was introduced, the application of fiberglass parts had grown to over 10,000 square feet, including the radome, wing leading- and trailing-edge panels, flaps, fairings, and control surfaces. Beginning in about 1962, composite sandwich parts made from fiberglass-epoxy materials were applied to aircraft such as the Boeing 727. Major operational issues for composite structures, such as lightning protection, were satisfied by the bonding of aluminum foil on the inner surfaces and aluminum flame spray on the outer surfaces of structural parts. The construction technique used for composites at that time consisted of tailoring the glass fabric to the required shape, pouring liquid resin onto the fabric, spreading and sweeping the resin to impregnate the fabric, vacuum bagging the part and tool, and curing in an oven or autoclave. This wet layup method was very labor intensive.

The next major advance in composites was a transition to graphite composite secondary aircraft structures, such as wing control surfaces, wing trailing and leading edges, vertical fin and stabilizer control surfaces, and landing gear doors. The obvious benefits of lightweight, strong composites have historically been tempered by issues regarding fabrication costs, potential degradation in characteristics due to environmental effects, impact damage resistance and repairability, and potential environmental effects of composites following aircraft accidents.

The transition from manufacturing aluminum aircraft components to composite structures involved the fabrication of filaments of graphite, fiberglass, or DuPont Kevlar material arranged in a matrix of epoxy, polyimide, or aluminum. The filament materials are imbedded in a matrix at specified angles in successive layers, and they can develop very high strength and stiffness. Potential weight savings come about because of the high strength-to-weight and stiffness-to-weight properties of the composite material. Cost reductions come about from the fewer number of pieces that make up the components and from the fewer number of fasteners required for assembly. The fabrication of composites was initially accomplished with hand layups similar to those used in the fiberglass construction of boats or automobiles. Currently, advanced fabrication techniques, including tape placement and stitching technology, are being applied by industry.

Research contributions of the Langley Research Center have played a key role in the widespread acceptance and application of emerging composite technology for both civil and military aircraft. Langley is the Agency's Center of Excellence for Structures and Materials in recognition of its long history of research into innovative composites, polymers, metallics, and structures for aircraft and spacecraft. By conducting fundamental and applied research with its industry partners, Langley has accelerated the use of composites and the confidence in the safety and economic feasibility of such applications.

Langley Research and Development Activities

The Langley Research Center has been conducting composites research with industry since 1970. The initial impetus for more aggressive focused research on composite structures came in 1972 during meetings of industry, universities, and government representatives involved in a project known as RECAST. One of the highlights of the study was the recognition that a major obstacle to large-scale applications of composites technology was the high initial costs of introducing the new materials because there was no large volume of production due to limited applications; no widespread applications were being used because the total cost was too high. To break this cycle, the RECAST participants suggested three approaches. First, components of advanced composites should be fabricated and tested under realistic service conditions; second, the application of composites to new designs should be encouraged; and third, in-depth studies should be undertaken to develop the technology and provide databases for designers. In response to these recommendations, NASA included composites in its Advanced Transport Technology Program as well as other research involving spacecraft, engines, and basic research. Early leaders of the composite research at Langley included Richard R. Heldenfels, Roger A. Anderson, William A. Brooks, Jr., George W. Brooks, Robert Leonard, Richard A. Pride, and Eldon E. Mathauser. Key researchers included Marvin B. Dow, H. Benson Dexter, Michael F. Card, John G. Davis, Jr., and Martin M. Mikulas, Jr.

One of the first efforts in the Langley composites research program was to reduce potential risk and build industry confidence through a series of contracts for the development, fabrication, and testing of aircraft secondary structures. Secondary aircraft components are relatively lightly loaded, and not critical to the safety of flight. Langley started the NASA Composites Flight Service Program in 1972 and installed over 300 experimental composite components on commercial transports and rotorcraft. The research was focused on assessing the potential environmental impacts on composite characteristics during typical flight service operations. Working under Langley contracts, Boeing designed and fabricated graphite-epoxy wing spoilers on twenty-seven Boeing 737 aircraft, Lockheed applied seven Kevlar fuselage fairing panels on three L-1011 aircraft, and Douglas applied graphite-epoxy material for the upper, aft rudder segment on ten DC-10 aircraft. Douglas also used a boron-aluminum composite skin for a panel on the aft pylon adjacent to the engine on three DC-10s. In addition to these civil applications, Langley also sponsored a boron-epoxy composite reinforcement for the aft aluminum tailcone of an Army CH-54B helicopter, and a boron-epoxy reinforcement for the aluminum center wing box of two Air Force C-130 transports. By the end of 1977, these flight experiments had involved considerable flight time and yielded valuable experience in composites technology and design. For example, the graphite-epoxy of the 108 spoilers on the 737 aircraft had accumulated over 921,000 flight hours in 4.5 years. Overall, the 142 composite components accumulated in excess of 1 million flight hours around the world with 17 operators. No significant incidents occurred nor damage detected in any of the flight components. Maintenance was reported as less than that required on similar standard aluminum parts. Several instances occurred in which the graphite-epoxy spoilers received sufficient damage in service to require repairs. The repairs were made by removing the spoilers on the aircraft, cutting out the damaged area, replacing honeycomb core as needed, and replacing graphite-epoxy plies. The repair process was straightforward and easily accomplished. The Langley program tracked the performance of these and the other composite parts in its Flight Service Program for over 15 years, and some of the parts were still in operational service at the end of the 1990s. By 1991, over 5.3 million flight hours had been achieved on 350 composite components.

When the NASA Aircraft Energy Efficiency (ACEE) Program began in fiscal year 1976, the Langley Research Center focused its composites research for aircraft into two main areas: supporting base technology efforts and the ACEE Composites Program.

Environmental Exposure Effects

In early technology studies within the Base Technology Program, Langley researchers conducted efforts on environmental effects on materials, characterization of material quality, development and validation of design and analysis methods, structural durability, impact sensitivity, and potential hazardous electrical effects of carbon fiber.

The issue of potential operational environmental effects on the behavior of composite materials and aircraft components was the subject of great concern for both airline manufacturers and airline operators. The question of long-term environmental durability for composites was viewed as the major undetermined issue for widespread acceptance and application. Led by Richard A. Pride, Langley researchers conducted extensive studies involving in-flight service experiences and ground-based outdoor exposures of composite materials at various worldwide locations. The focus of these studies was the extent of composites degradation due to ultraviolet light effects and moisture gained by diffusion. Individual composite panel specimens were mounted in racks and deployed on rooftops of airline buildings at a number of airports around the world so that maximum exposure to the airport environment occurred. The test panels were deployed domestically at Langley, Seattle, San Francisco, San Diego, Honolulu, and internationally at

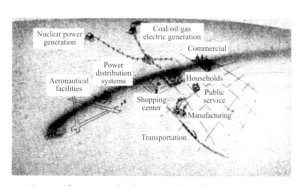

Areas of concern for free graphite fiber dispersion following an aircraft crash and burn incident.

Frankfurt, Germany, and Sao Paulo, Brazil. After exposures of either one or three years, individual panels were removed from the racks and shipped to Langley for testing and valuation. At Langley, the panels were weighed to determine moisture absorption, and scanning electron micrographs were made to evaluate the composition of the specimen. Flexure, compression, and shear stress tests were also performed. No significant degradation was observed in residual strength tests after 3-year outdoor exposures for all panels tested. These results, presented at a major NASA conference at Langley on Advanced Transport Technology in 1978, coupled with the industry flight tests of the ACEE Program, provided significant confidence for future applications of composites. Additional tests were conducted after 5, 7, and 10 years of outdoor exposure with no significant reduction in strength.

A major issue regarding the large-scale application of composites in the early 1970s was the potential effect of carbon fiber on electrical components. Laboratory tests and the accidental release of long free fibers from a carbon fiber plant had caused widespread concern that the properties of carbon fibers could have a unique adverse economic impact on the Nation. Carbon fibers are electrical conductors, and free fibers in contact with an unprotected electrical circuit can cause shorts, electrical arcing, and resistive loading. Fibers that are confined in a plastic matrix do not pose any electrical hazard. However, concern existed over ways by which free carbon fibers could be released into the atmosphere in the aftermath of an aircraft crash and fire. The uncontrolled release of carbon fibers might occur if the binding matrix material was burned away cleanly and the fibers became airborne following a crash.

Concern over the potentially disastrous effects of free graphite fibers reached the highest national levels (including the White House), and the future of composite graphite structures was suddenly examined with intensity. In view of the widespread applications and plans for greatly expanded uses of composites within the aviation, automotive, housing, leisure, and other industries, this issue posed a threat that could have terminated any application of composites. In July 1977, the Office of Science and Technology Policy (OSTP) directed that several government agencies undertake immediate studies to justify or disprove the serious concerns regarding composites. A national program on carbon fiber effects was established in 1978, and responsibilities for activities in the program were delegated to nine individual agencies for specific application areas—for example, the Department of Transportation was assigned responsibility for the automotive issues, the Department of Energy was responsible for the vulnerability and protection of power generation, and NASA was charged with responsibility to determine the impact of graphite fibers released from civil aircraft. NASA was also charged with management support to OSTP for the program.

Responsibility for conducting the NASA study was assigned to the Langley Research Center under its Director, Donald P. Hearth. Richard R. Heldenfels, Director for Structures, then appointed Robert J. Huston as program manager of the Graphite Fibers Risk Analysis Program Office. Under Huston's leadership, a team of about 20 researchers worked for 3 years; they ultimately determined that the issue was not a problem. The Langley program investigated the problem in two areas. The first area was to quantify the potential problem of using composites on civil aircraft. The work included defining the ways by which carbon fibers could be released in the event of an aircraft crash and subsequent fire, the propagation of extremely fine fibers away from the fire site, and the vulnerability of electrical components, especially in other aircraft and in the surrounding area. The second research area, in parallel with this activity, was to develop materials that alleviate or eliminate the electrical hazard. The materials studies included modifications or changes in the binding system which would prevent the release of fiber following a fire and the development of nonconductive fibers to replace graphite.

Huston was assisted by deputy program manager Thomas A. Bartron, and technical element leaders Wolf Elber, Israel Taback, Vernon L. Bell, Jr., Richard A. Pride, Arthur L. Newcomb, Ansel J. Butterfeild, Jerry L. Humble, and Karen R. Credeur. The Program Office sponsored and coordinated 19 studies conducted by NASA Centers, private contractors, the aviation industry (including Boeing, Lockheed, and Douglas), and other government agencies. The responsibility of the industry was to provide data for the analysis with the unstated objective of ensuring they were fully briefed on progress and analysis. Langley contracts required industry to deliver detailed crash data on every jet transport crash worldwide. One of the companies (Lockheed) then turned the data into statistical rates on the probabilities of a crash burn incident, including where (enroute, x miles from a major airport, etc.), when (time of day, takeoff or landing), how (crash burn, fraction of structure consumed), and what (size of aircraft, fuel load). The Langley team then used the supplied data in its analysis. In addition to its technical leadership, NASA contributed the major funding required (about $10 million) for the in-house and contracted studies from its own research funds.

The results of the studies were reported in over 50 technical reports by NASA and other agencies. The scope of activities included probability and risk analyses, outdoor experiments, modeling of events, visits to potentially susceptible sites including hospitals, and nuclear power plants. In one study, for example, Pride directed an investigation of the realistic release of carbon fibers by burning about 45 kg of carbon fiber composite aircraft structural components in five individual large-scale, outdoor aviation jet fuel fire tests that included detailed measurements of the fiber physical and release characteristics.

The Langley investigation projected a dramatic increase in the use of carbon composites in civil aircraft and developed technical data to support the risk assessment. Personal injury was found to be extremely unlikely. In 1993, the year chosen as a focus for the study, the expected annual cost of damage caused by released carbon fibers was only about $1,000. Even the worst-case carbon fiber incident simulated (costing $178,000 once in 34,000 years) was relatively low-cost compared with the cost of a typical air transport accident. With regard to potential power distribution outages, one outage induced by carbon fiber was expected to occur for every 200,000 to 1,000,000 outages caused by lightning or tree contact.

On the basis of these projections, the NASA study concluded that the issue was a nonproblem—exploitation of composites should continue, additional protection of avionics was unnecessary, and development of alternate materials specifically to overcome this problem was not justified. Three independent assessments of the risk all predicted very low value damage to the public and local governments (relative to the cost of the crashed airplane itself). All three cost projections were 3 or 4 orders of magnitude under a risk level that would cause concern. The results of the study, presented in 1980 and 1981 in three public hearings, a formal NASA publication for OSTP (see bibliography), and a presentation to the Director of the Civil Preparedness Agency (now the Federal Emergency Management Agency), are regarded as a pivotal and extremely significant contribution to the Nation's application of composite materials to civil aircraft of the 1990s. The final OSTP report concluded "The economic loss risk from the accidental release of carbon fibers is so low as to be clearly acceptable on a national basis and does not justify follow-on work to develop alternate materials." The Langley Research Center clearly played a key role in eliminating one of the most serious obstacles to the growth and use of composite materials.

Aircraft Energy Efficiency Composites Program

Under the sponsorship of the NASA Aircraft Energy Efficiency (ACEE) Program, composite research and applications were investigated by The Boeing Company, Douglas Aircraft Company, and Lockheed Aircraft Corporation with coordination and technical oversight provided by Langley. The overall objective of the ACEE Composite Primary Aircraft Structures Program was to develop and conduct experiments that would lead to applications of composites for small, secondary aircraft components in the early 1980s followed by more complex larger scale structures through the 1990s, with the goal of providing weight reductions resulting in fuel savings over 15 percent.

In 1978, the Langley Aircraft Energy Efficiency Project Office was headed by Robert W. Leonard, and leadership for the NASA Composite Primary Structures Project Office was provided by Louis F. Vosteen. Langley planned a phased composite development research program that would incrementally lead to the design, fabrication, and test of a large-segment

Composite elevators in flight evaluations on Boeing 727 during ACEE Program.

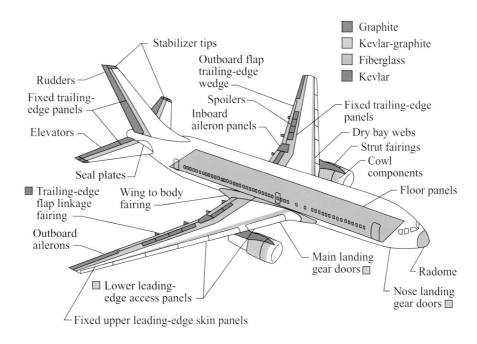

Use of composite materials on Boeing 767 aircraft.

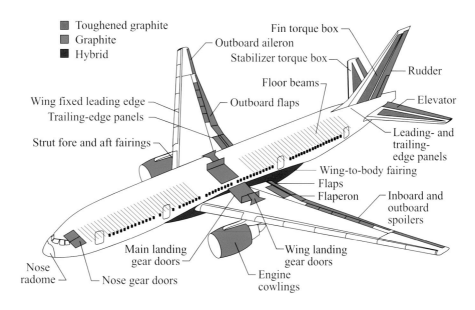

Use of composite materials on Boeing 777 aircraft.

wing and fuselage representative of future transports. The first phase involved secondary structures, including elevators for the Boeing 727, ailerons for the Lockheed L-1011, and rudder segments for the McDonnell Douglas DC-10. Later, medium-sized primary structures were created in the second phase of the program, including a horizontal stabilizer structural box for the 737 and vertical fins for the L-1011 and DC-10.

In addition to weight reduction for aircraft components (projected to be from 10 to 30 percent), it was anticipated that a significant reduction in component parts (40 to 60 percent) such as fasteners could be obtained. The principal role of the integrated studies was to define the specific technologies that would be required in order to proceed with a large primary composite structure such as the wing of future transports. Industry's experience in the studies would cover all critical aspects of composite applications including manufacturing, FAA certification, and flight assessments.

The research plan for the ACEE Composites Program called for the components to be flown on passenger-carrying aircraft in normal airline service; therefore, the new composite structures had to comply with FAA certification requirements; the industry also utilized production-quality tooling to manufacture the components. The benefits of composite components became evident in the ACEE Program: the DC-10 upper rudder segment saved about 30 percent in weight over the aluminum rudder; the L-1011 vertical fin saved about 25 percent in weight; and the Boeing 727 elevators used almost 50 percent fewer ribs and 70 percent fewer fasteners than conventional structures.

When Boeing started design work on the 767 in 1971, the aircraft had been conceived as an all-aluminum aircraft, but the timing of the NASA ACEE Composites Program permitted expanded experience for Boeing, which resulted in extensive applications of composites for the 767, as well as the 757. Even though no primary composite structures were utilized, the weight savings for the 767 was an impressive 2,000 lb. Applications of composites by McDonnell Douglas to its MD-80 and MD-11 transports followed. Numerous applications also occurred for derivative Boeing 737 and 747 aircraft. Stimulated by the successes of the ACEE activities, industry began efforts on advanced composite wings and primary composite structures. Boeing's experience base and further developments of composite technology led to incorporation of an even higher degree of composites for the Boeing 777. The first major use of composites for primary structures of a U.S. commercial transport was for the empennage of the 777.

The stimulation of the ACEE Program is believed to have accelerated the application of composites to commercial transports by approximately 5 to 10 years. NASA research and development in the ACEE era (1975 to 1986) produced over 600 technical reports. In addition to technology advances in performance prediction and manufacturing processes, a significant increase in confidence was obtained regarding issues such as durability, cost verification, FAA certification, and airline acceptance. The ACEE Program was primarily responsible for the impact of Langley contributions to the application of composites to commercial aircraft of the 1990s. However, composites research activities at Langley that followed ACEE, which ended in 1985, have had a marked influence on the potential near-term applications of composites in the new millennium. In particular, now that issues regarding the environmental durability have been successfully addressed for composites, the focus of research in

Composite upper aft rudder flown on McDonnell Douglas DC-10 in ACEE Program.

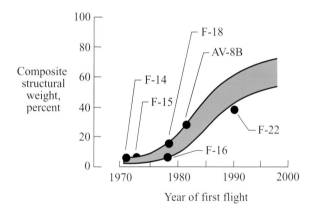

Use of composite materials on U.S. military aircraft.

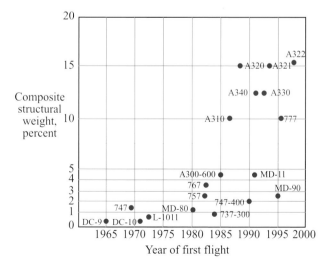

Use of composites in civil commercial transports.

the late 1980s and 1990s has turned to the all-important issue of cost. Whereas military applications of composites have been very aggressive (for example, the F-22 has about 38 percent of its structural weight in composites), applications to the commercial transports area have been relatively low. The most aggressive U.S. commercial transport application to date has been the Boeing 777, which has about 10 percent of its structural weight in composites. If commercial aircraft applications are to increase, cost impact factors must be significantly improved.

Without question, the ACEE Program provided the airframe companies with important technology, but the program ended without accomplishing its original goal of developing composite primary wing and fuselage structures. Without a NASA technology program, industry lacked the confidence to proceed with production of high-risk primary structures. The barrier issues were high acquisition costs and low damage tolerance. Cost data extrapolated from the ACEE development contracts showed that wings and fuselages would cost considerably more than aluminum structures. The industry position on production commitment was that composite primary structures must be demonstrated to cost less than aluminum structures. Low damage tolerance remained a characteristic of composite structures despite major efforts to develop and use toughened matrix resins. Industry wanted robust structures able to withstand the rigors of flight service with minimal damage.

Advanced Composite Technology Program

By 1985, research engineers at Langley were holding conferences to explore the potential of textile composites, based on approaches similar to those used in the textile industry, to provide barrier-breakthrough technology. By 1987, funds were available for a modest expansion of the Langley composites program. A NASA Research Announcement (NRA) was issued seeking proposals for innovative approaches to cost-effective fabrication, enhanced damage tolerance designs, and improved analysis methods. Forty-eight proposals were submitted by companies and universities, and 15 proposals were selected for contracts. Then, in 1988, NASA launched its Advanced Composites Technology (ACT) Program, a major new program for composite wing and fuselage primary structures. The program incorporated the existing NRA contracts with significant increases in funding for wing and fuselage hardware developments. A Structures Technology Program Office at Langley provided management for the ACT Program. Under the direction of Charles P. Blankenship, John G. Davis, Jr., was the Program Manager of ACT, and leading researchers included James H. Starnes, Jr., Marvin B. Dow, H. Benson Dexter, and Norman J. Johnston. The 15 previously mentioned contracts were awarded by Langley in 1989 to commercial and military airframe manufacturers, materials developers and suppliers, universities, and government laboratories. The program approach was to develop materials, structural mechanics methodology, design concepts, and fabrication procedures that offered the potential to make composite structures cost-effective compared with aluminum structures. Goals for the ACT program included 30–50 percent weight reduction, 20–25 percent acquisition cost reduction, and the scientific basis for predicting materials and structures performance.

Phase A of the Program, conducted from 1989 to 1991, focused on the identification and evaluation of innovative manufacturing technologies and structural concepts. Industry participants included Northrop, Lockheed Corporation, McDonnell Douglas Corporation, The Boeing Company, and Grumman Aerospace. At the end of Phase A, the leading wing and fuselage design concepts were selected for further development in Phase B of the Program from 1992 to 1995. Two major fabrication technologies emerged from Phase A as the most promising approaches to manufacturing cost-effective composite primary structures. These two approaches were the stitched textile preform and automated tow placement manufacturing methods. Each method emphasized rapid fiber placement, near-net-shape preform fabrication, part count minimization, and matching the technologies to the specific structural configurations and requirements. The objective of Phase B was to continue the evolution of design concepts by using the concurrent engineering process; selecting the leading structural concept; and designing, building, and testing subscale components. In this phase, Boeing and Lockheed focused on fuselage technology, while McDonnell Douglas focused on wing technology. Phase C of the ACT Program, begun in 1995, was to design, build, and test major components of the airframe and to demonstrate the technology readiness for applications in the next generation of subsonic commercial transport aircraft. The original program plan called for the contribution of Boeing to be a complete fuselage barrel with a window belt and a wing box at the wing-fuselage intersection. The structure was to have been pressure tested as part of the engineering verification process. Unfortunately, the funding for ACT was reduced and forced cancellation of the composite fuselage studies. McDonnell Douglas, meanwhile, focused on the successful development, fabrication, and testing of an advanced composite wing, as discussed later. The ACT Program ended in fiscal year 1997.

Textile Composites

In the 1980s, researchers looked to textile composites as breakthrough technology. Supporters argued for new concepts that would use knitting, weaving, braiding, and through-the-thickness stitching for reinforcement and use existing U.S. textile manufacturing technology for cost-efficiency. An outstanding summary by Dow and Dexter of progress and details of textile composite research by NASA during the period from 1985 to 1997 is recommended to the reader (see bibliography).

Under the leadership of Marvin B. Dow, Langley conducted and sponsored extensive research on woven, braided, knitted, and stitched (textile) composites in the NASA ACT Program in the period from 1985 to 1997. The major objective of the studies was to develop textile composites technology approaches that would provide a paradigm shift in cost and damage tolerance to overcome barrier issues. One such barrier issue is the impact performance of textile composites. Low-velocity impacts from tools, hail, runway debris, and ground equipment can damage resin matrix composites with carbon fibers. With sufficient kinetic energy, these impacts can damage the composite without readily visible evidence and can significantly reduce the strength. Current regulations require composite structures to carry ultimate load with nonvisible impact damage. Textile composites are potentially more resistant to impact damage than traditional laminated composites fabricated using prepreg unidirectional tape. In 1994, Clarence C. Poe, Jr., of Langley conducted studies of conventional tape laminates and textile composites, providing detailed design information on their characteristics.

Research by H. Benson Dexter in 1994 on braided composite materials demonstrated that a braided-woven stiffener wing concept could meet damage tolerance goals and be designed and fabricated with a cost-effective process. Braiding is an automated process for obtaining near-net-shape preforms for fabrication of components for structural application. Stiffeners, wing spars, floor beams, and fuselage frames are examples of potential applications of cost-effective braided composites. Test results on wing panels fabricated from stitched skins and stitched-stiffener preforms obtained at Langley and McDonnell Douglas indicated that damage-tolerance requirements could be met. Accordingly, stitched panels with braided stiffeners were tested to assure that braided stiffeners also satisfied damage requirements.

Braid-stiffened wing-panel preforms were fabricated by Langley from dry-stitched skin and braided stiffeners obtained from Fiber Innovations, Inc., Norwood, Massachusetts, followed by a resin film infusion (RFI) process by McDonnell Douglas. Wing panels were intentionally impacted on the skin side midway between stiffeners, directly beneath a stiffener, or at the flange edge of a stiffener. Impact energies were selected to produce the onset of visual damage. All impacted panels exceeded the impact design goal and failed without any skin-stiffener separation.

One major breakthrough in Dow's program was the use of advanced stitching methods to fabricate large composite structures. Various types of textile composites were thoroughly tested, but it was stitching, combined with RFI, that showed the greatest potential for overcoming the cost and damage tolerance barriers to wing structures. Assembling carbon fabric preforms (precut pieces of material) with closely spaced through-the-thickness stitching provided essential reinforcement for damage tolerance. Also, stitching made it possible to incorporate the various elements—wing skin, stiffeners, ribs and spars—into an integral structure that would eliminate thousands of mechanical fasteners. Although studies showed that stitching had the potential for cost-effective manufacturing, the critical need was for machines capable of stitching large wing preforms at higher speeds.

A primitive single-needle stitching machine, resembling a scaled-up version of a household sewing machine, was the first prototype used by Langley to determine the benefits of stitched composites. This initial research identified that stitched composites offered better levels of damage tolerance than conventional laminated composites. This single-needle sewing machine was used in exploratory research on stitched composites. In 1994, a computer-controlled single-needle stitching machine capable of stitching dry high-performance textile materials (such as graphite and glass) was designed and built for the Materials Division at Langley. The stitching machine was capable of stitching a planform area of 4 by 6 ft with thicknesses greater than 1.5 in. using a lock stitch, and programming stitching in any direction (including curves) within the planform area. The machine was capable of stitching with

Lower-stitched wing cover for 42-ft-span structural test wing.

a wide variety of needle and bobbin threads, such as polyester, nylon, DuPont Kevlar, and carbon. A wide variety of preform sizes were fabricated and delivered to McDonnell Douglas for RFI processing to produce test specimens for evaluation at NASA Langley.

In the stitched-RFI process, layers of dry carbon fabric are stacked to form the wing structural elements and are stitched with through-the-thickness Kevlar threads. RFI of the preform with epoxy resin followed by autoclave curing completes the process of making an integral wing cover.

Results obtained with test panels and a small wing-box test article indicated that the process produced composite aircraft parts with outstanding damage tolerance. The process has the potential for major reductions in the labor content of manufacturing composite wing primary structures. However, demonstrating a stitching machine with the size and speed required for cost-effective fabrication of full-scale composite wings for commercial transport aircraft was critically important.

One of the first demonstration sections was a 12-ft-long wing stub box that was fabricated by McDonnell Douglas and tested at the Langley Research Center in July 1995. The wing stub box demonstrated that the stitching-RFI concept could be used to make the thick composite structures needed for heavily loaded wings. The successful test of the stub box proved the structure and damage tolerance of a stitched wing.

NASA awarded Boeing (subsequent to the merger of Boeing and McDonnell Douglas) a contract to develop a large machine capable of stitching entire wing covers for commercial transport aircraft. This high-speed, multineedle machine, known as the Advanced Stitching Machine (ASM), was designed and built under the NASA ACT Wing Program. Under subcontract to Boeing, Ingersoll Milling Machine Company, Rockford, Illinois, was selected to design and build the ASM. The advanced stitching heads of the ASM were designed and built by Pathe Technologies, Inc., Irvington, New Jersey. Concurrent with the development of the large stitching machine, NASA and Boeing proceeded with a building block approach to demonstrate the design and manufacture of stitched-RFI wing structures.

Ingersoll's machine was capable of stitching a contoured wing preform 50-ft long and 8-ft wide. Following extensive checkout tests, the machine was dismantled, moved, and reassembled at the McDonnell Douglas stitching facility in Huntington Beach, California. When the stitching was completed on the machine, the still flexible wing skin panel was put into an outer mold line (OML) tool that provided the shape of the outside surface of the wing. A film of resin was laid on the OML form, followed by the composite skin panel and the tools that defined the inner mold line. These elements were put into a plastic bag from which the air was drawn out, creating a vacuum. The materials were then placed in an autoclave, where heat and pressure were applied to let the resin spread throughout the carbon fiber material. After heating to 350° F for 2 hours, the wing skin panel took on its final hardened shape.

Panels were stitched on the ASM to be used as test articles in a full-scale ground test of a composite wing representative of a transport aircraft. The Stitched-RFI Composite Wing Program was successfully completed with ground testing of a 42-ft-long wing box. The box was tested in the Langley Structures and Materials Laboratory under the leadership of Dawn

Pretest photograph of 42-ft-span wing structure at Langley.

Tests of 42-ft-long wing box.

Jegley in 2000, and the box failed at 97 percent of design ultimate load (145-percent design limit load). Boeing is seriously considering using this technology in the next generation of aircraft.

Boeing named its new Stitched Composite Development Center after NASA Langley researcher Marvin B. Dow in honor of his contributions to stitched composites research and, specifically, to the ASM. Dow spent the last 25 years of his 40-year NACA/NASA career in pursuit of the application of advanced composite materials on commercial transport aircraft. He is the first NASA employee honored in the naming of a corporate facility. His work on composites led to the early flight testing of graphite-epoxy rudders on the McDonnell Douglas DC-10 commercial transport aircraft, the ACEE structures for the DC-10, Boeing 737, and C-130 aircraft, and his pioneering and visionary research on textile reinforcement concepts such as weaving, braiding, knitting, stitching, and resin transfer processes introduced the world to innovative new fabrication techniques. The ASM—made possible by Dow's long-term dedication—is expected to revolutionize the way aircraft wing structures are fabricated in the future.

Fundamental Research and Technology in Composites

In addition to the foregoing activities, Langley's contribution to understanding composite failure mechanisms has been widely recognized. In the late 1970s, a series of landmark tests of composite panels under impact were conducted by Marvin D. Rhodes in the Structures and Materials Laboratory. The results stimulated design, analysis, and test activities, led by James H. Starnes, to reduce impact sensitivity and understand new failure modes in stiffened plates and shells. Langley was also a key contributor to toughened resin research led by Norman J. Johnston and Terry St. Clair. Contractual work, sponsored by Langley, led to industry development of resins used in today's structural applications. In yet another area of research, Charles E. Harris and Clarence C. Poe, Jr., led critical research efforts on fracture mechanics that included analysis methods and databases. Much of the work just described has been recognized by citations to Langley throughout Military Handbook 17 on composites.

Composites for General Aviation

The general aviation community has long been a user of composites technology, especially for small personal-owner aircraft and home-built aircraft. Led by innovative designers such as Burt Rutan, this sector of aviation has enthusiastically embraced the benefits of composites technology, and although NASA research has not been directed specifically at this class of aircraft before the AGATE program, Langley has ensured that appropriate communications with the small aircraft community regarding NASA technology has occurred through briefings at national meetings, such as the Experimental Aircraft Association's Oshkosh convention.

Beech Aircraft (now Raytheon Aircraft Company) made extensive use of composites in the Beech Starship, as well as new business aircraft, the Premier I and the Horizon. These applications have made use of information and results from the ACEE, ACT, and AGATE

Certified composite aircraft, Lancair Columbia and Cirrus SR20.

Composite Programs. The general aviation industry is now the leader in the use of composites in production aircraft. The FAA is currently in the certification process for 19 new aircraft with significant use of composites. The Lancair Columbia 300 and the Cirrus SR20, which have benefited from Langley's AGATE Program, are the two most recent all-composite GA aircraft to receive FAA certification. The NASA Small Business Innovation Research (SBIR) Program has played a major role in numerous technologies used on these aircraft, including the development of low-cost composite manufacturing processes.

Led by the efforts of Bruce J. Holmes and William T. Freeman, Jr., one of the most significant accomplishments of general aviation research at Langley was the 1998 publication entitled *Material Qualification Methodology for Epoxy-Based Prepreg Composite Material Systems.* This publication documents the breakthrough process that allows airframe manufacturers to procure certified composite materials from vendors in the same manner that they were able to procure metals for decades.

In the decades since the introduction of synthetic composite materials for use in aerospace applications, the cost of materials qualification has inhibited expanded uses. Much of this cost has resulted from the extensive testing required by the FAA. Each airframe manufacturer intending to apply a composite material to a product has been required to submit detailed materials property reports to the FAA, regardless of whether they or other manufacturers had previously certified the same materials. Long ago, resulting from sustained statistical confidence in the ability of materials suppliers to meet common production standards, industry and FAA dispensed with such testing requirements for aluminum and other metals.

The previously mentioned NASA publication outlines a materials qualification method that has been accepted by the FAA and eliminates the need for repeated tests to qualify composite materials. Specifically, it provides the method by which composite material vendors can market composites that comply with FAA certification requirements. This qualification process eliminates the need for airframers to qualify composite materials for their aircraft certification programs. Airframe manufacturers dramatically reduce the costs associated with using composite materials by buying materials that are already certified or approved by the FAA. As a result, the cost of FAA certification of new composite airframes is reduced by more than $500,000 per material, and the time required for certification of a new airplane is reduced by more than 2 years. These reductions in certification time and costs will make the use of composite materials a viable choice for small and large companies and can help generate the market forces necessary to foster the revitalization of the general aviation industry.

Applications

The legacy of the ACEE Program and its significant contributions to the acceleration, acceptance, and application of advanced composites has become a well-known example of the value of Langley contributions to civil aviation. In the best tradition of NASA and industry cooperation and mutual interest, fundamental technology concepts were conceived, matured, and efficiently transferred to industry in a timely and professional manner. With the participation and guidance of Langley, industry was able to address numerous high-risk issues that posed serious obstacles to advances in the state of the art and applications. Widespread use of composites today by military aircraft and the continuing increase of composites used by civil aircraft are very visible reminders of the impact of this important technology contribution by the Langley Research Center.

FLUTTER

Background

Flutter is a dynamic aeroelastic phenomenon that involves the interactions of elastic and inertia forces of the structure with the aerodynamic forces produced by the airflow over the vehicle. It is a self-excited oscillation of the aircraft structure, where energy is absorbed from the airstream. When the elastic structure of the aircraft is disturbed at speeds below the flutter speed, the resulting oscillatory motions decay. However, when the structure is disturbed at speeds above the flutter speed, the oscillatory motions will abruptly increase in amplitude and can ultimately lead to catastrophic failure of the structure. In some instances, flutter oscillations are limited to just a single airplane component such as the wing, whereas in other instances the oscillations may be considerably more complex and involve coupling of wing, fuselage, and empennage vibrations.

The process of ensuring that an airplane is flutter free, commonly referred to as "flutter clearance," involves carefully planned analytical and experimental studies of the complex aeroelastic interactions that the aircraft will experience throughout its flight envelope with sufficient margins beyond the expected flight conditions. If a significant flutter tendency is discovered within the operational envelope, modifications to the aircraft structure must be made. The most common modification is to increase the most critical structural stiffness, which usually results in an increase in structural weight. This increase in weight is commonly referred to as the "flutter weight penalty." The civil and military aircraft industries conduct extensive analyses of flutter characteristics by using company-owned facilities and computer codes during aircraft development programs. Many of the design teams consult with Langley flutter experts and conduct proprietary or cooperative studies using the unique transonic aeroelastic testing capability provided by the Langley Transonic Dynamics Tunnel (TDT).

Flutter clearance testing in the TDT for military aircraft configurations has become a typical element in most aircraft programs, and the emphasis is placed along the developmental requirements for the specific aircraft program at that time. Unlike military airplane testing, TDT testing of civil aircraft frequently has a research element included in the test program in addition to developmental requirements. Many of these research activities include in-depth assessments of analytical codes, developing and evaluating advanced flutter control mechanisms, and determining the impact on aeroelastic phenomena of advanced aerodynamic or structural concepts such as airfoils for next-generation aircraft. Thus, civil aircraft flutter testing at Langley is typically more closely coupled to fundamental research than military aircraft studies. Tests of this type ensure that flutter or other undesirable aeroelastic problems that may exist for a new design are identified early enough in the design-development cycle that a solution (fix) can be identified in a timely manner with minimum impact on cost and schedule. In addition, wind-tunnel tests such as those described herein reduce the number of more costly flight flutter tests.

Transonic Dynamics Tunnel

Aeroelastic testing for flutter characteristics of civil aircraft using dynamically scaled aeroelastic models has taken place for decades in many subsonic wind tunnels within industry and academia. However, aeroelastic problems at higher subsonic speeds, near the transonic speed range, became more critical and increasingly difficult to predict as the performance and flight envelopes of aircraft expanded. In response to requests for a dedicated facility for testing large flutter models at relatively high Reynolds numbers and transonic speeds, NACA converted its existing Langley 19-Foot Transonic Pressure Tunnel into a new aeroelastic testing facility with a 16- by 16-ft test section that could operate at Mach numbers up to 1.20 with variable pressure conditions in either air or a heavy gas known as dichlorodifluoromethane (DuPont Freon 12 gas). Design of the new facility began in 1954, and the new Langley Transonic Dynamics Tunnel (TDT) began research operations under the management of Robert W. Boswinkle, Jr. and his assistant, D. William Connor, in early 1960. The first research tests by Jerome T. Foughner, Jr., and Norman S. Land began on February 5, 1960, with air as the testing medium. In March 1960, calibration tests were run with Freon 12 gas. Stagnation pressures in the TDT vary from near-vacuum to atmospheric conditions, which simulate variations in flight altitude. Testing in a heavy gas provides aeroelastic model scaling advantages because the density of Freon 12 gas is approximately four times that of air, and it has a speed of sound of about half that of air. As a result, scaled models for flutter testing can be made heavier than a scale model that would be tested in air. This approach makes the task of building a scale model with sufficient strength and appropriate structural frequencies much easier. In addition, the lower speed of sound of Freon 12 gas results in a model having lower frequencies of vibration; thereby more reaction time is provided for the test crew to back off from a potentially catastrophic test condition.

Today, the TDT is the world's premier wind tunnel for testing aeroelastically scaled models at transonic speeds. Operational since 1960, the tunnel has been the site of a wide variety of investigations ranging from flutter clearance tests to fundamental research on aeroelastic phenomena for military and civil aircraft. The scope of tests has included

1. Flutter clearance aimed at reducing risk and defining potential flutter problems and potential solutions through studies of aircraft components as well as complete configurations

2. Parametric variations of aircraft parameters in risk reduction tests to help guide flight tests

3. Studies to analyze and solve aeroelastic problems of specific configurations

4. Code calibration tests conducted in conjunction with flutter clearance tests to obtain data for validation and extensions of flutter prediction methods

In the 1980s, environmental concerns regarding the impact of Freon 12 gas caused NASA to convert the test medium for heavy gas testing in the TDT to R-134a, an inert gas with properties similar to those of DuPont Freon 12 gas.

Several types of model mount systems are used for tests in the TDT. Sidewall mount systems provide the capability of testing semispan wing models, which are generally easier to build and less expensive than full-span models. Conventional sting-support mount systems

Langley Transonic Dynamics Tunnel.

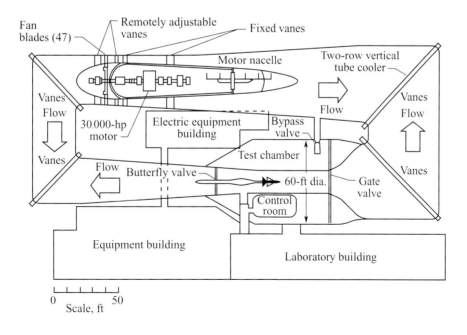

Plan view of TDT.

are also utilized for tests of full-span models or aircraft components. The most unique model mount system, however, is the cable mount system developed by Wilmer H. Reed III, which is most compatible with aeroelastically scaled full-span model testing. For this system, a full-span model is supported in the test section by a system of two cables routed through a system of pulleys. Additional cables are also provided for a "snubber" system that can be manually tightened during a model instability to prevent loss of the model. In a typical test program, it is customary to first "fly" a cheaper rigid or dummy model on the cable mount system to demonstrate the stability of the model configuration on the cable mount system prior to testing the expensive, flexible flutter model.

The TDT is equipped with several features that accommodate the unique challenges of flutter testing. For example, the tunnel is equipped with a group of four bypass valves connecting the test section area (plenum) to the opposite leg of the wind-tunnel circuit downstream of the drive fan motor. When opened, the bypass valves cause a rapid reduction in the test section Mach number and dynamic pressure. This feature is available for use when model flutter instabilities result in motions that could damage a model. In addition to potentially saving a model from catastrophic destruction, the rapid reduction in tunnel flow conditions reduces the inertial force of the model debris that might impact the tunnel drive motor fan blades. An additional feature of the tunnel is a model debris catch screen located upstream of the tunnel fan blades. The tunnel is also equipped with a pair of vanes on each side of the test section entrance cone. These vanes can be oscillated over a range of frequencies and amplitudes to generate sinusoidally varying vertical flow velocities for use in gust response studies. High-speed motion-picture cameras and video recorders and cameras are available to capture the rapidly occurring aeroelastic events so they can be viewed and analyzed later in slow-motion detail. The tunnel is also equipped with state-of-the-art instrumentation for high-frequency measurements and data acquisition and analysis. Finally, a sophisticated gas pumping and handling system is available for processing, reclaiming, liquefying, and storing the R-134a for reuse.

Flutter testing in the TDT requires the use of special models. A reduced-size, dynamically scaled aeroelastic model is essentially a mechanical analog of the full-scale aircraft. If the appropriate model-to-full-scale scaling relationships are used to design and construct a model, then its behavior during wind-tunnel tests can be used to accurately predict full-scale behavior. For example, if the flutter velocity is obtained for a properly designed, constructed, and tested model, then that value can be used with confidence to predict the full-scale flutter velocity.

For dynamically scaled aeroelastic models, there are several nondimensional parameters that must be identical for both the model and airplane to produce meaningful results. First, the geometry of the model must be the same as that of the full-scale aircraft. For instance, the angle of wing sweep and wing taper ratio must be identical between model and aircraft. The size of the model (the length scale factor) and the test conditions—fluid density, Mach number, velocity—at which the model is to represent the airplane are dictated by the size and operating envelope of the wind tunnel chosen for the test.

For flutter models, the three most important parameters in addition to size and geometry are Mach number, reduced frequency, and mass ratio. The Mach number is a speed-related parameter that is associated with the compressibility characteristics of the test or flight medium. If compressibility effects are deemed important, then the model must be tested at the same Mach number as the airplane. Reduced frequency can be thought of as a time-related parameter. Satisfying the requirements of this parameter ensures that the relative time scale for the model and airplane are the same and that the time required for events on the model can be correctly scaled to full-scale time. The ratio of model natural frequencies to full-scale frequencies depends on this parameter. Mass ratio is an altitude-related parameter that relates fluid density and structural mass. The mass of the model relative to the mass of the full-scale aircraft is determined by this parameter. The structural stiffness of the model is determined once the natural frequency and mass requirements are defined because they are interrelated.

Reynolds number, related to the fluid viscous, or fluid friction effects, is also an important test parameter. Matching this parameter between model and full scale is usually impossible; therefore, customary practice is to try to test at as high a Reynolds number as possible. Because the value of Reynolds number is directly proportional to model size and fluid density, the large size of the TDT and the high density of the R-134a test medium offer the possibility for relatively large Reynolds numbers for tests. For instances where the effects of the gravitational force are important, the requirements of a parameter known as the Froude

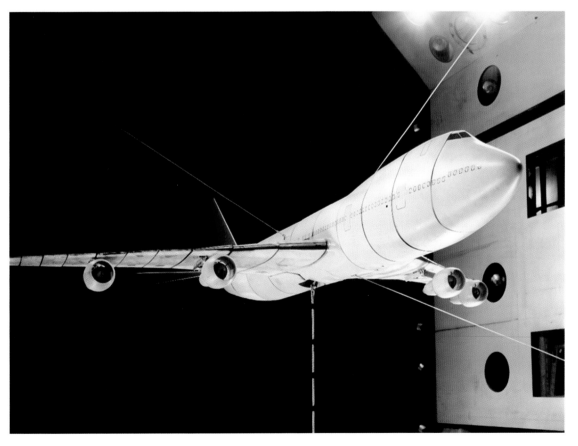

Flutter model of Boeing 747 aircraft with typical spar-pod construction.

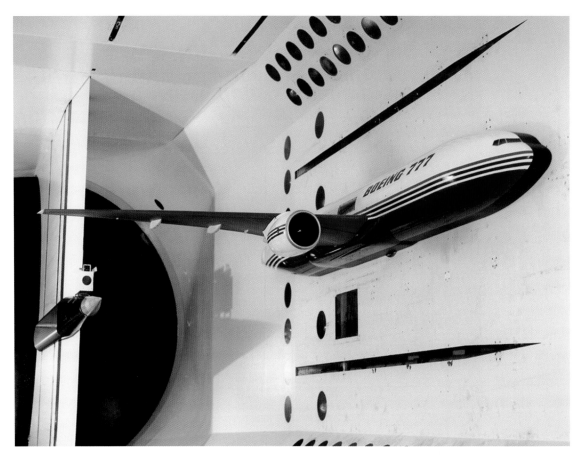

Model of Boeing 767 aircraft with continuous skin construction.

number must be satisfied. When compressibility effects are important, simultaneously satisfying the scaling requirements of Froude number and the other three parameters is generally impossible. This can be accomplished, however, by testing an approximately 0.25-scale model in heavy gas in the TDT. This feature is yet another unique one of this facility.

Flutter models of full-scale aircraft fall into essentially two categories: low-speed models and high-speed models. For low-speed models, compressibility effects are not important and the customary practice is to match only the reduced-frequency and mass-ratio parameters. Froude number simulation for these models is also possible. Models of this type are often fabricated by using what is referred to as spar- and segmented-pod construction. A central metal spar is designed to have the appropriately scaled level and distribution of structural stiffness. This spar is enclosed by a series of very lightweight pods, often fabricated from wood, that provide the proper external geometry. Because the span of a wing is segmented into a number of such pods, each pod is only connected to the spar at one or two points and not connected to adjacent pods. Thus, the pods do not contribute appreciably to the structural stiffness. Typically, the mass of the spar and pods is not sufficient to simulate the scaled mass of the full-scale structure and/or fuel; therefore, metal weights are attached inside the pods to provide proper inertia characteristics.

For high-speed flutter models, matching Mach number—in addition to matching the reduced-frequency and mass-ratio parameters—is necessary. Although spar-pod construction is still used in some instances for models of this type, the trend is toward using continuous skin models because differential movement between adjacent pods creates a steplike irregularity in the surface contour that might cause undesirable aerodynamic interference effects for some configurations at transonic speeds. A continuous-skin model might be constructed by laying a fiberglass skin of varying thickness over a lightweight honeycomb core that has been shaped to the proper planform and airfoil section geometries. The skin is bonded to the honeycomb core to form a sandwichlike structure, and the fiberglass skin primarily contributes the structural stiffness. The thickness of the skin is varied to account for required variations in structural stiffness along the wingspan and chord. To achieve proper inertia characteristics, metal weights are imbedded within the honeycomb core.

In its operational history, the TDT has been used for over 550 tests of military and civil aircraft. The following examples discuss some of the more important contributions of Langley research using the facility for civil aircraft.

Applications to Civil Aircraft

Lockheed Electra Aircraft

The first TDT test focusing on a particular full-scale design was conducted in 1960 and used a model of the four-engine turboprop Lockheed Electra commercial transport. The relatively new Electra, having been introduced into airline service in the fall of 1958, could carry 98 passengers more than 2,000 miles while cruising at speeds up to 400 mph. Because a number of accidents, some unexplained, involving the Electra had severely damaged the public's confidence in airline transportation, a virtual crisis had developed within the air transportation industry. The TDT began operating just in time to assist in understanding the causes of some of the accidents that had befallen this relatively new airplane.

Soon after its introduction to the civil transport fleet, the Electra suffered a number of accidents, with the wreckage of two widely publicized fatal accidents raising concerns about the structural integrity of the airplane. On September 29, 1959, a Braniff Electra with 5 crew members and 28 passengers enroute from Houston to Dallas disintegrated near Buffalo, Texas without survivors. Investigation of the aircraft wreckage revealed that the left wing had failed and separated from the airplane in flight. The outboard engine nacelle on the failed wing displayed evidence that the propeller and gearbox had twisted over 30° out of alignment with the wing. Although the cause of the accident remained unidentified, catastrophic flutter was among the candidate factors. Then, on March 17, 1960, a Northwest Airlines Electra carrying 6 crew members and 57 passengers from Minneapolis to Miami crashed in Indiana with a startling similarity to the Texas accident. Its right wing was found over 11,000 ft from the crash site, indicating that it had also been torn from the airplane. Again, the outboard engine nacelle of the failed wing panel showed the same twisted characteristics as the earlier accident. With over 130 Electras operating in the civil fleet at the time, immediate action was required to ensure that these airplanes operated safely. Consequently, cognizant authorities immediately reduced the cruise speed of the airliners while the investigation attempted to identify the cause of the fatal crashes. Meanwhile, public and congressional concern over the safety of the Electra and commercial aviation in general rapidly increased with a demand for an explanation of the causes of the crashes and assurance that the safety of the flying public was guaranteed during continued operations. The Electra problems, therefore, became a problem for the entire air transport industry.

As suspicions of flutter-induced structural failure continued to grow within the investigation groups, key managerial interactions between industry, the Civil Aeronautics Board (precursor of today's National Transportation Safety Board), and Langley concluded that flutter tests of an Electra model in the newly commissioned TDT would be beneficial to explaining the cause of the accidents. The purpose of these tests would be to determine whether the airplane might have experienced propeller-whirl flutter as Lockheed flutter engineers were beginning to suspect. Propeller-whirl flutter, first identified in the late 1930s, is characterized by a wobbling motion of the propeller resulting from gyroscopic coupling of the rotating-propeller–engine system with the elastic wing through flexible engine nacelle supports. No airplane had encountered it previously, but the advanced Electra design with its large, high rpm (revolutions per minute) turboprop engines might have just the combination of parameters necessary to produce propeller-whirl flutter. Langley's Philip Donely, I. Edward Garrick, John C. Houbolt, Robert W. Boswinkle, Jr., and Dennis J. Martin led Langley's involvement in the investigation.

An existing 1/8-size full-span Lockheed model that had been used previously in the Electra flutter clearance program was modified to meet the needs of the study. Among the

Powered model of Lockheed Electra mounted in Langley Transonic Dynamics Tunnel for flutter tests.

modifications were the incorporation of windmilling propellers and the facility to adjust engine mount stiffness. The model was mounted on a Boeing-developed vertical-rod support system that allowed for a limited simulation of free-flight conditions. Lockheed Aircraft Corporation, Boeing Airplane Company, and NASA engineers participated in the tests. Nine different tunnel entries occurred between May 1960 and December 1961. In addition to tests of the full-span model, studies were conducted with an isolated propeller-nacelle model and a sidewall-mounted semispan wing-nacelle model. In addition to the experimental activities in the TDT, staff members Wilmer H. Reed III and Samuel R. Bland developed mathematical methods for analysis of the propeller-whirl phenomenon and helped validate refined models for the prediction and elimination of such problems in the future.

The TDT test results showed that propeller-whirl flutter could, in fact, occur for the Electra, but only if the engine mount stiffness was reduced below the nominal design value (as might be caused by a structural failure during a hard landing or an encounter with extremely severe turbulence in flight). During the model tests, no flutter was observed for the model in the basic as-designed condition. However, when the NASA and industry team reduced the scaled stiffness of the engine mounts on the outer engine nacelles, the whirl-flutter mode was observed. It was predicted that the fatal resonance could build up and tear the full-scale airplane apart in a matter of seconds. The problem was solved by increasing the structural stiffness and damping designs of the engine mounts and nacelle. Based on these results from the TDT, the engine mounts on all Electra aircraft were modified and strengthened, and the modified Electra (known as the Super Electra II) entered service in

Electra model following catastrophic flutter.

1961. The modified Electra, and its military derivative Navy P-3 Orion patrol aircraft, have since operated successfully without flutter issues.

The Electra test was an extraordinarily difficult challenge for a new facility with a newly assembled staff. The challenge required marshalling the efforts of practically everyone associated with the facility to ensure its success. The dramatic investigation of the Electra in the TDT had many impacts. First, the airline industry and Lockheed were provided a graphic and accurate definition of the causes and cures for the crashes. The solution to the problem provided a badly needed boost to the public's confidence in air travel and, no doubt, played a key role in the continued expansion of commercial aviation. The success of the TDT investigation, conducted in the international spotlight with intense scrutiny, properly portrayed the professionalism, dedication, and value of the Langley staff and facilities.

Boeing 747 Aircraft

A flutter model of the Boeing 747 was tested twice during separate entries in a cooperative NASA and Boeing study in the TDT during 1967–1968. The investigations, led by Langley's Moses G. Farmer and Irving Abel, were focused on determining the effects of the relatively large engine cowls of the high-bypass engines on flutter characteristics of the aircraft. The 4.6-percent scale, full-span model was tested on two different mount systems in the TDT—the Boeing-developed vertical-rod mount system that had found extensive use in

Researcher Irving Abel with Boeing 747 flutter model.

low-speed flutter model tests, and the newer Langley-developed cable mount system that had become the system of choice for TDT tests. Model parameters for the tests included nacelle aerodynamics, engine-pylon stiffness, mount system, and mass ratio. The aerodynamic effects of the nacelles on flutter characteristics were determined by replacing the engine nacelles with "pencil nacelles" that simulated the inertia and center-of-gravity characteristics of the engine nacelles.

Results from the tests indicated that the aerodynamic forces for the simulated high-bypass-ratio engines reduced the flutter speed by about 20 percent. The flutter characteristics were greatly dependent on the outboard engine lateral frequency. The effects of mount systems on flutter speed were small.

Lockheed L-1011 Aircraft

In 1969, Langley and Lockheed collaborated for cooperative tests of the Lockheed L-1011 in the TDT. The objectives of the tests included flutter clearance as well as general research on the effects of supercritical airfoils on flutter characteristics. Five tests used L-1011 models, the first being conducted in January 1969 and the last in October 1969. The first four were flutter clearance tests and utilized full-span cable-mounted models. The fifth test was of a research nature and used semispan sidewall-mounted L-1011 wing models to evaluate the

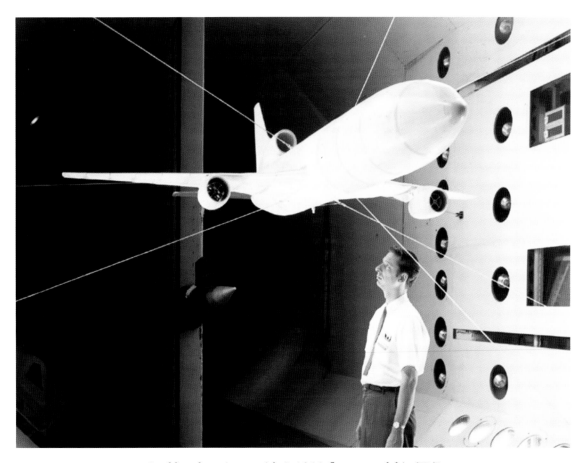

Lockheed engineer with L-1011 flutter model in TDT.

effects of the supercritical airfoil shape on flutter characteristics. The actual L-1011 aircraft did not incorporate a supercritical airfoil, but Lockheed's interest in future applications of supercritical technology led them to furnish a conventional-airfoil wing and a supercritical-airfoil wing for the test. This investigation was the first such experimental study of the impact of supercritical airfoil on flutter. Several TDT engineers played important roles in the L-1011 tests, including Moses G. Farmer, Rodney L. Duncan, Perry W. Hanson, and Robert V. Doggett, Jr.

DC-10 Aircraft

The TDT was used in November 1969 and July 1970 to evaluate the flutter characteristics of the unique split-rudder empennage configuration of the DC-10. The proposed rudder design was split into two spanwise sections, rather than being the single section rudder found on most airplanes. This test, directed by Maynard C. Sandford, used an empennage and aft-body model of the DC-10 on a sting mount. Specific objectives of the program were to determine the flutter characteristics of the vertical tail with a split rudder configuration and compare those results with the flutter characteristics of a vertical tail with a conventional single section rudder design. The results of this TDT study showed that the split rudder had a beneficial effect on flutter by requiring less structural stiffness to prevent flutter than that needed for a conventional single section rudder.

Maynard C. Sandford and empennage and aft-fuselage flutter model of McDonnell Douglas DC-10.

Gulfstream American III Aircraft

A model representative of the Gulfstream III configuration with a proposed supercritical wing was tested twice in the TDT in 1978 by a team of NASA and Gulfstream American Corporation engineers led by Charles L. Ruhlin. This joint NASA and Gulfstream program used a 1/6.5-scale semispan model of the Gulfstream III wing. The wing was mounted to a rigid half-body fuselage so that the effects of fuselage aerodynamics could be properly accounted for. The wing could be configured with three different wingtip arrangements: a nominal wingtip, a wingtip with a winglet, and a normal wingtip ballasted to simulate the winglet mass properties. Specific test objectives were to determine the effects of the winglet on the flutter characteristics of a supercritical wing, compare the results with analytical predictions, investigate possible angle-of-attack-induced flutter issues, and examine the effects of aeroelastic deformations on aerodynamic characteristics of the supercritical wing. Transonic flutter characteristics were measured for each configuration over a Mach number range from 0.60 to 0.95. Although some tests of the winglet effects on flutter had been performed previously with simple research models, this was the first such study of those effects using a wing model of an advanced civil transport airplane.

The shape of the transonic flutter boundary observed for all three configurations tested was consistent with what has been observed for many other configurations in the past, that

Patricia Cole inspects semispan model of Gulfstream III in TDT.

is, a gradual decrease in flutter speed with a minimum occurring at a transonic Mach number (0.82 in this instance) followed by an increase in flutter speed as Mach number increases. However, the magnitude of the flutter speed was different for the three configurations. The flutter speeds of the ballasted tip and winglet configurations were lower than those of the normal tip configuration throughout the test Mach number range. A comparison of these data showed that most of the reduction resulting from the addition of the winglet was due to winglet mass effects rather than winglet aerodynamic effects. Calculated flutter boundaries obtained by using doublet lattice unsteady aerodynamic theory correlated well with the experimental results up to Mach 0.82.

Boeing 767 Aircraft

Two 1/10-scale models representative of the Boeing 767 were tested in the TDT in August 1979. This cooperative Boeing and NASA study was led by Charles L. Ruhlin of Langley. Both a low-speed model and a high-speed model were tested. A low-speed flutter model is designed without consideration of Mach number, or compressibility, effects; a high-speed flutter model is designed with Mach number effects taken into consideration.

The objectives of the low-speed-model test were to study the effects of mass-density ratio (an altitude-related parameter) on flutter and to provide experimental data for correlation with and evaluation of analytical flutter prediction methods. This model was tested with and without a wingtip-mounted winglet. The analytical data correlated reasonably well with the experimental results, although there was some discrepancy in the conditions at which a change in flutter mode of vibration occurred.

The objectives of the high-speed-model tests were to determine the effects of Mach number on the wing flutter boundary, to determine the effects of a wingtip-mounted winglet on the wing flutter boundary, and to correlate the experimental data with analytical results. The wing was tested without a winglet, with a winglet, and with a tip mass equal to the mass of the winglet. Results were obtained for variations in simulated wing fuel loading and engine mount stiffness. The results showed that the addition of the winglet significantly reduced the wing flutter speed and that winglet aerodynamic effects caused most of this reduction in flutter speed. This result was different from the Gulfstream III results previously described, where winglet mass effects were the primary cause of the reduction in flutter speed.

Subsequently, the high-speed flutter model was used in a cooperative effort between NASA and Boeing to investigate and understand the various aeroelastic phenomena associated with advanced high-speed transport configurations and to provide a database to evaluate unsteady aerodynamic theories and aeroelastic analysis methods. Key Langley participants in these studies were Stanley R. Cole and Donald F. Keller. In addition to flutter and buffet, the study specifically addressed the nonlinear phenomenon known as limit cycle oscillations (LCOs). LCO, which is related to flutter, is a limited-amplitude, self-sustaining oscillation that may occur at transonic speeds when shock waves are present on the airfoil. These waves move back and forth and interact with the boundary layer in complex manners to force the wing to vibrate. Data from tests such as this one provided important insight to

*Stanley Cole with representative Boeing 767 model mounted
for general research on limit cycle oscillations in TDT.*

aid in the understanding of LCO and to assess analytical methods being developed to predict its occurrence.

NASA Propfan Test Assessment Airplane

Although this airplane was a one-of-a-kind vehicle, its TDT test is noteworthy and significant. As part of the NASA Propfan Test Assessment (PTA) Program, a 1/9-scale flutter model of the flight test vehicle, a Grumman Gulfstream II airplane with an advanced turboprop mounted on the left wing, was tested in August 1985. The full-span model was supported on the two-cable suspension system to provide for the simulation of rigid body freedoms. Results using this model, which was built by Lockheed-Georgia, showed that the flight test airplane was safe from flutter throughout its intended operating boundary; this ensured that it would not be necessary to restrict the airplane research flight envelope because of flutter. In 1987 the National Aeronautics Association awarded the Collier Trophy to the Advanced Turboprop Program, of which this test was an important part. Several members of the TDT test team were included as members of the award team in recognition of their significant contributions to flutter clearance of the flight test research airplane.

Propeller Test Assessment configuration in TDT with Langley's Michael Durham.

Boeing 777 Aircraft

A dynamically scaled semispan aeroelastic model of the Boeing 777 wing was tested in the TDT in late July 1992 as part of the flutter clearance program. The primary NASA test engineers were James R. Florance and Moses G. Farmer. A rigid fuselage half-body simulated the interactive airflow and the effects between the fuselage and wing. The model engine nacelle was designed to simulate air mass flow through the aircraft engine, and the model was designed so that the amount of simulated fuel in the wing and the stiffness of the engine pylon could be changed remotely; thus, testing was expedited. Model angle of attack could be remotely controlled as well.

Ten configurations were tested throughout the simulated flight envelope of the aircraft without obtaining flutter. Parameters that were varied included wing fuel, engine pylon stiffness, and the stiffness of the structure that attached the wing to the fuselage. To create a configuration for which flutter would occur within the TDT operating envelope, a mass was installed in the wingtip and results were obtained for correlation with predictions. The measured flutter boundary agreed fairly well with preliminary analytical predictions for this configuration. The test results were used to calibrate Boeing's analytical flutter codes used during the flutter safety certification of the 777 aircraft.

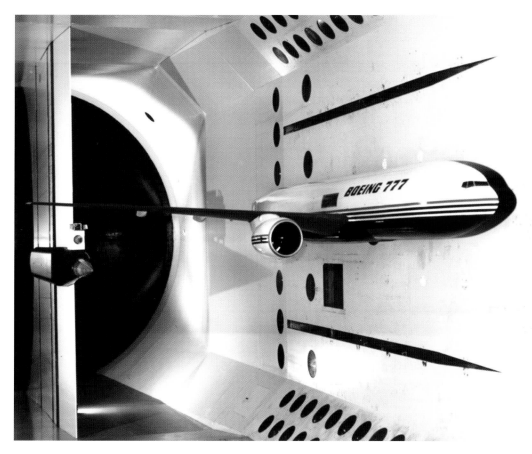

Boeing 777 flutter model mounted for TDT tests.

Gulfstream V

In 1994, Langley and Gulfstream Aerospace Corporation teamed for a cooperative flutter study with emphasis on code calibration and the effect of winglets on flutter characteristics. Three TDT entries were made under the Langley leadership of Donald F. Keller. A semispan model of the Gulfstream V was used, with a wing structure consisting of an aluminum plate of varying thickness to which balsa wood was bonded and contoured to form a supercritical airfoil. A winglet was mounted at the wingtip, and a fuselage half-body fairing was used to provide more realistic wing-root aerodynamics. The baseline configuration consisted of the wing, root fairing, and winglet. The model was also tested without the winglet and without the winglet but with a tip boom in place to simulate the winglet mass with negligible aerodynamic effects. The test program also included an advanced design winglet.

Flutter results for the three configurations indicated that the winglet effects on flutter were mostly caused by the mass of the winglet rather than its aerodynamic effects, a result similar to that found previously for the Gulfstream III design but different from that found for the Boeing 767 model.

The approach in this test differed from the usual flutter clearance studies. The model was essentially geometrically correct but had a simple structural representation. Consequently, it

Donald Keller with Gulfstream V model during winglet flutter investigation.

was considerably less expensive to design and fabricate as compared with most flutter clearance models. The primary purpose from the flutter clearance point of view was to acquire high quality experimental flutter data for correlation with analytical results obtained by using advanced analysis methods. The experimental data were used to "calibrate" the analysis that was used in the design and certification of the airplane. This approach clearly proved quite successful, as the Gulfstream V turned out to be an outstanding design that would go on to be awarded the Collier Trophy in 1997.

Cessna Citation X Aircraft

Business jet aircraft must be designed so that flutter will not occur within the flight envelope with a 20-percent safety margin. Traditionally, wind-tunnel model tests have played an important role in the flutter certification process of new designs. The objective of the cooperative study with Cessna Aircraft Company was to provide wind-tunnel flutter data for use in ensuring that the wing of the Citation X would be safe from flutter.

Flutter models of the Cessna Citation X business jet were tested on three occasions in the TDT during 1993 and 1994. In the first test program during February 1993, a NASA and Cessna team led by Langley's José A. "Tony" Rivera, Jr., and Moses G. Farmer conducted tests of a 1/4-scale semispan aeroelastic model of the Citation X wing. A rigid fuselage half-body

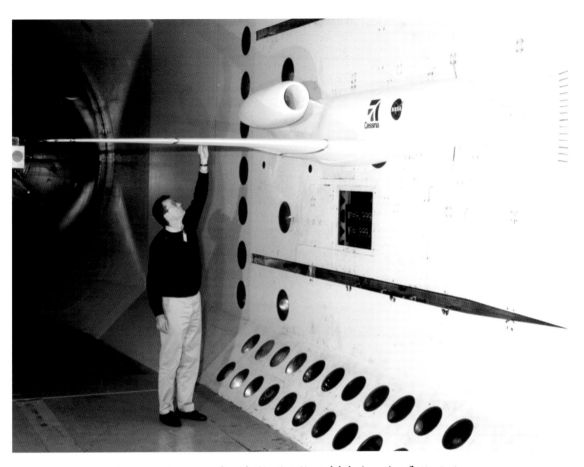

Cessna's Craig Mundt with Citation X model during wing flutter tests.

and flow-through nacelle were used to simulate their interference effects on flow over the wing. The wing model included an aileron that could be tested undeflected or deflected. Eight configurations were tested to obtain data to correlate with flutter and aileron-reversal analyses. A wingtip-mounted aerodynamic exciter was used extensively during the test to track frequencies and estimate damping as the flutter boundaries were approached. For nominal aileron actuator stiffness, flutter analyses by Cessna predicted that the flutter boundary would be outside the full-scale aircraft flight envelope with a 20-percent margin. The experimental flutter points obtained for this configuration in the TDT correlated well with the analytical results, and they indicated that the Citation X wing would be safe from flutter.

In January and February of 1994, additional testing of a 1/7-scale sting-mounted, full-span aeroelastic model of the Citation X was conducted in the TDT for a range of Mach numbers from 0.60 to 0.97. The Langley leaders for this series of tests were Donald F. Keller and Moses G. Farmer. Based on the analyses and results of the previous flutter tests of the semispan-wing model, the empennage surfaces of the Citation X configuration were considered the critical structural components for flutter. The rotational stiffness and mass balance of the elevator and rudder were changed to simulate hydraulic-system-failure conditions and control-surface center-of-gravity variations, respectively. Eight configurations were tested,

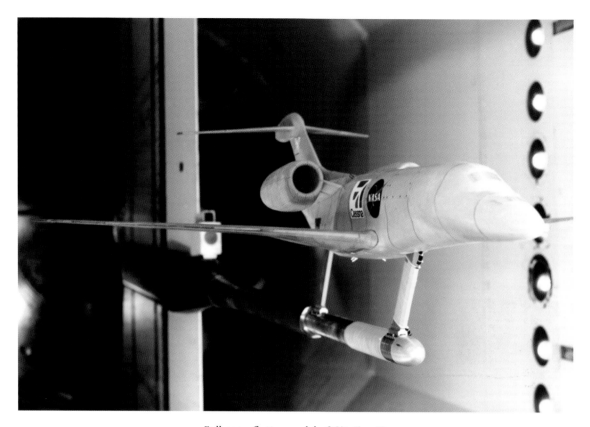

Full-span flutter model of Citation X.

and flutter or lightly damped oscillations were only encountered outside the scaled operating envelope. In general, flutter analyses performed before the test correlated well with the experimental results.

The test results were used by Cessna to provide guidance during the flight flutter clearance program for the Citation X and aided the NASA and Cessna team in understanding aeroelastic phenomena encountered during the clearance program. The experimental flutter results were also useful for the validation and calibration of analytical flutter codes.

Learjet Model 45 Aircraft

In May 1995, Langley and the Learjet Corporation teamed to conduct flutter model studies of the new Learjet 45 business jet. These tests were part of the airplane flutter clearance program. Learjet furnished a 1/6-scale sting-mounted, full-span aeroelastic model that had flexible lifting surfaces and a rigid fuselage. This model was tested twice in the TDT. Stanley R. Cole, James R. Florance, and Elizabeth Lee-Rauch were the Langley project engineers for the first test; Langley's José A. "Tony" Rivera, Jr., and Donald F. Keller led the test team for the second test. The primary objectives of the tests were to ensure that flutter would not occur within the scaled flight envelope with a flutter safety margin of 20 percent, evaluate the impact of free play and jammed control surfaces on flutter characteristics, measure the transonic flutter conditions for a modified wing configuration, and obtain data to evaluate the application of linear flutter prediction codes for transonic Mach numbers. The

Stanley Cole with flutter model of Learjet 45 in TDT.

test was very successful with all these objectives being met. The nominal vehicle was shown to be flutter free up to speeds 20 percent beyond the dive speed and dive Mach number. Component-failure configurations, such as excess control-surface free play and control-surface mass balance variations, were shown to be flutter free up to the dive speed and dive Mach number. In addition, transonic flutter was measured for a modified wing configuration to evaluate linear flutter prediction codes. Compared with the experiment, the linear flutter predictions were approximately 10 percent conservative. These valuable data were used by Learjet to minimize the risk and flight test time for flutter clearance flight tests of the Learjet 45 aircraft.

DEEP-STALL AVOIDANCE

Background

As aircraft configurations continued to advance into the 1950s, designers began to recognize the potential advantages of "T-tail" configurations, wherein the horizontal tail was moved to the top of the vertical tail for enhanced efficiency and reduced weight. By arranging the vertical and horizontal tails in a T, designers could locate the horizontal tail in a relatively benign flow field. In this location, the flow downwash from the wing would not reduce the stabilizing effects of the horizontal tail at the relatively low angles of attack associated with cruise conditions. This advantage was also obtained during the landing

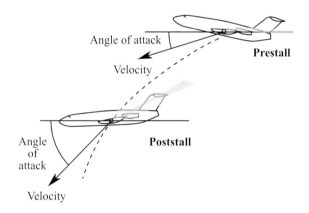

Wake flow patterns before and after entry into deep-stall condition. Note impingement of low-energy stalled wake on horizontal tail in poststall, deep-stall situation.

A British aircraft BAC 111, similar to this, experienced a fatal deep-stall accident.

approach, when the downwash effects became even stronger because of the deflected wing trailing-edge flaps. In addition to placing the horizontal tail in a region of less downwash, the T-tail position provides more tail length (with a swept vertical tail); thereby less tail area is used for the required tail contribution to stability. Also, the endplating effect on the vertical tail makes the vertical tail more effective and permits a reduction in vertical fin size. As a result of the increased efficiency of the horizontal and vertical tails, the surface areas could be reduced relative to a tail size for the conventional low-tail configuration and thereby result in a significant weight savings.

In the early 1960s, four new T-tail jet transports (the de Havilland Trident, the Boeing 727, the BAC 111, and the McDonnell Douglas DC-9) emerged within the highly competitive transport market. These aircraft shared many common configuration features in addition to the T-tail arrangement: aft-fuselage-mounted engines and all-moving (variable-incidence) horizontal tails, for instance. In Britain, the de Havilland Aircraft Company, Ltd. (who later merged with Hawker Siddeley Aviation, Ltd.), developed the Trident transport, which first flew on January 9, 1962. In the United States, Boeing brought forth its new model, the 727, which first flew on February 9, 1963. The BAC 111 first flew later that year on August 20, 1963. The Douglas DC-9 provided additional competition with a first flight that occurred a few years later, in February 1965.

The BAC 111 suffered a major setback during early flight testing of the prototype on October 22, 1963; the aircraft was destroyed and crew members lost their lives in a fatal accident during tests to evaluate the stall characteristics of the configuration. The accident investigation board conducted an exhaustive investigation of the aerodynamic, stability, and control characteristics of the BAC 111 and concluded that the cause of the accident was an unrecoverable deep-stall phenomenon, which was precipitated by the geometric and aerodynamic characteristics of the configuration. In particular, wind-tunnel tests indicated that at high angles of attack near and above those associated with wing stall, the low-energy wakes of the stalled wing and fuselage-mounted engine nacelles impinged on the horizontal tail and significantly reduced its stabilizing effect. Also, the low-energy wakes severely reduced the effectiveness of the horizontal tail as a longitudinal control. These characteristics manifest themselves as an insidious poststall condition in which the angle of attack of the aircraft would increase to very large values (in excess of 40°) in response to the loss of stability, and the pilot would be unable to recover from the condition because of the loss of horizontal tail control effectiveness. During this entire sequence, the attitude of the aircraft fuselage would vary over a relatively small angular range, and the uncontrollable aircraft would descend steeply in an almost horizontal, wings-level attitude with a high rate of descent to an unsurvivable crash.

The BAC 111 design was subsequently modified to incorporate a stick pusher, modified leading-edge camber, and powered elevator controls to prevent the aircraft from entering high-angle-of-attack conditions. As news of the BAC 111 accident and its causal factor spread throughout the technical community, other design teams raced to examine the characteristics of their own T-tail aircraft. For example, Douglas immediately returned to the wind tunnel and conducted additional testing for the DC-9, which had not entered flight testing. Douglas had followed conventional wisdom regarding preliminary assessments of stall

Hawker Siddeley Trident jet transport.

characteristics of conventional configurations during the DC-9 development program. The transport industry approach to wind-tunnel testing did not include high-angle-of-attack testing much beyond stall, and few studies of very-high-angle-of-attack characteristics had been conducted. However, when Douglas engineers examined the newly acquired high-angle-of-attack data, they found that the baseline DC-9 configuration would exhibit locked-in deep-stall characteristics similar to those exhibited by the baseline BAC 111. Following in-depth analysis of the aerodynamic data, Douglas designed an under-wing leading-edge fence (which they named a "vortillon" which is short for vortex generating pylon) that provided additional flow energy at the tail for nose-down recovery at and slightly above the stall angle of attack. In addition to analyzing wind-tunnel data, Douglas also conducted some rudimentary piloted flight simulations before deciding on final modifications for the DC-9. The final modifications developed to prevent the DC-9 from entering a dangerous deep stall included the vortillons (which assisted in immediate poststall recovery, but had little effect at the deep-stall condition), an increase in the span of the original horizontal tail, a stick shaker, visual and aural stall warnings, and a standby power system that provided full nose-down elevator capability for deep-stall recovery. (The original aerodynamic tab system was not capable of providing sufficient elevator angle at very high angles of attack.) These modifications, which were incorporated prior to the first flight of the DC-9 on February 25, 1965, proved effective in preventing deep stall for the DC-9 throughout its service life.

Even after the BAC 111 experience and the international concern and research activities it stimulated, the deep-stall phenomenon continued to cause problems in civil aviation. For example, deep stall was found to be responsible for crashes experienced with the Hawker Siddeley Trident transport. On June 3, 1966, one of the first production Trident aircraft crashed during its first flight as a result of entering a deep-stall condition, with all four crew members killed. The aircraft was carrying out the first of a series of production test flights to qualify for a Series Certificate of Airworthiness. After completing a large part of the required tests, the stall tests were begun. Three approaches to stall were made to check the stall warning and stall recovery systems. The fourth stall test was made at an altitude of 11,600 ft in the landing configuration and with the stall warning and recovery systems inoperative. The Trident entered a deep stall with the nose going up to a 30°–40° attitude. The aircraft turned to the left, the right wing dropped, and the plane went into a flat spin to the right. The investigation board concluded: "During a stalling test, decisive recovery action was delayed too long to prevent the aircraft from entering a superstall (deep stall) from which recovery was not possible." Later, on June 18, 1972, another Trident entered a deep stall immediately after takeoff from Heathrow airport in severe weather and crashed, with a loss of 118 lives.

Langley Research and Development Activities

Immediately following the BAC 111 crash, Langley responded by mapping out a research program directed at understanding the physical phenomena and factors responsible for the deep-stall problem. Langley's Edward C. Polhamus visited England and was briefed on the BAC crash and analysis data. Upon his return, the staff of the Langley 7- by 10-Foot High-Speed Tunnel formulated and conducted a generic research program with systematic variations of T-tail configurations to provide industry with appropriate design guidelines, analysis procedures, and wind-tunnel test techniques to avoid the potential for unacceptable deep-stall behavior for T-tail aircraft. Under the leadership of Robert T. Taylor and Edward J. Ray, a parametric wind-tunnel study was immediately begun with generic configurations that included a range of some of the more critical configuration features, such as the relative locations of the engine nacelles and the horizontal tail. The data resulting from the studies served not only to provide insight into the causes and cures of the problem, but the method of approach and analysis techniques provided designers of future aircraft with a general understanding and sensitivity to the deep-stall problem.

The wind-tunnel testing at Langley was augmented by extensive piloted simulator studies at the Langley and the Ames Research Centers to establish potential pilot recovery procedures, recognition cues of the deep stall, and assessments of various modifications designed to limit angle-of-attack excursions during stall testing. At Langley, the simulator and analytical studies were led by Martin T. Moul, Lindsey J. Lina, and Raymond C. Montgomery. With a representative DC-9 cockpit, the researchers were able to define levels of satisfactory recovery and an index for aerodynamic control design, as well as give recommendations for deep-stall recovery criteria.

Applications

The Langley researchers dedicated themselves to provide timely, valuable dissemination of the results to all sectors of the civil aircraft industry. In addition to active interchanges with interested industry representatives, the results of the studies were highlighted at several national symposia in 1965. With a rapid growth in the popularity of the aft-mounted engines and T-tail arrangement incorporated by both large jet transports as well as business jets, the data and procedures generated in the Langley program have had a significant impact on industry's awareness of the potential danger, and industry has adopted a general approach to design and testing for stall and poststall characteristics. Armed with this information, industry has been able to design aerodynamic and flight control concepts to prevent the occurrence of deep stalls. Because this pioneering work was conducted with representative generic configurations, it provided a fundamental explanation of the phenomenon and general sensitivity and approach to avoid this catastrophic problem. Collectively, the results of this research provided an intrinsic tool for easy understanding and direct application throughout industry.

Cessna Citation, a current T-tail aircraft, designed to avoid potential for deep stall.

SPIN TECHNOLOGY

Background

The related subjects of stalling and spinning have received the continuous attention of aircraft designers throughout the history of manned flight. High-performance military aircraft must be capable of extended flight at high angles of attack near or beyond stall during strenuous maneuvers without unintentional loss of control or unrecoverable spins. Commercial civil transports, business jets, and general aviation aircraft must exhibit a high degree of stability and controllability for the low-speed, near-stall conditions associated with landing and takeoff. In addition, both military and civil aircraft must display satisfactory recovery characteristics from inadvertent stalled conditions, with no tendency to enter unrecoverable poststall conditions such as an unrecoverable deep stall. General aviation aircraft in the light, personal-owner category must display benign, easily controlled motions during stall maneuvers, with no tendency to enter dangerous inadvertent spins, particularly at low altitudes with insufficient height for recovery.

Stalls and spins involve complicated balances between the aerodynamic and inertial forces and moments acting on the vehicle. Unfortunately, the complexities of separated aerodynamic flows and the high dependence of poststall aerodynamics on details of aircraft configurations result in a formidable design problem. The prediction of spin and spin-recovery characteristics has been especially difficult during aircraft development programs, and designers have been challenged since the first recorded spin and spin recovery occurred in 1912 when Lieutenant Porte of the British Royal Navy intentionally spun and recovered his Avro biplane.

The principal motions of stalling and spinning involve four distinct phases of flight: the approach to stall, the stall and incipient spin, the developed spin, and spin recovery. During the approach to stall, as airspeed is reduced and angle of attack is increased, some aircraft may exhibit large-amplitude rolling or pitching motions, wing-dropping tendencies, unconventional or ineffective responses to

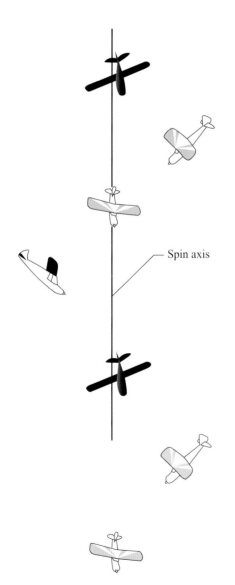

Spin axis

Sketch of position of aircraft while descending in relatively steep, developed spin to left.

control inputs, or longitudinal or directional instabilities. If the motions occur in a rapid and disorienting matter, the pilot may inadvertently lose control of the aircraft and enter the incipient-spin phase. The incipient spin may also be entered intentionally by the pilot through applications of rudder-elevator-aileron controls. In the incipient-spin phase, the flight path of the aircraft changes from horizontal to nearly vertical, the angle of attack increases beyond the value at stall, and the rate of rotation increases from zero to the rate exhibited in the fully developed spin. If the loss of altitude is to be kept to a minimum, the pilot must quickly recognize the out-of-control situation and apply corrective controls. If the pilot delays the inputs or applies the wrong control combinations, the aircraft may enter the developed-spin phase.

In the developed-spin phase, the attitude, angles, and motions of the aircraft tend to be repeatable from turn to turn, and the flight path is approximately vertical. The spinning motion is sustained by a balance of the aerodynamic and inertial moments acting on the aircraft. The spin consists of a spinning motion about the airplane center of gravity plus translatory motion of the center of gravity; however, the motion is primarily rotary. The developed spin can be very smooth and steady, or it may be quite oscillatory, violent, and disorienting to the pilot. In addition, the spin may be relatively steep, characterized by a nose-down attitude, an angle of attack ranging from slightly above the stall angle of attack to about 30°, and a relatively large spin radius (distance of the center of gravity of the aircraft from the spin axis). The developed spin may also be fast and "flat," with a relatively horizontal fuselage attitude, an angle of attack approaching 90°, and the spin axis passing almost vertically through the center of gravity of the aircraft with a spin radius of near zero.

Spin recovery is accomplished by upsetting the balance of aerodynamic and inertial moments acting on the aircraft by movement of the aerodynamic control surfaces. The specific control inputs required for satisfactory spin recovery for a particular aircraft depend on certain critical aircraft mass and aerodynamic properties, and the most effective control sequence varies for different types of airplanes (for example, fighters and personal-owner aircraft). Recoveries from steep spins tend to be less difficult because the aircraft aerodynamic controls retain a limited degree of effectiveness slightly beyond the stall. However, recovery from a flat spin is normally extremely difficult because the aircraft controls are ineffective at such high angles of attack.

Because unrecoverable spins may be encountered during initial aircraft stall/spin flight tests, spin test aircraft are commonly equipped with emergency spin-recovery parachute systems, which can be deployed to terminate the spinning motion and reduce the aircraft angle of attack to below stall conditions. The parachute is then jettisoned by the pilot and conventional flight resumed.

Unfortunately, when inadvertent loss of control and spin entry occur at low altitudes, the pilot may not have enough altitude to terminate the poststall motions and complete the near-vertical recovery maneuver before impacting the ground. Sadly, this scenario occurs frequently in fatal civil aircraft accidents for personal-owner aircraft that are piloted by relatively inexperienced individuals, with minimum exposure to out-of-control maneuvers and spins.

From a technical perspective, stalls and spins are very complicated because of a single factor—aerodynamics. The aerodynamic characteristics of most aircraft configurations become extremely nonlinear and ill behaved at angles of attack beyond stall. Thus, the prediction and analysis of stall/spin behavior have not been amenable to theoretical methods. After decades of experience and national leadership in the area of stall/spin technology, researchers at the Langley Research Center have evolved a series of dynamically scaled model test techniques to provide the information required for the prediction of airplane spin and spin-recovery characteristics. Historically, the quality of correlation of results from dynamic model tests with full-scale aircraft results has been extremely good for military aircraft that employ wings with relatively sharp leading edges (which are relatively insensitive to Reynolds number effects at high angles of attack), swept wings, and/or fuselage heavy loadings. For these configurations, isolated problems have arisen when fuselage cross-sectional shapes have shown Reynolds number effects. Langley has developed artificial model modifications to correct for many of these effects for military aircraft models.

Unfortunately, the quality of correlation between dynamically scaled free-flight models and full-scale personal-owner general aviation aircraft has frequently been poor. For these configurations, the relatively low Reynolds numbers involved in model tests can sometimes produce erroneous predictions. The fundamental aerodynamic problem is that the relatively large radius of the wing leading edges and the high-lift airfoils used for general aviation aircraft tend to be extremely sensitive to Reynolds number. In particular, the wing of a subscale model at low Reynolds number will generally not produce as much lift at high angles of attack, and it will also stall at a lower angle of attack. Many times, this effect results in the model predicting a more docile, steeper spin than that exhibited by the full-scale aircraft. Without corrections for this Reynolds number phenomenon, the designer may be surprised by a full-scale aircraft with unsatisfactory characteristics that were not adequately predicted by model tests. In summary, spin and spin-recovery predictions for personal-owner aircraft based on model tests should be approached with caution.

Langley Research and Development Activities

NACA researchers at Langley conducted some of the earliest studies of aircraft stalling behavior with a Curtiss JN4H Jenny in 1919. In the 1930s, the pioneering efforts of Fred E. Weick of Langley were directed toward providing a safe, easy-to-fly design that would be free of the dangers associated with stalling and spinning. Weick and his associates developed the highly successful W-1A experimental airplane, which exhibited radically improved stalling characteristics compared with other aircraft of the day. Weick later designed the famous Ercoupe aircraft, which utilized limited elevator travel, two-control operation, a nose-down inclination to the thrust axis, and a carefully tailored wing stall progression in such a manner that the entire wing could not be stalled. The configuration is still in existence today as a popular antique, and an Ercoupe has never had a spin accident.

World War II, and the national focus on military aircraft, virtually eliminated all NACA research on stall/spin characteristics of personal-owner type aircraft. Essentially all NACA resources were devoted to providing support to high-priority military aircraft development programs, and Langley's facilities, such as the Langley Vertical Spin Tunnel, were busily engaged in military studies. Hundreds of military aircraft configurations were tested in the specialized facilities at Langley; although the focus was not on civil research, the potential for future applications to civil aircraft of the data generated in the military studies was recognized. After World War II, the large influx of surplus aircraft into the personal-owner marketplace resulted in an alarming number of stall/spin accidents, largely because of the inexperience of new pilots, the high wing loadings of the aircraft, and aggravated roll instability at the stall due to power effects on high-lift systems. In this period, stall/spin accidents accounted for over 48 percent of all fatal accidents. Interest in improving the abysmal safety record inspired new research efforts within NACA, with a particular emphasis on stalling behavior and leading-edge devices. In addition, researchers involved in spin recovery research attempted to summarize and collate the vast amount of data generated during the war years in an attempt to provide design guidelines for light aircraft. During the late 1950s, however, the pace of research related to general aviation in NACA slowed to the extent that no new breakthroughs were forthcoming in the area of stall/spin technology. In fact, research was virtually nonexistent, and communications with industry and its needs were

Piper PA-30 Twin Comanche aircraft mounted in Langley 30- by 60-Foot (Full-Scale) Tunnel for investigation of power-on stall characteristics.

extremely limited. The situation was further aggravated by the fact that in the postwar years, military aircraft configurations became markedly different from general aviation configurations (for example, wing airfoils, wing sweep, and mass loadings); thereby, any meaningful transfer of military stall/spin research results to the civil sector was prevented.

Research activities picked up again in the early 1960s with a series of landmark flight studies of the handling qualities of representative single- and twin-engine general aviation aircraft by the Dryden Flight Research Center. The flight investigations identified poor stalling behavior for several of the aircraft tested; this stimulated follow-on wind-tunnel studies of a series of twin-engine full-scale aircraft in the Langley 30- by 60-Foot (Full-Scale) Tunnel. Lead Langley researchers for these studies included Marvin P. Fink, Delma C. Freeman, Jr., and James P. Shivers. Some of the twin-engine aircraft had been found to exhibit abrupt wing-drop tendencies at stall in flight. The tunnel tests showed that this unsatisfactory behavior was caused by asymmetric local upwash caused by the conventional mode of propeller rotation (clockwise viewed from the rear). When the propellers were used in

*James Bowman, Jr., James Patton, Jr., and Sanger Burk with low-wing spin
research aircraft along with radio-controlled model, and spin-tunnel model of configuration.*

opposite modes (both rotating down at the wingtip), the asymmetric stall was alleviated. In addition to providing designers with key information, these studies helped to provide a foothold for general aviation research in the NASA aeronautics program.

The most progressive era of NASA stall/spin research for general aviation configurations was conceived and initiated by James S. Bowman, Jr., James M. Patton, Jr., and Sanger M. Burk at Langley in 1972. Together they conceived, planned, and implemented a research program that was subsequently augmented with numerous associates at the Langley and Ames Research Centers. Initially, the program focused on the validation and interpretation of design guidelines for spin recovery, but a rapidly growing research program quickly expanded the scope of activities. Also, lines of communication with the general aviation industry were established, and a mutual trust was cultivated that permitted practical research to be conducted despite a liability-sensitive environment. In 1976, a workshop was held at Langley to discuss and focus the NASA efforts as recommended by industry, academia, and other government agencies. Several NASA advisory committees and the General Aviation Manufacturers Association (GAMA) advocated for more NASA funding for the area. In response, the resources were augmented, and for the next 6 years a concentrated effort was conducted at Langley with support from Ames and academia. Over 100 technical papers were subsequently published by NASA and its contractors and grantees to document the results of the program, and a major workshop was held at Langley in 1980 to disseminate the results to the industry. The data transmitted included advancements in the area of aerodynamics at high angles of attack, factors affecting the spin and spin recovery, stall/spin prevention concepts, model/flight test procedures, emergency spin-recovery systems, and analytical techniques.

In the early 1980s, the emphasis on other NASA priorities and competition for limited resources necessarily curtailed the research program. NASA funding for general aviation stall/spin research was sharply reduced, and the research activities were reduced accordingly. Nonetheless, cooperative research with industry has continued to the current day and has resulted in progress in several areas, especially for advanced unconventional designs and the design of inherently spin resistant wings.

Langley 20-Foot Vertical Spin Tunnel

Following the initial operations of a 15-foot-diameter spin tunnel that became operational in 1935, Langley designed and developed the Langley 20-Foot Vertical Spin Tunnel and initiated operations in 1941. The Langley Spin Tunnel is a closed-throat, annular return wind tunnel that operates at atmospheric conditions. A fixed-pitch fan and drive motor located above the test section are controlled by a system that permits rapid changes in fan speed, which results in rapid flow accelerations in the test section. Models used in free-spinning tests are designed and fabricated according to specific scaling relationships (relative density and Froude number) similar to some discussed in an earlier section on aeroelasticity. To study spin characteristics, the dynamically scaled free-flying models are hand launched with prerotation into the vertically rising airstream. The tunnel operator varies the tunnel speed so that the spinning model remains in equilibrium in the field of view of multiple video cameras installed around the test section. Images of the test are stored on a laser disk

Langley 20-Foot Vertical Spin Tunnel and adjacent office building.

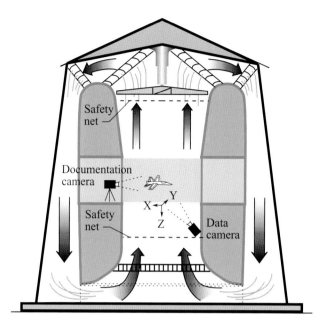

Cross-sectional view of Langley Vertical Spin Tunnel.

and later analyzed by using a computer code that is capable of calculating the six-degree-of-freedom position and attitude of a model at a sample rate of 60 Hz. The resulting motion time histories are then used for quantifying spin modes as well as calibrating spin simulations. Direct observation of the model is possible during tunnel operations via panoramic control room windows. The spin-recovery characteristics of the model are studied by using remote actuation of the model aerodynamic control surfaces. The size of emergency spin-recovery parachutes for flight test aircraft is also determined by using specialized tests of scaled parachutes attached to the model.

In addition to free-spinning tests, the facility permits the measurement of aerodynamic forces and moments during spin conditions with a unique rotary-balance apparatus. In this testing technique, the model is attached to a strain-gauge balance similar to those used for conventional wind-tunnel tests; however, in this technique the model is forced into continuous spinning motions and the balance signals are transmitted via slip rings to data reduction equipment. Data obtained with this technique are used for theoretical studies of spins, and the apparatus has also been used to provide electronically scanned pressures on models during spinning motions.

The rotary-balance test technique had been used in the Langley spin tunnels during the 1930s and early 1940s; however, the pressures of free-spinning tests in the Langley tunnel during World War II precluded the use of this testing capability and the test apparatus fell into disrepair. With new resources to invigorate its program in the 1970s, Langley contracted Bihrle Applied Research, Inc., to refurbish and upgrade the testing capability. The upgrade included state-of-the-art digital data acquisition equipment and pressure measurement instrumentation. Data obtained on the rotary balance cannot be obtained in conventional static wind-tunnel testing because, during a spin, each location on the model is subjected to

*Typical model mounted on rotary-balance apparatus for aerodynamic measurements
during simulated spin. Airflow is vertical from bottom of picture to top.*

a different local flow angle due to the rotational kinematics of the spin. In addition, the trends of forces and moments with variations in rotation rate are generally very nonlinear for spin conditions. A new rig with significantly enhanced capabilities became operational in the tunnel in 1992.

Radio-Controlled Models

One of the thrusts of the Langley General Aviation Spin Program was to develop and evaluate a low-cost testing technique using radio-controlled models for the prediction of stall/spin characteristics. Such a technique would provide industry, and interested individuals, with a method that could be utilized in lieu of spin-tunnel tests in the design stages of aircraft development activities. As a nationally recognized expert in radio-controlled model technology, Langley technician David B. Robelen designed, fabricated, and flew several scale radio-controlled models and correlated model flight results with those obtained from spin tests of the corresponding full-scale aircraft. Robelen led the development of innovative, low-cost hobby-type instrumentation that used sensors to permit measurement of control positions, angle of attack, airspeed, angular rates, and other variables. His efforts even included the design and use (deployment and release) of emergency spin-recovery parachute systems for models. Through the use of special camera tracking equipment and recorders, relatively sophisticated data were generated in the model tests.

Emergency Spin-Recovery Parachutes

Parachutes have been commonly installed on spin test aircraft for backup in the event that an unrecoverable spin is encountered during flight tests. The challenges involved in the design and operation of parachute systems include a determination of the minimum parachute size required for satisfactory recovery, the parachute riser line length, and the design of the mechanical parachute deployment and release mechanisms. Prior to the NASA program, a generally accepted approach to system design for general aviation was not available, and numerous fatal accidents had occurred during spin tests of general aviation aircraft because of improper parachute geometry, deployment, or jettison characteristics. The parachute canopy distance for emergency spin recovery is particularly critical. If the distance from the aircraft to the parachute (riser plus suspension line length) is too short, the parachute will probably collapse in the low-energy stalled wake of the aircraft and have little effect on the spin. On the other hand, if the length is too long, the parachute will trail over to the spin axis, rotate with the aircraft, and be ineffective in terminating the spin. The range of information provided by the NASA program also included design approaches for the engineering of mechanical deployment/jettison systems under the leadership of Charles F. Bradshaw. Extensive testing by Langley researchers led by Bowman, Burk, and Robelen using spin-tunnel model tests, radio-controlled models, and full-scale aircraft tests provided critical information on the design of parachute systems. Langley test pilots used the Langley-developed parachute system to terminate unrecoverable spins 28 times on 4 different aircraft during flight tests without failure or incidents. This valuable, life-saving information on emergency spin-recovery systems was quickly transferred to the general aviation industry and further disseminated to the public at seminars and national meetings such as the annual Oshkosh Convention.

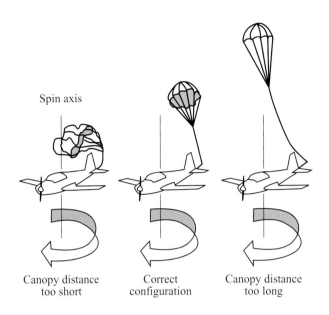

Impact of parachute canopy riser line length on spin recovery.

Pyrotechnically deployed spin parachute developed in Langley program.

Flight Tests

The final, definitive answers in any analysis of stall and spin behavior are provided only by flight tests of the full-scale aircraft. Obtaining these answers, however, involves potentially hazardous conditions, requiring careful planning, the provision of emergency spin-recovery and pilot egress systems, and careful procedural policies for success. Stall/spin flight tests have traditionally been a high-risk area for general aviation manufacturers, particularly in the area of emergency systems. The NASA program, therefore, included a concentrated effort to develop and refine flight test technology.

Four spin research airplanes shared the Langley flight test activities in the program. These aircraft resembled production aircraft, but they were extensively modified for research with special instrumentation and mass loadings. The modified research aircraft included a Grumman American AA-1 Yankee, a Beechcraft C-23 Sundowner, a Cessna 172 Skyhawk, and a Piper prototype T-Tail. Over 2,500 spins were accomplished with the aircraft, including about 8,000 spin turns. Each airplane was equipped with wing booms that supported sensors for measurements of angle of attack, angle of sideslip, and airspeed. Motion-picture cameras were mounted internally within the wing structure, coupled with innovative mirrors used to photograph wool tufts in visualizing the airflow over the wing surface. In addition to conventional telemetry data, the aircraft carried onboard instrumentation. Numerous geometric modifications were made to each aircraft to assess the effects of various components on spin-recovery characteristics. Each aircraft was equipped with a pyrotechnically deployed emergency recovery parachute system. One of the airplanes was outfitted with an innovative hydrogen-peroxide thruster system, which utilized small thrusters at the wingtips of the airplane to provide a selected level of moments about the aircraft axes. The test site for the

Langley's chief test pilot, James Patton during flight test program.
Note symbols denoting successful operations of spin-recovery parachute system.

Modified AA-1 Yankee research aircraft in flight.

flight studies was the NASA Wallops Flight Center, located on Virginia's Eastern Shore. Close communication was maintained with general aviation industry flight test teams regarding the operational procedures and hardware used in the Langley effort. Industry teams visited the test site at Wallops and evaluated the overall approach to testing. Many of the program elements, such as parachute system design, have been implemented and adopted for industry use.

Tail Damping Power Factor

Following World War II, the immediate focus in stall/spin technology for general aviation aircraft was the developed spin and recovery from the spin. The NACA researchers who labored in the Spin Tunnel during the war years began to collate and summarize data from about 100 model tests that might be applicable to general aviation aircraft. General results obtained in spin-tunnel tests indicated that certain critical parameters dominated the spin and recovery characteristics for configurations similar to general aviation designs. These parameters included the relative density (aircraft density relative to air density), mass distribution (with extremes of fuselage heavy or wing heavy), and tail design. These data were analyzed and used to develop conservative engineering design guidelines for satisfactory spin characteristics.

The Langley data emphasized that tail design was very important and that designers should consider the tail geometry as a first-order parameter from spin and recovery perspectives. During spins, a dead-air region exists over much of the vertical tail because of the stalled wake of the horizontal tail. Therefore, to have good rudder effectiveness for spin recovery, a substantial amount of rudder area must be outside this dead-air region, either above or below it. Also, a substantial amount of fixed area should be beneath the horizontal tail to retard, or dampen, the spinning motion. These geometric properties were combined in a parameter known as the tail damping power factor (TDPF), which quantified the attributes of a specific tail design through a mathematical equation that estimated the measure of spin damping provided by the fixed area beneath the horizontal tail and the control power provided by the unshielded part of the rudder. With the passage of time, these guidelines were extrapolated and eventually evolved into a criterion for satisfactory spin recovery based solely on tail geometry; this approach provided the only existing spin design information for many years.

Several reports of general aviation aircraft with unacceptable spinning behavior were brought to the attention of Langley researchers. These unsatisfactory aircraft had been designed with the TDPF criterion, yet they displayed dangerous characteristics. At the other extreme, several cases were reported wherein aircraft did not meet the TDPF design criteria yet they had extremely good spin characteristics. In a national atmosphere of liability issues and civil lawsuits, it was imperative that NASA analyze the situation and assess the validity of its tail-based TDPF criterion. Accordingly, the initial effort of the Langley program in the early 1970s was to determine the validity of the criterion and the effects of other configuration variables on spin and recovery.

A systematic series of studies was conducted by Langley in which the tail surfaces of a modified AA-1 Yankee aircraft were changed to produce configurations predicted to have either satisfactory or unsatisfactory behavior according to the existing TDPF criterion. Four different tail configurations were tested on spin-tunnel models, radio-controlled models, and the actual research airplane. The results of the study showed that the criterion provided good engineering practice for the design of tail features that were highly desirable for spinning. However, the extrapolation of this criterion to predict the spin-recovery characteristics for a complete, specific configuration using only a consideration of tail design could result in erroneous predictions; this was in agreement with the earlier reports of deficient predictions by the general aviation community.

From a technical perspective, this Langley investigation was a major contribution because the so-called criterion was properly examined and evaluated and designers were made aware of the many configuration features that could overpower the effects of tail

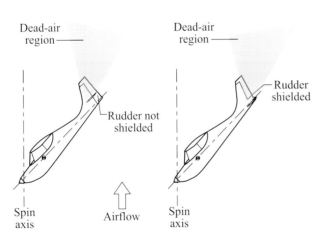

Sketches of good tail design (left) and poor tail design (right) for spin recovery.

Some tail configurations tested on radio-controlled model of modified AA-1 aircraft.

configuration on spin characteristics. As discussed in the next section of this document, the effect of the wing was particularly noted to be important. The effects of power, mass loading, center-of-gravity position, and fuselage cross-sectional shape were also determined. These effects were so powerful that configurations with apparently ideal tail configurations (such as T-tail designs) could have unacceptable spin recovery. In addition to the foregoing studies of aircraft configuration effects, Langley test pilots examined the effect of control inputs and recovery procedures for each of the four full-scale research aircraft. Researchers and the test pilots participated in numerous workshops, training symposia, and formal meetings with the civil pilot community to disseminate their findings with regard to recovery procedures and the human factors involved in spinning. This exchange with private pilots has been extremely important and beneficial, especially in view of the current lack of formal requirements for spin training for pilots of general aviation aircraft.

Applications

The results of Langley's research on spin and spin-recovery characteristics of general aviation aircraft have formed a fundamental core of knowledge that has been used throughout the industry in the general awareness and approach to designing for satisfactory behavior. By providing data, operational experiences, and critical assessments of various test techniques to general aviation manufacturers, home-built aviation enthusiasts, and private pilots, Langley's efforts have made substantial contributions to the safety and well-being of this sector of the civil aviation community. The contributions continue to this day, including applications by industry for the latest emerging generation of advanced personal-owner aircraft.

In 1974, Langley and Piper Aircraft Corporation conducted a joint assessment of the use of radio-controlled models for stall/spin evaluation of general aviation aircraft, and in 1975 Langley and the Beech Aircraft Corporation teamed for a joint program to assess the accuracy of radio-controlled model tests for the YT-34C aircraft, which was then being used as a

Radio-controlled model of YT-34C aircraft used in Beech study of spin characteristics.

*Beechcraft Model 77 Skipper, one of first industry applications
of radio-controlled model test technique for spin studies.*

spin trainer by the U.S. Navy. Spin tests of the configuration had previously been made in the spin tunnel with a 1/15-scale model, and over 1,200 spins had been made with two proto-type aircraft. These tests provided a large database for comparison with the radio-controlled model results. Langley's contributions to the YT-34C program had been made earlier when spin-tunnel tests indicated that the original aircraft configuration would have a very flat, unrecoverable spin mode. This result led to YT-34C modifications prior to the first aircraft spin test. After flight and spin-tunnel tests, the final YT-34C configuration was modified to include dual ventral fins and long triangular strakes on the aft fuselage, forward of the horizontal tail. With this configuration, the YT-34C provides exceptional spin characteristics. Unfortunately, the results of the YT-34C radio-controlled model tests were viewed with concern. The model spin-recovery characteristics correlated very well with the aircraft results when the spin modes of the model and aircraft were similar. However, the radio-controlled model did not develop the same spin mode as the aircraft. Possible explanations of the differences included the potential impact of Reynolds number and other scaling issues.

Despite the unsettling results of the YT-34C radio-controlled model tests, Beech included spin-tunnel and radio-controlled model tests in its development program for the Beechcraft Model 77 "Skipper" in the mid-1970s. The Skipper was a T-tail, two-place trainer used primarily for initial exposure for pilots and the acquisition of private pilot's certificates. The aircraft also incorporated the Langley-developed GA(W)-1 airfoil for improved performance. The 1/5-scale radio-controlled model of the Skipper was the first use of an instrumented radio-controlled model in an aircraft development program by any general aviation company. Beech used instrumentation and a general approach to testing gained through its experience with the Langley-sponsored T-34 program. Two radio-controlled models used in the test program performed a total of 638 spins in the Skipper program. Beech also

*Researcher Charles Fremaux (left) and technicians Ronald Hermansderfer
and James Hassell conduct tests of Columbia 300 model. Note auxiliary
leading-edge flaps on wings for correction of Reynolds number effects.*

committed to conducting spin-tunnel tests of a 1/11-scale model in the spin tunnel. This spin-tunnel test was the first fee-paid test ever run in Langley's spin tunnel, and the first such test conducted with general aviation personnel as participants in the tunnel test operations.

The results of the radio-controlled model and spin-tunnel model testing for the Skipper closely matched each other, but they did not completely match the full-scale aircraft results. Specifically, the aircraft would only spin if the ailerons were held against the spin. In contrast, the spin-tunnel model would not spin with ailerons against the spin, but would always spin with ailerons with the spin. The angle of attack of the developed spin for both the radio-controlled and spin-tunnel model was about 15° less than that of the aircraft. Based on these results, Beech concluded that the value of dynamically scaled model tests for this class of aircraft is limited to an indication of trends and not quantitative results.

As a result of concern over potential aerodynamic Reynolds number effects, Langley made these results known to industry and provided consultation for the interpretation of model tests. As would be expected, the potential existence of Reynolds number effects for general aviation type configurations could impact the results obtained from spin-tunnel and rotary-balance tests, which are also conducted at very low values of Reynolds number. Because the source of difficulty is associated with wing aerodynamics, Langley's staff has attempted to artificially modify the wing shape to accommodate scale effects. The success obtained by using this approach has been marginal to good.

An example of the impact of Reynolds number scaling and attempts to circumvent the problem involved a cooperative study between Langley and the Lancair Company for the Lancair Columbia 300 aircraft. In 1997, representatives from Lancair approached Langley for consultation regarding spin and spin-recovery testing of the prototype Columbia 300 aircraft. Lancair requested assistance in the determination of the emergency spin-recovery parachute required, the approach and value of dynamic model testing, and wing design for spin resistance (to be discussed in the next section). As a result of mutual interests, a cooperative experimental program was initiated to conduct spin-tunnel tests of a model of the Columbia 300 for correlation with full-scale results and to provide information on the parachute size required for satisfactory emergency recovery for the spin test aircraft. Under the direction of Charles M. Fremaux and Raymond D. Whipple, free-spin tests were initiated in the Langley 20-Foot Vertical Spin Tunnel.

Lancair had obtained spin test results for the full-scale aircraft prior to the tunnel entry, and the Langley-Lancair team could quickly correlate the results with the model data. For the baseline configuration, the developed spin for the model occurred at substantially lower angles of attack than for the full-scale aircraft; this was in general agreement with the other general aviation results previously discussed. No doubt, the cause of the poor correlation was the limitation of the aerodynamic characteristics of the model wings due to the low Reynolds number of the tunnel tests.

In an effort to simulate the higher lift capability of the full-scale aircraft wings, the Langley researchers modified the wing of the model to incorporate leading-edge flaps on the outer wing panels. With this modification, the spin mode exhibited by the model more closely approximated that of the full-scale aircraft and permitted the sizing of the emergency spin-recovery parachute to proceed with confidence.

SPIN RESISTANCE

Background

Despite decades of research and development on spin and spin-recovery characteristics, stall/spin accidents continued to plague the military and civil communities up to the 1970s. In the 1970s, however, two concepts suddenly dominated research activities and resulted in dramatic improvements in the stall/spin behavior of aircraft configurations. One engineering concept was the technical approach of using emerging advanced flight control systems for automatic spin prevention and spin recovery. For years automatic flight control systems could recognize the loss of control and incipient-spin conditions more quickly than the human pilot and could apply corrective controls before the aircraft could enter a developed spin. In fact, if the control loops were tight enough, the control system could be tuned to prevent the incipient spins; this would provide carefree maneuvers and flight operations for the pilot. This concept was particularly appealing for advanced military aircraft configurations, which were frequently flown in the hazardous high-angle-of-attack environment. Unfortunately, the flight control systems used prior to the 1970s did not utilize the flight parameters necessary for automatic spin prevention. If a unique auxiliary spin-prevention system had been implemented during that time period, it would have operated very infrequently, and the probability of failure or maintenance problems were major issues that blocked the implementation of the concept. However, in the 1970s, flight control systems of advanced military aircraft began using feedback from virtually all flight parameters; this permitted the design and integration of automatic spin-prevention systems into the normal flight control system. Such systems have had a profound beneficial impact on current military aircraft and significantly improved the flying qualities of high-performance aircraft at high angles of attack and spin resistance, as well as avoiding the loss of pilot lives and the cost of aircraft destroyed in accidents.

The second engineering concept that emerged in the 1970s involved a change of emphasis in stall/spin research for personal-owner civil aircraft. Because most stall/spin accidents for this class of aircraft occurred at low altitudes, where the altitude was insufficient to even obtain a developed spin before ground impact, it became obvious that the major research thrust should be changed from an emphasis on the developed spin and spin recovery to an emphasis on spin avoidance and increased spin resistance. In other words, the historical approach of concentrating on the developed spin was finally recognized as working the wrong end of the stall/spin problem. Thus, Langley researchers involved in the General Aviation Stall/Spin Program began to turn their efforts toward concepts that might be utilized to achieve these goals.

Langley Research and Development Activities

Several approaches might be used to increase the spin resistance of personal-owner light aircraft. For example, commercial civil transports have successfully used pilot stall-warning systems, such as stick shakers, for many years to provide an awareness of stall proximity. Some T-tail transports have used automatic stick pushers to actively prevent inadvertent stalls to avoid entry into potentially dangerous deep-stall conditions. High-performance military fighters successfully use complex control system feedbacks and schedules which permit strenuous maneuvers at high angles of attack. Another approach to providing spin resistance was used by Weick to design the spin-proof Ercoupe aircraft mentioned in the previous section. His approach involved restricted control surface deflections and limited center-of-gravity travel. Finally, research prior to the 1970s had indicated that the selection of wing airfoils and wing stalling characteristics had significant potential for improved spin resistance; and several aircraft programs within the civil sector indicated that canard-type configurations could be designed to be inherently stall proof. Each approach to improve the spin resistance of an aircraft involves consideration and trade-offs of various levels of complexity, cost, and compromise in the performance and utility of the aircraft.

For a comprehensive discussion of the details of Langley's efforts in spin resistance for civil aircraft (including extensive references), the reader is referred to the excellent paper by H. Paul Stough III and Daniel J. DiCarlo listed in the bibliography section of this document.

Control System Concepts

Control system concepts for increased spin resistance are very attractive for personal-owner aircraft because pilots of this class of vehicle are usually not as experienced as professional commercial or business pilots. Therefore, their ability to recognize and correct for inadvertent stalls and spin entry (particularly during disorientation) would be significantly enhanced by automatic control systems. Unfortunately, relatively inexpensive personal-owner aircraft cannot reasonably be implemented with expensive, maintenance-intensive control systems, especially concepts similar to those used by military aircraft.

Researcher Dale Satran inspecting full-scale powered model of AA-1 research aircraft during tests of automatic stall-prevention concepts in Langley 30- by 60-Foot (Full-Scale) Tunnel.

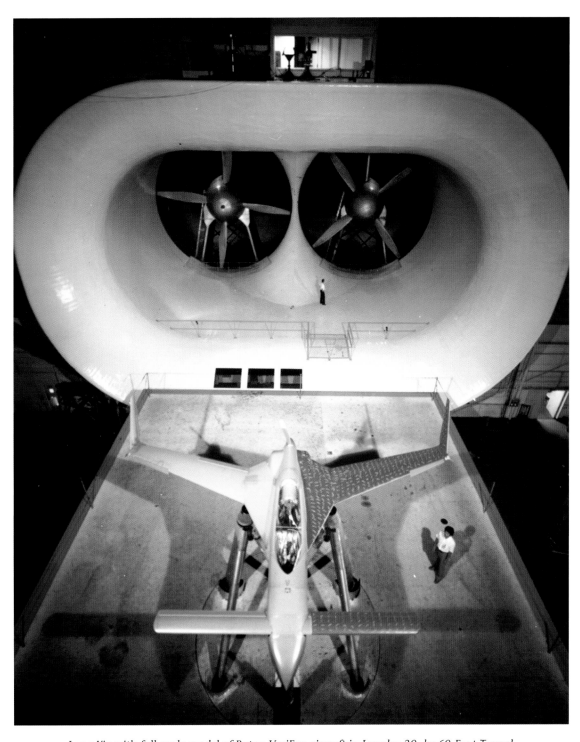

Long Yip with full-scale model of Rutan VariEze aircraft in Langley 30- by 60-Foot Tunnel.
Note outer wing extended leading-edge-droop modifications on aft main wing.

In the mid-1970s, Langley researchers led by Eric C. Stewart and Dale R. Satran participated in joint studies with academia to develop and assess active control concepts that might be suitable for personal-owner aircraft within the cost and maintenance constraints associated with this class of aircraft. Analytical studies, piloted simulator investigations using a General Aviation Cockpit Simulator at Langley, wind-tunnel tests in the Langley 30- by 60-Foot (Full-Scale) Tunnel, and flight investigations were conducted in individual programs with Mississippi State University and Texas A&M University to assess stall-deterrent systems that used angle-of-attack sensors and automatic longitudinal control concepts. Although the results of the research studies indicated that such automatic control concepts were extremely effective in the prevention of stalls, the relative cost, maintenance, and certification issues limited interest in this approach to spin resistance.

Canard Configurations

It has long been recognized that aircraft with canard surfaces might be designed for inherent (passive) stall and spin resistance. For a typical canard configuration, the canard tail surfaces are mounted forward on the fuselage and are designed to stall before the aft-mounted main wing. The mechanism of canard stall (and the associated loss of canard lift and the effectiveness of canard-mounted elevators) results in an inherent limiting of angle of attack to values lower than that required to stall the main wing. Langley's interest in pursuing the potential benefits of canard configurations for spin resistance led to a cooperative study with noted aircraft designer Burt Rutan to obtain detailed aerodynamic, performance, and stability and control characteristics of his homebuilt VariEze canard configuration in the early 1980s. As a firm believer in the advantages of canard-type aircraft, Rutan has embodied the concept in most of his designs. The scope of this cooperative study included wind-tunnel force and free-flight studies of a subscale VariEze model and wind-tunnel force, moment, and pressure studies of a full-scale VariEze model. The program was initiated and managed by Joseph R. Chambers and Joseph L. Johnson, Jr., and the Langley 30- by 60-Foot (Full-Scale) Tunnel was the site of the investigations. Key Langley researchers in the studies included Long P. Yip, Dale R. Satran, and Paul F. Coy.

A full-scale VariEze aircraft was fabricated from a commercial homebuilt kit by the Langley fabrication shops and prepared for testing in the 30- by 60-Foot Tunnel. Extensive aerodynamic measurements, pressure instrumentation, and flow visualization studies provided data to help quantify the stallproof character of the VariEze configuration. The thick high-lift airfoil of the unswept canard surface stalled well before the swept aft wing. Augmented by free-flying model tests in the 30- by 60-Foot Tunnel, the information gathered in the joint program has provided a broad database for the understanding, engineering analysis, and design of advanced canard configurations. One of many highlights of this research program was an assessment of the effects of a discontinuous wing leading-edge droop on the outer main wing of the VariEze. The outer wing droop eliminated tip stalling of the main wing at extremely high angles of attack; thereby large-amplitude wing-rocking motions of the configuration were eliminated for centers of gravity beyond the aft limit. The discontinuous-droop concept was a key factor in other Langley research projects on wing design for increased spin resistance as discussed in the next section.

Free-flight model of VariEze aircraft undergoing flight tests to evaluate stall resistance.

The database provided by other Langley studies of canard civil configurations included a wind-tunnel study of the potentially degrading effects of power for a tractor propeller canard configuration and the attributes of "Three-Surface" configurations that use a forward-mounted canard as well as a conventional aft-mounted tail.

Spin-Resistant Wing Design

The fact that the aerodynamic characteristics and stalling behavior of the typically unswept wings of personal-owner aircraft often dominate the spin resistance of these configurations has been well-known for many years. Certain stalling characteristics (especially abrupt leading-edge flow separation) produce sudden, asymmetric wing drop and highly autorotative rolling moments, which can result in rapid rolling and yawing motions that precipitate spin entry. Wing leading-edge devices such as slots, slats, and flaps can significantly improve the autorotative resistance of unswept wings at stall, and early research at Langley by the NACA demonstrated the effectiveness of these devices. However, many of these devices proved to be impractical because of complexity, maintenance requirements, cost, and degradation of aerodynamic cruise performance.

In the late 1970s, NASA researchers at the Ames and Langley Research Centers began to reassess the effectiveness of various leading-edge devices on stall control for unswept wings. Initial cooperative efforts by T. W. Feistel of Ames and R. A. Kroeger of the University of Michigan were directed at avoiding the abrupt and precipitous drop in lift curve associated with relatively small increases in angle of attack above stall displayed by wing configurations that were prone to autorotate. As a goal, their efforts involved the use of separate leading-edge slat segments to control the shape of the lift curve, eliminate the sudden drop in lift curve at stall, and produce a "flat-top" lift-curve shape to angles of attack far beyond the stall. These initial efforts proved very promising. The results indicated that, with auxiliary slats on the inner and outer wing segments (no slat on the middle wing section), the shape of the lift curve for rectangular wings representative of those used by general aviation aircraft was essentially flat to an angle of attack of approximately 32°—far in excess of values that were believed to be adequate for spin resistance. The value of maximum lift obtained was about the same as for the unmodified wing, but the flat top of the lift curve indicated that favorable, more benign stalling characteristics would be expected. In addition, the effectiveness of conventional ailerons was noted to be significantly improved with the leading-edge modifications.

Inspired by these fundamental studies, Langley researchers under the direction of Joseph R. Chambers undertook studies to more fully explore the impact of various leading-edge modifications on aerodynamics and to extend the studies to explore the impact on autorotative characteristics and aircraft stall/spin behavior. The scope of these initial tests in 1977 consisted of static and dynamic wind-tunnel tests of a subscale wind-tunnel model of the NASA AA-1 experimental research aircraft used in the general aviation stall/spin program as discussed in the previous section "Spin Technology." Sanger Burk led the first wind-tunnel tests to develop wing configurations that attempted to provide the flat-top lift-curve characteristic displayed by the Ames and University of Michigan studies. In collaboration with Chambers and his assistant, Joseph L. Johnson, Jr., Burk examined a series of leading-edge modifications, including a "discontinuous" leading-edge configuration in which the airfoil of the outer wing panel was extended and drooped. The Langley team projected that this obligation would have a minimal impact on the cruising performance of the wing and might be a more acceptable modification if it improved stalling characteristics and increased spin resistance.

During the initial test program for the discontinuous leading-edge modification, Burk reported difficulty in achieving a flat-top lift curve. Instead, he obtained data showing a lift curve that exhibited a first break in linearity at stall, followed by an increasing lift-curve slope with increasing angle of attack to extreme angles of attack well beyond stall—on the order of 40°. After examining these remarkable data and associated flow visualization results, the Langley team realized that the unique lift-curve variation was indicative of a wing stall progression that started at the trailing edge of the midspan position and progressed forward as angle of attack was increased to stall (the first stall break in Burk's data). However, the increase in lift-curve slope beyond stall was caused by the fact that the outer wing panel continued to produce lift to extreme angles of attack, as would be expected from a low-aspect-ratio (about 1) unswept wing. Using flow visualization tests, Burk was able to show that the leading-edge discontinuity produced vortical flow that prevented the low-energy stalled flow of the inner wing from progressing spanwise and stalling the outer wing. Thus, the discontinuity worked as an aerodynamic fence to prevent outer panel stall. When the discontinuity was eliminated with a fairing, the lift curve exhibited by the model reverted to the sudden, undesirable break displayed by the baseline unmodified configuration.

Armed with these extremely promising results, Burk and technician David B. Robelen used an existing 1/5-scale radio-controlled model of the AA-1 aircraft in early 1978 in the first flight tests to evaluate the impact of the discontinuous leading edge on spin resistance. During these radio-controlled model flight tests, the basic unmodified configuration easily entered spins following deliberate prospin control inputs. With the discontinuous outboard leading-edge modification, the spin resistance of the model was significantly improved. The model exhibited only a very slow steep rotation from which recovery could be achieved immediately by removing prospin control inputs.

Following additional exploration with the radio-controlled model, the Langley researchers were ready for full-scale flight test validation and assessments by Langley test pilots. When high-priority approval for the proposed flight test program was given by then Division Chief Robert O. Shade, the Langley fabrication shops completed (in a period of only about a week) a wood and fiberglass leading-edge modification for the full-scale aircraft, NASA 501, which was concurrently undergoing spin technology testing at the NASA Wallops Flight Facility. A project team that was led by engineer Daniel J. DiCarlo and included H. Paul Stough III, Langley Chief Test Pilot James M. Patton, Jr., and research pilot Philip W. Brown directed the tests at Wallops. Initial research flights of the modified aircraft by Patton on June 6 and 7, 1978, validated the results previously obtained with the radio-controlled model. The marked improvement in the airplane stall/spin characteristics with the leading-edge modification correlated extremely well with the model results. Subsequent flight tests of the aircraft with the discontinuity faired over indicated that the improved spin resistance provided by the modification had disappeared; this showed that the discontinuity was a key feature of the modification and also in agreement with the results of the model tests.

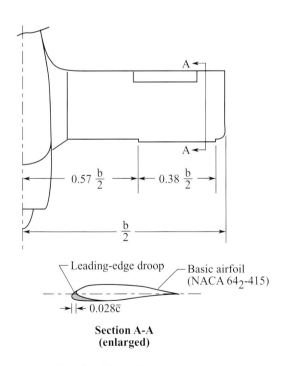

Sketch of discontinuous outer wing leading-edge droop on AA-1 configuration.

The very positive results of these initial tests resulted in a complete shift in emphasis of the Langley General Aviation Stall/Spin Research Program from the developed spin and spin recovery to the topic of spin resistance and the evaluation of wing configurations that significantly enhanced aircraft characteristics. The scope of full-scale aircraft configurations that had been included in the original Langley program proved to be invaluable for this research on spin resistant wings. The AA-1 configuration used for the early tests incorporated a rectangular (untapered) untwisted wing. Langley's other research aircraft included a modified Beech C-23, which incorporated a rectangular twisted wing; a modified Piper PA-28 T-tail aircraft with a tapered twisted wing; and a Cessna C-172 high-wing

Airplane	Number of spins/Attempts, percent, for—	
	Basic airplane	**Modified airplane**
AA-1 (Yankee)	$\frac{185}{193} = 96$	$\frac{0}{31} = 0$
C-23 (Sundowner)	$\frac{127}{129} = 98$	$\frac{7}{134} = 5$
PA-28R (Arrow)	$\frac{173}{209} = 83$	$\frac{13}{244} = 5$
C-172 (Skyhawk)	$\frac{97}{164} = 59$	$\frac{0}{36} = 0$

Summary of results for spin attempts for four NASA research aircraft.

Cessna 172 research aircraft with outer wing leading-edge-droop modification.

configuration with a tapered twisted wing. The availability of these flight-test aircraft provided Langley researchers with a broad range of configuration variables for the wing studies.

Aircraft models ranging from subscale to full scale were tested in both static and dynamic flight conditions in the Langley 20-Foot Vertical Spin Tunnel, the Langley 30- by 60-Foot (Full-Scale) Tunnel, the Langley 12-Foot Low-Speed Tunnel, and the Glenn L. Martin Tunnel at the University of Maryland. Rotary-balance testing and radio-controlled model tests rounded out this unique set of facilities and research tools for the task at hand. Throughout the 1980s, Langley researchers conducted extensive research on the geometric variables involved in the discontinuous leading-edge concept, and a detailed database was developed to define the most effective location of the leading-edge discontinuity, the impact of airfoil variations, and other key geometric features. Unique flow visualization tests using fluorescent light techniques in the Glenn L. Martin Tunnel provided considerable insight into the flow mechanisms involved in the stalling behavior of the aircraft, and an overall approach to design assessments of the lift-curve variations produced by wing leading-edge modifications was developed.

Throughout this Langley research effort, consistent results were obtained regarding the impact of the discontinuous wing leading-edge modification on spin resistance. Tested on a wide range of configurations, the concept was truly effective in increasing spin resistance with a minimal impact on aircraft cost, performance, or other key factors. One of the most impressive measurements of the effectiveness of this wing modification on spin resistance was obtained by examining the frequency of spin entry following the intentional application of prospin control inputs by the pilot for each of the four NASA research aircraft. The basic airplanes entered spins in 59 to 98 percent of the intentional spin-entry attempts, whereas the modified aircraft entered spins in only 5 percent of the attempts and required prolonged, aggravated control inputs or out-of-limit loadings to promote spin entry. These impressive results are indicative of the powerful influence that wing aerodynamics can have on the spin resistance of personal-owner aircraft, and they offer considerable promise that simple, inexpensive wing designs can significantly improve the safety of this class of aircraft.

Applications

The international leadership of the NASA Langley Research Center in the area of spin resistance has produced contributions that have been widely utilized within the military and civil aircraft sectors. Langley's contributions to military aircraft of the 1990s are documented in NASA SP-2000-4519 *Partners in Freedom*. Because spinning is not a major concern for commercial civil aircraft, the industry approach of providing adequate stall warning and (sometimes) active angle-of-attack limiting has proven to be satisfactory and very successful. Thus, few technical interactions have occurred between Langley and the commercial transport industry in this area. However, the continuing national effort to reduce the number of accidents and fatalities due to inadvertent spin entries for personal-owner aircraft has resulted in extensive Langley and industry cooperative interests and assessments of Langley-developed technology.

Although Langley's research activities and sponsored studies indicated that it might be possible to limit the angle of attack of personal-owner aircraft to values below stall, thereby avoiding inadvertent spin accidents, the issues of cost, complexity, and maintainability presented formidable barriers to the implementation of this technology. As a result, none of the personal-owner aircraft of the 1990s incorporated the active controls approach to providing increased spin resistance.

Aerodynamic data provided by Langley research on canard configurations represent a significant design resource for industry. The relative lack of popularity of canard-type aircraft, because of other considerations, has limited the applications of this particular approach to spin resistance at the present time. This experience emphasizes that the ultimate application of technology depends on a broad spectrum of user requirements (i.e., performance, cost) beyond safety issues such as spin resistance.

Unquestionably, the most important contribution of the Langley Research Center in the area of spin resistance for civil aircraft has been the development and demonstration of the discontinuous wing leading-edge droop. During the course of NASA research studies, daily communications with interested industry observers were commonplace, and the flight-test studies conducted within the NASA program were especially effective in demonstrating first-hand the improved aircraft characteristics noted with the wing modifications. For example, following the first significant flight tests of the modified AA-1 research aircraft in 1978, Grumman American Aviation Corporation personnel and a test pilot conducted flight tests of the modified aircraft at Wallops. In 1982, industry flight evaluations of the NASA PA-28 with the wing modification were performed by Piper. Cessna and Beech also conducted flight evaluations of the same aircraft in 1983. In addition to the dissemination of results to the industry via company visits, cooperative projects, and technical symposia, Langley ensured that this information was provided to other organizations, such as the FAA, the homebuilt aircraft community, and emerging aircraft companies. In 1983, the FAA Kansas City Office visited Wallops and participated in an assessment of the modified PA-28 with a view toward certification requirements.

Industry applications of the spin-resistance technology developed by Langley immediately faced a challenge because of the lack of FAA certification requirements for spin-resistant aircraft. At the time Langley initiated its research program, the stall/spin certification standards for personal-owner aircraft considered two types of aircraft spin behavior for aircraft in the so-called Normal Category (nonaerobatic). Specifically, the stall/spin certification requirements had been defined for either a spinproof aircraft (characteristically incapable of spinning) or aircraft capable of recovery from a one-turn spin. The provision for spinproof aircraft had been essentially unused by industry because the absolute nature of the regulation made compliance a very lengthy and technically difficult process. On the other hand, compliance with the one-turn spin and recovery forces the aircraft configuration to be spinnable. Thus, regulations had not been included in the certification procedures to provide manufacturers with an incentive to develop a spin-resistant aircraft.

In reaction to a continuing concern over stall/spin accidents, in October 1981 the General Aviation Manufacturers Association (GAMA) hosted a workshop on General Aviation Stall/Spins that highlighted the need for certification requirements that would promote the development of aircraft with spin-resistant characteristics. After the workshop, in 1982 the GAMA proposed to the FAA that a new certification category be developed for spin-resistant aircraft. However, before such a regulation could become effective, the FAA required the formulation of specific criteria. Langley researchers led by Stough, DiCarlo, Patton, and Brown and others participated in joint flight tests and analysis using NASA's research aircraft, that formulated spin-resistance criteria in cooperation with industry and FAA partners. GAMA subsequently used these data as the basis for its proposed spin-resistance certification standards that were submitted to the FAA on May 2, 1985. FAA representatives who had experienced the remarkable characteristics displayed by the modified NASA research aircraft were key participants in the development of these criteria, and they championed the development and acceptance of the proposal by the FAA. Subsequently, the new regulation emerged from an extensive review process as Amendment 23-42 to the Federal Aviation Regulations (FAR) Part 23 dated February 4, 1991, which officially incorporated criteria to allow for spin-resistance certification.

Initial efforts to apply the discontinuous wing leading-edge concept were undertaken by several emerging general aviation companies. Under the leadership of Joseph L. Johnson, Jr., Langley responded to numerous proposals from these companies for cooperative studies of the application of the concept. Research efforts at Langley were led by Long P. Yip, Holly M. Ross, and David B. Robelen. In addition to the Rutan and Langley VariEze application discussed earlier, several new aircraft configurations incorporated the concept. Unfortunately, for other reasons, many of these aircraft never progressed to flight certification and production.

One of the first NASA and industry cooperative programs conducted during the mid-1980s focused on a radical new high-wing, canard, turboprop pusher configuration known as the OMAC Laser 300. Long P. Yip led a NASA and OMAC test team during wind-tunnel tests in the Langley 12-Foot Low-Speed Tunnel to assess the overall stability and control characteristics of the configuration, with emphasis on high-angle-of-attack characteristics and stall/spin resistance. The results of the tests indicated that the configuration would have unacceptable longitudinal stability at high angles of attack, and an extension to the wing trailing-edge flap was designed to minimize this problem. The discontinuous leading-edge droop installed on the outer portion of the main wing also benefited longitudinal stability

OMAC Laser 300 prototype in flight.

Model of OMAC 300 in Langley 12-Foot Low-Speed Tunnel.
Note leading-edge droop and extended chord of wing trailing-edge flap.

and kept the flow attached in the region for angles of attack up to about 35°. In addition to the spin resistance provided by the droop concept, the canard configuration provided a nose-down pitching moment at stall, enhancing the stall resistance of the aircraft. Although a prototype of the aircraft was flown, the Laser 300 was never certified or produced.

The DeVore 100 Sunbird aircraft, a two-place, high-wing, single-engine pusher configuration, was designed with the droop concept. Cooperative DeVore-Langley wind-tunnel and radio-controlled model tests indicated that an abrupt, uncontrollable roll departure at stall was eliminated by the droop and that the modified configuration would exhibit extreme spin resistance. A prototype of the Sunbird aircraft was first flown in October 1987. Unfortunately, the Sunbird aircraft did not enter production.

The Questair Venture, a low-wing, tractor-propeller, kit-built aircraft incorporated the discontinuous droop concept as a result of cooperative wind-tunnel and radio-controlled model tests with Langley in 1987. Designed as a relatively short-coupled, high-aspect-ratio aircraft with emphasis on high cruise speeds, the Venture incorporated an NACA five-digit airfoil that was expected to have poor stalling characteristics.

As a result of several cooperative studies with Langley (involving graduate students onsite at Langley), the aeronautical engineering staff of the North Carolina State University (NCSU) was aware of Langley's discontinuous outer-wing-droop concept and brought the concept to the attention of Questair with a proposal to form a cooperative Langley, NCSU, and Questair team to develop and assess the discontinuous droop concept for the Venture aircraft. Yip and Ross led the activities at Langley, and John N. Perkins of NCSU and his graduate students contributed to the cooperative study.

The researchers faced two technical challenges in the project. First, the Venture incorporated a high-aspect-ratio wing (10.4), which was expected to exhibit different stall progression characteristics than those exhibited by the lower-aspect-ratio wings (about 7.0) previously involved in Langley's research. This feature would probably require a different leading-edge-droop configuration to control stall progression. The second challenge was created by the fact that the design of the Venture was focused on high-speed capability. Thus, any modification to the wing had to result in a minimal impact on aerodynamic performance. Yip and Ross found that a single leading-edge-droop segment would not provide the necessary spin resistance for the high-aspect-ratio wing configuration. A Langley contractor, D. V. Rao of ViGYAN, Inc., had conducted research on a new wing-slot stall-control concept for high-aspect-ratio wings, and Yip and Ross included the concept in their study. The team subsequently found that the combination of leading-edge droop and wing slot operated synergistically to provide significantly more spin resistance than could have been obtained with each individual concept for this particular wing design; the Venture incorporated a single outboard-droop segment together with a small slot for spin resistance. The challenge of minimizing performance penalties due to wing modifications for spin resistance had been previously addressed by Pat King, a Langley graduate student, who used the Eppler airfoil design code in an optimization study to design wing-droop shapes with minimal impact on aircraft drag. D. Bruce Owens, an NCSU graduate student, applied the technique to the Questair wing and developed an appropriate droop shape.

Long Yip and David Robelen prepare radio-controlled model of DeVore Sunbird for flight tests.
Note discontinuous leading-edge-droop segments on outer wing.

The basic Venture wing was expected to exhibit unpredictable and abrupt stall characteristics, and the original prototype aircraft displayed unsatisfactory stall behavior. The pilot for this aircraft reported unpredictable roll offs at stall and generally unacceptable characteristics. When the wing-droop–slot modification was incorporated, however, the aircraft exhibited a gentle, very controllable stall with no tendency for wing drop. In carefully controlled performance tests, the penalty in cruise performance was found to be imperceptible—about 1 knot. Lateral control was shown to be effective throughout the entire stall maneuver, even with full elevator deflection. The Questair Venture was subsequently produced and sold in kit form.

The Schweizer SGM 2-37A motorglider, which first flew in 1986, incorporated two spanwise segments of wing leading-edge droop to improve stall characteristics. The development of this unique wing modification was stimulated by cooperative studies of Langley and the University of Maryland to further explore the stall progression and spin resistance of high-aspect-ratio wings with discontinuous leading-edge modifications. With an unusually high aspect ratio of 19, this aircraft required multiple-droop segments, as predicted, based on oil flow studies in the Glenn L. Martin Tunnel at University of Maryland.

As part of a cooperative research program between the Langley Research Center and the Smith Aircraft Corporation, wind-tunnel tests involving the discontinuous wing leading-edge droop were performed on a 1/6-scale model of a proposed general aviation trainer

Concept to Reality

*Model of Questair Venture aircraft in Langley 12-Foot Low-Speed
Tunnel during tests to develop spin-resistant wing configuration.*

configuration in the Langley 12-Foot Low-Speed Tunnel. Although the full-scale aircraft program never proceeded into certification or production, this activity is noteworthy because of the innovative application of the discontinuous-droop concept. One focus of the aircraft development program was to develop wing leading-edge modifications that would tailor the stall/spin characteristics of the aircraft. The configuration was designed to be a trainer aircraft with two different training roles. The first role was to provide an aircraft in which a student pilot could learn spin-entry and spin-recovery techniques. The second training role was to provide a spin-resistant aircraft that could be safely flown by student pilots without fear of inadvertent spins. It was thought that the two very different types of training could be accomplished with one aircraft design by modifying the wing leading edges differently to alter high-angle-of-attack characteristics. The leading-edge modification for the spinnable version would be used to provide a more gentle, controllable stall without allowing the aircraft to attain too high an angle of attack, which could make entering a spin more difficult and harder to recover from. For these reasons, the leading-edge modification would need to be relatively small and kept on the outboard wing only. In contrast, the spin-resistant configuration should have a leading-edge modification that protects the outboard wing to very high angles of attack to provide good roll damping past the stall. The cooperative wind-tunnel test program identified candidate leading-edge modifications for the trainer configuration, but the aircraft program was canceled before production.

Model of Smith Aviation Corp. trainer in Langley 12-Foot
Low-Speed Tunnel with outer-wing leading-edge droops.

On June 14, 1994, the Advanced Aerodynamics and Structures Jetcruzer 450, a single-engine, pusher-propeller, canard, six-seat transport became the first aircraft to receive FAA certification as spin resistant. On October 23, 1998, the Lancair Columbia 300 and the Cirrus SR20 advanced aircraft, both of which employ discontinuous outboard-wing leading-edge droop to enhance spin resistance, received FAA certification using selected spin-resistance certification requirements. Although neither aircraft was certified as fully spin resistant, they both exhibited an exceptional level of safety in the stall/post-stall regime. Furthermore, the aircraft were found to provide a definite increased level of safety in safeguarding against loss of control and low-altitude stall/spin accidents that have been so prevalent in general aviation.

Other applications of the discontinuous-droop concept included a military application for the U.S. Marine Corps Exdrone delta-wing remotely piloted vehicle. As discussed in *Partners in Freedom*, the incorporation of droop to the outboard wing significantly improved the departure resistance of the vehicle and greatly improved its operational viability. This unique and unusual transfer of technology from the general aviation community to the military is extremely noteworthy.

Cirrus SR20 with outboard drop concept.

NASA Lancair 300 research aircraft with outboard leading-edge droop.

After 20 years of research and development, the extremely promising concept of inherent spin resistance through a specific approach to wing design has reached fruition and applications. Hopefully, additional applications and experiences in the future will validate the potential benefits on safety and result in an attendant reduction of fatal accidents in the general aviation community.

FLIGHT SYSTEMS

Background

Efficient and safe flight operations within the international air transportation system continue to challenge the technological capabilities of the aerospace community. The dramatic increase in demand for air travel by the public and business sectors in the 1990s led to increased airport congestion, and the unacceptable nature of commercial and private aircraft accidents demanded even more options for improved safety, especially with most of the accidents attributed to human error. The scope of these challenges includes many of the operating problems issues discussed in previous sections, such as wind shear and runway operations during inclement weather conditions. Technological solutions to these issues require a careful integration of advanced concepts for aircraft flight systems including advanced cockpit displays, flight management concepts, avionics architecture and integration, and system health monitoring concepts.

The Langley Research Center is widely recognized for its international leadership and research contributions to advanced flight systems for commercial and general aviation aircraft. By utilizing carefully coordinated efforts including ground-based activities (such as piloted simulators and avionics laboratories) and sophisticated flight-test assessments of new technology using unique research aircraft, the Center has maintained its leading-edge perspective in this area.

In recognition of the special challenges to the relevance and implementation of new flight system technologies, Langley maintained a close partnership and working relationship with regulatory agencies such as the FAA and with industry. Emphasis in the Langley program was placed on cooperative studies with the FAA and industry partners so that the transfer of technology into aerospace applications was facilitated and encouraged. A key strategy in this process was the use of aircraft flight demonstrations of the potential improvements provided by new concepts to prove the technology in the actual environment and to increase significantly the probability that it would be introduced into production aircraft. One major outcome of this NASA, FAA, and industry relationship is the installation of an awareness and sensitivity by the Langley researcher to factors—such as cost, certification issues, and integrated system effectiveness—that might limit the extent of applications of emerging concepts. With this approach, Langley has successfully contributed critical technology that has been implemented into civil aircraft of the 1980s and 1990s.

Langley Research and Development Activities

The most significant impetus to the establishment of a formal flight systems expertise at the Langley Research Center was a national awareness of the challenges facing the rapidly growing U.S. air transportation system in the late 1960s. During that time, signs of the emerging congestion of airports, the impact of adverse weather, and the potential benefits of advanced technologies to improve the efficiency and reliability of flight operations were already apparent to leaders in Congress and to the research community. Under the leadership of John P. Reeder, George B. Graves, Jr., and others in the early 1970s, Langley researchers formulated the plans for a research program whose objectives were directed toward the improvement of air operation efficiencies around and at the Nation's airports. The research project, known as the Terminal Configured Vehicle (TCV) Program, included research on advanced, nonstandard approach paths for noise abatement and increased runway acceptance rates, displays of traffic information in the cockpit, use of optimal fuel-efficient flight paths, data links with air traffic controllers, high-speed runway turnoffs, and optimization of air operations using the Microwave Landing System (MLS).

Reeder's vast experience and expertise gathered in years of extensive piloting experience with a multitude of different military and civil aircraft, together with his role as Chief of Flight Research at Langley, enabled him to provide the strong technical management, advocacy, and critical outside contacts required for the initiation and success of the TCV Program. The highly successful initiation of the program, its early accomplishments, and the impact

John Reeder, principal advocate and leader of Terminal Configured Vehicle (TCV) Program.

on the aeronautics community were directly related to his leadership, international recognition, and personal dedication. In 1982, the scope of the TCV Program was expanded to focus on the larger perspective of air transportation system problems, rather than individual aircraft technologies. The newly formulated program was named the Advanced Transport Operating Systems (ATOPS) Program under the management of Jeremiah F. Creedon. Over a 20-year life span, various projects sponsored by the TCV and ATOPS Program offices brought leading-edge technologies into the spotlight as potential breakthroughs and critical problem-solving mechanisms for some of the most critical issues facing the U.S. air transportation system. As a result of outstanding and sustained technical expertise, dedication, and professionalism, the highly successful efforts of Langley researchers and their technical partners provided critical contributions to U.S. civil aircraft of the 1980s and 1990s.

The technical contributions and ultimate applications of concepts and results of the TCV and ATOPS Programs were primarily directed at commercial transports. However, along with these highly acclaimed contributions, other Langley researchers contributed advanced flight system technologies that significantly advanced the state of the art for general aviation aircraft. One of the major stimuli for these contributions was the NASA Advanced General Aviation Technology Experiments (AGATE) Program, under the leadership of Bruce J. Holmes. As discussed earlier in the introduction, the extraordinary visionary perspective of Holmes on the impact of advanced technology and its ability to revitalize the faltering general aviation industry in the United States is considered one of the critical ingredients to the current health of the industry. The coalition of industry partners formed under the auspices of this remarkable program provided significant leaps in technology levels and potential applications for flight systems of advanced general aviation and business aircraft in the late 1990s. As the new millennium began, flight systems technology was being rapidly incorporated into emerging new general aviation aircraft.

Langley Boeing 737 Research Aircraft

Because the focus of the TCV Program involved tightly integrated interactions between aircraft, aircrews, and air traffic controllers, it was relatively obvious to Langley researchers that a representative transport aircraft would greatly facilitate the technology assessments, technology transfer, and acceptability of their research efforts. At the time of the inception of the program, Langley did not have an appropriate research aircraft, and after considering several candidate aircraft, the Center acquired the original prototype Boeing 737-100 aircraft for its research vehicle. The aircraft, which had first flown on April 9, 1967, had been equipped with special instrumentation for FAA certification testing, which added to its research value. After the aircraft was purchased by NASA from The Boeing Company for $2.2 million on July 26, 1973, the aircraft was modified by Boeing to NASA requirements and delivered to Langley on May 17, 1974, where its aircraft designation was NASA 515 and its initial name was the Research Support Flight System (RSFS). The first flight of the Langley RSFS occurred on June 7, 1974. Later, the name of the aircraft became the Terminal Configured Vehicle (TCV) aircraft, then the Transport Systems Research Vehicle (TSRV). Over the next 20 years, this remarkable aircraft would be involved in some of the most important leading-edge civil research ever conducted by the Langley Research Center.

During initial discussions with Boeing regarding TCV-related research, Reeder had pointed out that most of NASA's display studies had been accomplished with only one side of the cockpit reconfigured for research; however, in commercial operations, the entire crew must work together for flight deck management. As a small team of NASA and Boeing engineers thought through this issue, they explored the requirements and approaches that might be used for both crew members to share the workload. Boeing engineers suggested that safely integrating a second cockpit into the aircraft might be feasible, and with the participation of Langley engineers led by Eugene L. Kelsey, an innovative approach was adopted. The new research aircraft was modified from its original 737 configuration to incorporate a second cockpit in the forward part of the main cabin for studies of advanced flight deck technology. The aft-flight deck was essentially a computer-controlled, auxiliary cockpit that could be used to study new concepts in a realistic, two-crew environment. The pilot and copilot stations were provided with primary flight displays and a navigation display. Initially, the aft cockpit was equipped with four monochrome cathode ray tube (CRT) displays, but the sophistication of the cockpit display technologies rapidly advanced as the aircraft contributed to research programs conducted by Langley, FAA, and industry. As a result of the versatility provided by the aft cockpit, research pilots could evaluate the effectiveness of advanced displays and controls from the aft cockpit while safety pilots monitored flight operations from the conventional forward cockpit. Many research projects conducted with the aircraft emphasized operations in instrument flight rules (IFR) conditions; therefore, the lack of visibility to the outside world did not adversely impact the research objectives. The computers that ran the experimental systems and the data instrumentation equipment were located behind the aft cockpit in the cabin area. Research stations were also provided for observers and other project participants.

The scope of research conducted by Langley with its TSRV aircraft is legendary within the accomplishments of aeronautical research at the Center. Details of the history of the aircraft, as well as the objectives and accomplishments of numerous cooperative studies conducted with the U.S. aerospace industry, the FAA, and the military are discussed in Lane Wallace's outstanding publication, NASA SP-4216, *Airborne Trailblazer*. Wallace's book covers research efforts that used the aircraft during such diverse studies as demonstrations of the U.S. MLS, effect of weather conditions on runway friction, aerodynamic flight tests of drag reduction and high-lift technology, advanced cockpit displays, wind-shear research, data link for air traffic control communications, flight management concepts, and the satellite-based global positioning system (GPS). Throughout its operational life, the primary pilots for the TSRV aircraft were Lee H.

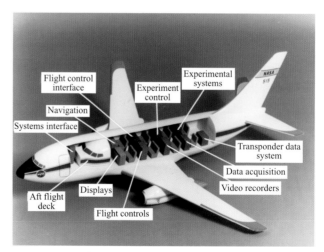

Cutaway view of model of TSRV aircraft showing aft cockpit layout.

NASA Boeing 737 TSRV research aircraft became operational at Langley in 1974.

Person, Jr., and Kenneth R. Yenni. From 1974 until 1995, Person and Yenni flew the aircraft in over 20 different research projects.

In the mid-1990s, Langley decided to finally retire its Boeing 737 and to replace it with a more modern Boeing 757 aircraft. The Boeing 737 was formally retired from NASA service at a ceremony held in the Langley aircraft hangar on September 19, 1997, with representatives from Boeing, the FAA, and other organizations in attendance. Later that same afternoon, Langley pilots Harry A. Verstynen and Philip W. Brown flew the veteran research aircraft to Seattle, Washington, where it has been retired to the Boeing Museum of Flight.

Langley dedicated its new Boeing 757 Airborne Research Integrated Experiments System (AIRES) on November 23, 1998. NASA bought the Boeing 757-200 for $24 million in 1994 from the Eastern Airlines bankruptcy sale. The aircraft is continuing the work begun by its predecessor in state-of-the-art technologies such as electronic cockpit displays, flight management systems, and flight safety devices. The aircraft is being used to conduct research to increase aircraft safety, operating efficiency, and compatibility with future air traffic control systems. It is a vital research tool in support of the Agency's Aviation Safety and Aviation Systems Capacity Programs.

Cockpit Displays for Commercial Transports

One of the most critical contributions of the Langley Research Center to civil aircraft has been the conception and development of advanced cockpit displays, especially the development and acceptance of flat-panel displays and the "glass cockpit." Langley researchers conducted pioneering research that led to worldwide applications of advanced displays in vehicles ranging from large commercial transports to personal-owner general aviation aircraft.

When Congress terminated the national Supersonic Transport (SST) Program in 1971, it authorized Boeing to continue research on technology related to electronic cockpit displays and digital flight controls. When NASA approached Boeing to acquire the prototype Boeing 737, it was apparent that common interests existed in advanced electronic display technology. In the early 1970s, typical commercial aircraft had more than 100 cockpit instruments, and together with ever-increasing numbers of indicators, crossbars, and symbols they competed for cockpit space and pilot attention. From Langley's perspective, advanced electronic displays that could process raw aircraft system and flight data into an integrated, easily understood picture of the aircraft situation, position, and progress offered the potential to significantly reduce the pilot workload and enhance guidance capabilities. A formal request to NASA from the Department of Transportation to support Boeing's follow-on development was accepted by Langley, and agreements with the FAA were formalized to permit testing of FAA-owned display equipment. Following the acquisition of the 737 for the TCV Program, the research flight deck (aft cockpit) was designed to accommodate advanced flight displays. Using advanced CRT displays, Langley researchers first developed promising display concepts in the ground-based TSRV simulator, then proceeded to assess the more promising concepts using the actual TSRV aircraft.

Led by Reeder, a team of Langley researchers defined a program that would lead to pioneering efforts in new flight systems technologies. Initial key team members included Robert

TSRV forward cockpit display in original layout. Note electromechanical gauges and dials; control and command panel added on glare shield to engage and transfer control to and from aft research flight deck.

T. Taylor, Thomas M. Walsh, Samuel A. Morello, George G. Steinmetz, Charles E. Knox, and Roland L. Bowles.

Under the leadership of Morello, initial studies of advanced displays during the 1970s centered on the impact of electronic displays on the pilot's ability to fly complex, curved approaches to airports. During that same period, Boeing began design of its new Boeing 757 and 767 transports, including extensive cost-benefit studies of advanced technologies for potential applications to these new aircraft. In recognition of the potential benefits of advanced technologies being researched at Langley within the TCV Program, Boeing sent a contingent of its engineers to Langley, from 1974 to 1979, to work with the TCV Office and to maintain awareness of emerging technology. When the leaders of this group with "hands-on" Langley experience in the area of advanced cockpit displays returned to Boeing, they were subsequently assigned leadership positions in the emerging transport programs and were extremely influential in the decision-making processes for Boeing's selection of advanced cockpit displays.

As Boeing and its airline customers considered the cost of ownership for CRT displays versus conventional electromechanical instruments, Langley's TSRV aircraft provided opportunities for a significant number of airline pilots and operators to become familiar with the

Research deck (aft cockpit) of TSRV configured with CRT displays.

benefits of the advanced CRT display technology. As a result of the advocacy of certain Boeing personnel that had participated in the Langley program and the management pilots for the customer airlines that had flown in the TSRV, Boeing decided to incorporate advanced CRT technology into the cockpit of its new aircraft in 1978, and United Airlines and Eastern Airlines were among the first airlines ordering the Boeing 757 and 767 with advanced electronic flight displays. Newer Boeing versions of existing aircraft, including the Boeing 747 and 737, were also upgraded to electronic displays. The technology has also been applied to the Boeing 777. The widespread implementation of electronic displays and flight management computers in virtually all new commercial transports and business jets is indicative of the value and benefits provided by the new cockpit technology.

Langley's unique role in the conception and transfer of advanced cockpit displays, from 1974 to 1978, is often overlooked by the aviation community; however, the intense cooperative studies undertaken by the Boeing and Langley team provided the key technical demonstrations and industrial advocacy to simulate a major advance in U.S. aviation technology.

Flight Management Systems

Associated with the fundamental and applied research conducted at Langley on glass cockpit concepts, extensive studies were also initiated on innovative new Flight Management Systems (FMSs). The objectives of these broad research studies were directed at improving the efficiency and safety of aircraft operations. The scope of research studies included takeoff and performance monitors, cockpit displays of traffic information, and efficient flight profiles.

Langley researchers Charles E. Knox, Dan D. Vicroy, and David H. Williams led an aggressive study of the potential impact of more efficient flight profiles on fuel efficiency. Emphasis during the studies was on more efficient profile descent paths because commercial jet engines operated most efficiently at high altitudes but consumed excessive fuel during the descent and approach phases prior to landing. Although the FAA had recognized and tried to improve air traffic control methods and regulations to allow pilots to descend at their discretion, the application of manual calculations and air traffic metering resulted in operations that could be further optimized. In the late 1970s, the Langley researchers teamed with Boeing to study a new four-dimensional (4-D) FMS concept. In addition to the normal three-dimensional parameters of vertical and horizontal flight paths, the 4-D concept added time as a critical parameter. The pilots of aircraft equipped with a 4-D FMS had the ability to adhere to specific guidance for vertical flight paths as well as the ability to accelerate or decelerate for a specific arrival time. In principle, the air traffic controller would specify an altitude, speed, and time to cross the metering point, and the pilot would enter these parameters into the 4-D FMS, which would then calculate the most fuel-efficient flight path to the specified metering point at the specified time.

After initial conceptual studies using the Langley TSRV piloted simulator, the concept was evaluated in the actual TSRV Boeing 737 aircraft at the Denver Stapleton Airport, Denver, Colorado. With two NASA pilots and four airline pilots providing their critiques, the research flights took place in June 1979. The results of the study showed that pilots who flew without the 4-D FMS tended to descend from cruise altitude earlier to ensure arrival at the metering point at the correct altitude airspeed; thus, flight was prolonged at the inefficient lower altitudes. The arrival times between flights with and without the FMS differed only slightly; however, when the FMS was used, the profile descent used 28-percent less fuel. Unfortunately, numerous real-world issues needed to be faced, such as the potential impact of the mixing of different aircraft using different descent paths and speed profiles. Although the 4-D FMS concept offered considerable promise, the air traffic control infrastructure was not equipped to incorporate it while maintaining safe separation of air traffic.

Despite these and other issues, continued development of less complex three-dimensional (3-D) FMS systems by Boeing and its contractors led to the Boeing 767 being the first U.S. commercial aircraft to include an FMS as standard equipment (3 years after the Langley Denver profile flight test program). Continued development of Boeing's interest in 4-D FMS concepts led to a system modified by Smith Industries being incorporated in the advanced models of the Boeing 737, 767, and 747 aircraft. Although the pioneering efforts of Langley's researchers in airborne 4-D FMS systems were not directly applied to aircraft of the 1990s, the TSRV assessments and demonstrations stimulated industry interest in pursuing more efficient flight profiles. Ultimately, a concept, originally developed by Heinz Erzberger of the NASA Ames Research Center, using a ground-based Center Tracon Automation System (CTAS) was selected by the FAA for installation at major airports across the United States. The CTAS system incorporated the basic principles and objectives of the 4-D FMS, but it required no airborne equipment and took other air traffic into account.

Microwave Landing System and Global Positioning System Demonstrations

Beginning in 1937, the Instrument Landing System (ILS) was implemented to provide pilots with a radio signal giving precise lateral and vertical guidance for approach and landing. The ILS broadcasted a straight, narrow signal beam that provided a glide slope angle of 3° for approach. The pilot's task was to fly down the ILS beam, which was laterally centered on the runway. This system significantly improved the safety and reliability of air operations, especially in low visibility conditions. By 1949, the ILS system was the world standard for landing guidance systems. During the 1960s, however, the pressures of airport congestion and reduced noise requirements demanded that new concepts be explored to provide more operational versatility than the ILS. One of several limitations of the ILS was its lack of ability to accommodate multiple approaches to a runway, especially curved or segmented approaches that might be very desirable from a noise reduction perspective.

In 1972, the International Civil Aviation Organization (ICAO), an agency of the United Nations that oversees international civil aviation procedures and standards, began a formal selection process for a new standard for international precision and approach and landing guidance systems. ICAO solicited proposals for the new system from all its member countries. In 1973, the FAA awarded contracts to U.S. industry to evaluate two different concepts that employed a microwave frequency-based, scanning-beam principle to permit more flexible approach paths. In early 1975, a concept known as the Time Reference Scanning Beam was chosen by the FAA as the U.S. candidate for international standards. Other nations submitted different standards, including the United Kingdom, the Federal Republic of Germany, and France.

As competition for the international standards intensified, the FAA managers sought out capabilities that might make favorable impressions and impact the final ICAO selection process. Meanwhile, researchers at Langley had already begun to gather data with prototype MLS systems at the NASA Wallops Flight Facility. Langley's objective was not to demonstrate the U.S. microwave candidate, but rather to utilize MLS signals for curved and variable approach paths as part of TCV research. Langley researchers built MLS airborne receivers for use in the Center's de Havilland Twin Otter aircraft, and they were able to use the equipment for flight operations research. Langley researchers had also begun research on the most efficient locations for MLS antennas on aircraft using Langley anechoic chambers; as a result of these activities, Langley was positioned to contribute directly to the FAA interests.

In July 1975, Langley agreed to an FAA request that Langley demonstrate curved-path approaches and automatic landings to the ICAO decision-making group during 1976. An immense number of design and fabrication challenges faced the Langley team in preparing TCV Boeing 737 aircraft for the demonstration. By accepting the aggressive flight schedule, the Center came under a national and international spotlight. Extensive laboratory development efforts, sophisticated simulations, and flight test assessments (in early 1976) were conducted to ensure that the equipment was ready for the demonstrations.

The demonstration of the capabilities of the MLS system to the ICAO group occurred at the FAA's National Aviation Facilities Experimental Center (NAFEC). The demonstrations consisted of two basic curved MLS approaches followed by automatic landings. The flight included observers during the demonstration process, and the dramatic capabilities and the potential beneficial impact on international air operations impressed ICAO. However, following the demonstration, intense competition from the British-sponsored MLS competitor rose to new heights; the situation became critical when a close vote by the ICAO group selected the U.S. MLS system in 1977 for an international standard. Intense lobbying by the British resulted in an international controversy that culminated in the review by the FAA Administrator agreeing to a series of international demonstrations with the aid of the TSRV Boeing 737 aircraft.

The first international demonstration of the U.S. MLS system occurred in late 1977 at Buenos Aires, Argentina, with the Langley researchers designing two descending, curved-path approaches to the airport that minimize the noise impact on the heavily populated areas under the conventional ILS approach. Fifty-six automatic approaches and landings were made, and the ICAO representatives from the Organization of American States were extremely impressed. In December 1977, the second series of demonstrations occurred at the John F. Kennedy (JFK) Airport in New York City, pitting the U.S. MLS system against the British MLS system. The TSRV flew a total of 38 automatic approaches, emphasizing curved-path approaches that could make a tremendous difference in airport safety and capacity at a congested area such as JFK. The British demonstrator aircraft, on the other hand, was not as impressive, because it did not have an autoland system or the capability to fly curved-path approaches. The last MLS demonstration flown by the TSRV was for the ICAO final-decision panel in Montreal, Canada, in April 1978, with both the British and the U.S. systems to be demonstrated on separate aircraft. Again, the TSRV demonstrated curved-path approaches and an increase in glide slope angle to over 4°.

On April 19, 1978, the decision-making ICAO organization voted in favor of the U.S. MLS standard. Unfortunately, 20 years later, only a handful of MLS installations have now been completed. The FAA's adoption and implementation of the MLS system took so long that new emerging technology capability provided by the GPS overtook it.

In 1983, the Reagan Administration made the U.S. satellite navigation network, which was originally developed by the DOD, available for international civil use. The system, which is based on an array of satellites, offers more capability and flexibility than any other preceding aircraft navigation system. However, to ensure the superiority of U.S. military capability, the DOD permitted "selective availability" and intentionally degraded the accuracy of the satellites for civil use. The resulting degraded accuracy was only within 100 meters (without selective availability, the GPS accuracy is normally 15 meters), which would not be precise enough for a landing system. These position errors could theoretically be corrected, but significant questions remained in the aviation community regarding the accuracy of the system for precision approaches.

In an act of serendipity, Langley researchers and the TSRV aircraft engaged in a cooperative project with industry in 1990 that had an extremely significant impact on the outlook of GPS for aircraft navigation and landing. Led by Cary R. Spitzer, the ATOPS Office aggressively pursued the emerging technology. Honeywell, Inc., proposed a cooperative evaluation of a GPS concept it had developed as a potential landing aid for returning space vehicles such as the space shuttle. Langley suggested that the cooperative effort include integrating the GPS equipment with the existing TSRV autoland system. In late 1990, the ATOPS Program demonstrated, for the first time, that a GPS-guided autoland was possible for commercial aircraft. The results of these flight tests directly answered the question of whether GPS could be used for landings. From this, the new question that then emerged was what degree of accuracy could be achieved. In 1993, Langley conducted a cooperative effort with Ashtech, Inc., and Ohio University with a more accurate Differential GPS (DGPS) receiver, which provided 3- to 5-meter accuracy. The demonstration showed that it was possible to use GPS for a precision approach, flare, and rollout.

As the Nation continued to contend with a rapidly expanding and congested national air transportation system in the 1990s, the role of Langley demonstrations of the potential benefits of MLS technology and the relative accuracies of the emerging GPS navigational system played key roles in the formulation and outlook for future systems. Currently, the FAA is developing the Wide Area Augmentation System (WAAS) Program for use in precision flight approaches. WAAS corrects for GPS signal errors caused by ionospheric disturbances, timing, and satellite orbit errors and provides vital integrity information regarding the health of each GPS satellite. Accuracy of the new system is projected to be within 3 meters.

Data Link

Because of increasing congestion in the terminal area, it became difficult to break into the growing numbers of radio transmissions between pilots and controllers. Because of the necessary rapidity of control or instructions, errors were sometimes introduced that required repetitive commands and increased pilot workload. Langley researchers led by Charles E. Knox, Charles H. Scanlon, Marvin C. Waller, David H. Williams, and David A. Hinton conducted simulator studies and flight tests to develop and assess the impact of a two-way data link system between ground controllers and pilots. In the data link concept, messages would be exchanged and displayed on CRT screens in the cockpit and at the controller station. With the aid of a satellite network, the concept could also allow pilots to communicate with controllers from remote locations. Weather information and charts in the cockpit would also be accommodated.

After Hinton and others conducted a highly successful evaluation of a two-way data link system in the early 1980s with a light twin-engine aircraft and flight and simulator studies of single-pilot IFR flight operations, Langley researchers became encouraged to apply the concept to commercial transports. At the time, a form of a data link system was already in use by the airlines to provide airline dispatchers with the capability to relay company messages, weather, and flight plan information to pilots. However, using a two-way data link as the primary communication mode for air traffic control information would be much more of a challenge. In 1990, the researchers continued development of their concept by using a combination of CRT message screen concepts together with digitized voices for more effective transmissions. Using a touch-sensitive panel that allows for rapid pilot inputs, ground-based simulator studies were conducted to mature the concept, and flight tests with the TSRV aircraft using NASA and commercial airline pilot evaluations were conducted. The results of the demonstration were impressive. Several instances of confusion occurred with conventional voice communications between the controller and pilots, and messages had to be repeated many times. The Langley experiments were the first flight tests using data link as the primary source for air traffic control communications. After the research flights were completed in May 1990, over 60 airline representatives showed up at Langley to witness the operation of the data link system. Interest in the FAA on the use of data link as a method to reduce radio frequency congestion and control workload began to peak, and it was recognized that, if the data link were combined with a GPS, the position of airplanes could be automatically sent to the controllers so that they could view all the aircraft in their control area on an oceanic scale.

Stimulated by emerging air traffic control technologies and the demonstrated value of the Langley concept, the FAA in 1993 made plans for a traffic control data link system for transoceanic flights. The airlines were especially enthusiastic about the data link capability, and Boeing included such systems in new versions of the Boeing 747 and 767, as well as the Boeing 777. Langley's contribution of demonstrating the value of integrating information in a data-linked air traffic scenario was a critical factor in influencing the community and accomplishing the fundamental research required for the implementation of the FAA's GPS-based Future Air Navigation Services Phase 1 (FANS-1). Boeing equipped most of its long-range aircraft in the late 1990s with FANS-1, including the Boeing 747-400 and the 777.

Landing Flare Control Laws

One of the most critical aspects of commercial aircraft operations is the efficient and timely interspersing of aircraft landings. A key factor in these operations is the ability of aircraft to land, slow down, and taxi off runways. The challenges to efficient operations increase significantly in low visibility conditions, and autoland systems face precision requirements that are extremely difficult to meet. An important element involved in autoland systems is the provision of an automatic landing flare capability, which would theoretically provide more precision and allow aircraft to turn off active runways more rapidly. Early versions of flare control laws used in transport aircraft were based on the aircraft's altitude above the runway for initiation of the flare. Unfortunately, the effect of head winds and tail winds severely impacted the precision of the aircraft landing on the intended touchdown point.

In 1978, Boeing and Langley cooperated in a joint assessment of advanced flare control laws using the TSRV Boeing 737 aircraft. Led by Jeremiah F. Creedon (who later became the Director of Langley Research Center), Langley studies included two approaches: one based on the aircraft ground speed as measured by an inertial navigation system (INS) and the other, a flare trajectory law known as "path in space," which aimed the aircraft toward a specific point on the runway. Flight tests of the new flare control laws indicated that touchdown dispersions were much less than those required by the FAA; this offered the potential for significant improvements in airport capacity. Some industry observers doubted that the specific approach used in the Langley studies would work—the TSRV aircraft demonstrations quickly eliminated those concerns. Boeing subsequently incorporated autoland refinements similar to the path-in-space control laws for versions of the Boeing 757, 767, 747, and 737 aircraft.

Engine Monitoring and Control System

In its continuing development of new cockpit display concepts, Langley also directed efforts toward technical approaches that might provide more efficient and effective information on the status and health of engine systems on advanced transports. Taking advantage of the research display versatility provided by emerging advanced electronic displays, Terence S. Abbott of Langley initiated research in 1987 on new concepts for engine information known as the Engine Monitoring and Control System (E-MACS).

The E-MACS was a computer-based display concept that processed and displayed engine information such as engine pressure ratio (EPR), low-pressure engine compressor speed (N1), and high-pressure engine compressor speed (N2) in an efficient manner that permitted rapid evaluation and alerts to the pilot. Abbott's innovative approach to the integration of this information for rapid decision making included a unique arrangement of electronic vertical bar graphics to provide clear indications of the actual and commanded engine thrust levels, as well as the relative health and levels of the individual engine parameters. The E-MACS display provided an intuitive, rapid assessment of engine operations; this resulted in a dramatic increase in the number of parameters that could be monitored and absorbed by pilots in a given period of time.

Extensive ground-based simulator studies of the E-MACS concept were conducted by Abbott using NASA, airline, and Air Force pilots in 1988. Results of the evaluation were extremely impressive and demonstrated that the display concept would provide a vastly improved capability to minimize potentially dangerous pilot misinterpretations, or lack of recognition of engine faults. The pilots stated an overwhelming preference for the capabilities provided by the E-MACS format compared with standard instruments.

Flight assessments of the E-MACS concept on the TSRV Boeing 737 were conducted in 1991 with positive results. The first applications of the principles and approach used by Abbott's concept were by ARNAV Systems, Inc., a general aviation avionics manufacturer. ARNAV built on Abbott's pioneering efforts and made several improvements to the concept in developing its MFD 5000 Cockpit Management System in 1992.

Digital Autonomous Terminal Access Communication

In 1983, Langley researchers responsible for the development and operations of the advanced experimental research systems employed by the TSRV aircraft became aware of an innovative new approach to data system integration being developed at Boeing. Rather than using separate, dedicated connections between individual computers and data system components, the Boeing approach utilized an innovative, magnetic coupling principle in which components shared information on a single "data bus." In this approach, a far greater number of components could be integrated into aircraft systems. If this new concept was successful, the NASA TSRV research system could be upgraded with significantly more research potential. However, the Boeing concept required much more development and a demonstration of its potential benefits.

Langley's David C. E. Holmes obtained approval to pursue a joint effort with Boeing to demonstrate the effectiveness of the Digital Autonomous Terminal Access Communication (DATAC) concept on Langley's Boeing 737 aircraft. During 1984, Holmes and his coworkers designed the required hardware and software interfaces to permit flight assessments of a prototype DATAC system that was designed and fabricated by Boeing. The integration process included an intensive laboratory integration and checkout effort by a cooperative Boeing-Langley team at Langley. The DATAC system was installed in the TSRV aircraft in August 1984, and flight tests of the system demonstrated problem-free operations and reliability.

Subsequent interactions between Langley researchers and advanced design engineers from Boeing regarding potential new technologies for future Boeing aircraft included discussions of the benefits of the new DATAC system. In 1985, briefings by William E. Howell, Chief of the Langley ATOPS Program, to Boeing representatives regarding the highly successful integration of the DATAC concept provided the stimulus for Boeing's consideration to apply the concept to new aircraft. Ultimately, the fundamental DATAC architecture was incorporated into the Boeing 777. In addition, the nonprofit standards-setting organization Aeronautical Radio, Inc. (ARINC), adopted the DATAC as the basis of a new industry data bus standard for all future aircraft. The specification, ARINC 629, was instituted in 1989.

The DATAC experience is an example of numerous successful cooperative projects that utilized Langley's unique research facilities, aircraft, and technical expertise in providing significant contributions to advanced aircraft of the 1990s. Common technical interests, the availability of a unique research aircraft, and a highly dedicated and professional effort by Langley researchers provided critical links for this significant contribution for future aircraft.

Visit of Boeing 777 to Langley Research Center

In 1996, the new Boeing 777 was honored as the greatest achievement in aerospace in America during the previous year, and The Boeing Company received the prestigious Collier Trophy. As a gesture of thanks for NASA's technology contributions to its creation, Boeing

Langley's staff touring first Boeing 777 aircraft during a "thank you" visit to Langley in 1996.

flew the first 777 to Langley for a "thank you" visit on May 10, 1996. The aircraft and company officials participated in a formal ceremony that included speeches by officials of Boeing and NASA and a walk-through inspection by Langley employees.

Basic research performed at NASA's four research centers contributed significantly to the precedent-setting jet's design and commercial success. The Boeing 777 was designed for medium- to long-range passenger flights and was the largest twin-engine jet manufactured in the 1990s. Its first passenger-carrying flights were conducted by United Airlines in May 1995.

Langley-developed analytical technologies and facilities used by Boeing in the Boeing 777 development work included fundamental mathematical procedures for computer-generated airflow images, which enabled advanced computer-based aerodynamic analysis; wind-tunnel testing for flutter; knowledge of how to reduce engine and other noise for passengers and terminal-area residents; radial tire strength and durability testing at the Langley Aircraft Landing Dynamics Facility; increased use of lightweight aerospace composite structures for increased fuel efficiency and range; a digital data bus system; and a modern glass cockpit that uses computer technology to integrate information and display it on monitors in easy-to-use formats.

Cockpit Displays for General Aviation Aircraft

Since World War II, Langley has directed considerable research toward concepts that might provide general aviation pilots with improved cockpit displays for enhanced operating efficiency and increased safety. For example, extensive fundamental research has been contributed by Langley researchers on the problem of loss of orientation during flight in marginal weather conditions. Simulator and flight studies of the basic phenomena and critical parameters that cause loss of control and accidents in such scenarios were conducted in a program known as Single-Pilot IFR led by John D. Shaughnessy and Hugh P. Bergeron. Langley researchers also pioneered new and innovative approaches to displaying primary flight information for inexperienced pilots; thereby the time and cost of pilot training were reduced. An ultimate objective of this research thrust was to make flying a general aviation aircraft as simple as driving an automobile. Under the descriptive title of "Highway in the Sky," researchers developed advanced electronic displays that literally projected a highway-type display for the pilot.

An emerging vision of Langley researchers in the early 1990s was an airspace system that would provide a point-to-point, on-demand, personal air transportation system that was competitive in cost and safety with alternative travel modes. A safe and affordable small aircraft transportation system infrastructure brings the mainstream of business, commerce, trade, tourism, health care, and education opportunities to the Nation's small communities and rural areas. These areas will benefit from the highway-in-the-sky concept as America benefited from the Interstate Highway System. Under the sponsorship of the NASA Advanced General Aviation Transport Experiment (AGATE) Program, a national assessment of the technology was planned.

The 1996 Olympic Summer Games in Atlanta provided the backdrop for an early success story for Highway in the Sky. In partnership with the Atlanta Vertical Flight Association, Helicopter Association International, Georgia Tech Research Institute, NASA, and eight AGATE member companies developed the world's first free-flight system for use in Atlanta. Working together under the FAA-led Operation Helistar, the team created a highway-in-the-sky capability. This system was installed in 50 aircraft, and an additional 60 units were produced at the request of the White House to meet requirements for special security forces. The system provided public and private sector aircraft with free-flight access to the restricted airspace during the Olympics. Satellite-based navigation, digital radio data link communications, and advanced flat panel display technologies were integrated to produce a communication, navigation, and surveillance system providing pilots and controllers with graphical traffic, weather, moving maps, and Olympic venue status information in real time. The effort was accomplished in less than 7 months with a joint government-industry investment of less than $2 million. The commercial cargo operators using the system in Atlanta estimated that over $20 million was generated in revenues that would have been lost without the Helistar technologies. The Atlanta Olympics project set the stage and accelerated the pace for modernization of the Nation's emerging air traffic management free-flight system.

Weather Displays

In 1998, as part of a new NASA aviation safety initiative, Langley personnel studied the compelling need to provide real-time graphical weather information in the cockpit. Weather-related accidents typically comprise 33 percent of the commercial air carrier accidents and 27 percent of the general aviation accidents, and more detailed data for the pilot would significantly reduce such accidents. A concept known as the Aviation Weather Information (AWIN) system for commercial airliners and general aviation aircraft was formulated to provide weather information in the cockpit. Langley solicited U.S. companies to submit proposals for research, development, prototyping, and implementation of AWIN systems and components. Industry teams submitted more than 40 proposals in three weather information categories: a national and worldwide system, a general aviation system, and topical areas or specific components.

Langley initiated nine cooperative efforts with industry teams in which NASA and the industry participants shared in funding the proposed research. Collectively, these teams included over 40 different industry, university, and government organizations. At the beginning of the new millennium, a team led by Honeywell was developing a national and worldwide Weather Information Network (WINN) including strategic and tactical airborne displays, airborne and ground-based servers, and multiple providers of weather products and data link services. A prototype of this system was installed on a business jet and demonstrated to airlines during the summer of 1999. The Boeing Company is leading an "Aviation Weather Information (AWIN)" implementation team that is using both a Federal Express Boeing MD-11 and an Air Force C-135C transport to evaluate a complete weather information system with weather sources, terrestrial networks, and ground-to-air satellite communications. The graphic display of current and advanced weather products to the flight crew is being evaluated during normal transport operations.

Weather information systems for general aviation are being developed by teams led by ARNAV Systems and AlliedSignal (now Honeywell). During 1999, the ARNAV team conducted in-flight evaluations of four advanced weather products being developed by the National Center for Atmospheric Research (NCAR). Additionally, the ARNAV team initiated evaluation of electronic reporting of humidity, temperature, and icing conditions from short haul aircraft being operated by Federal Express. The AlliedSignal team is developing an affordable, open architecture Flight Information Services (FIS) system for general aviation. Another team led by AlliedSignal has developed a prototype low-cost sensor package for in-flight measurement and transmission of automated weather observations from small airplanes that must fly "down in the weather." In July 1999, both ARNAV and AlliedSignal were selected by the FAA to implement nationwide weather-in-the-cockpit information systems. Both systems utilize technologies that were developed with support from the NASA AGATE Program and the AWIN Project.

During 1999, Rockwell Science Center completed a prototype of a web-based system to improve general aviation preflight weather briefing and enroute situation awareness. Text and graphical weather information sources are integrated, and information is filtered, to display to the user only that which is route or time relevant (based on mission, equipment, flight rules, and pilot risk threshold). Rockwell Science Center is also developing a system that will integrate onboard, in situ, radar information with up-linked ground radar information. Honeywell Technology Center has developed a prototype route optimization tool that integrates both weather data and perception of weather hazards. The NCAR leads a team undertaking the development and phased evaluation of an operational weather hazard dissemination system for aviation operations in oceanic and remote areas. The intent is to provide a timely summary of potential weather hazards to airline dispatch centers, air traffic control centers, and flight crews of en route aircraft. Information transmission systems are currently being verified prior to initiation of tests on transports flying across the South Pacific.

Results of these cooperative efforts will be commercialized by industry and will be used by NASA as the basis for development of enhancements to improve the coverage, affordability, and ease of use of weather information systems. Widespread applications of this technology are expected to occur in the early twenty-first century.

General Aviation Cockpit Technologies

Since early 1998, a Beech Bonanza F33C owned and modified by Raytheon Aircraft has been serving as an "integration platform" test bed for validation experiments of new technologies being developed by the AGATE Team. The experiments have resulted in the first successful combination of a number of breakthrough technologies on a single aircraft. Flight

*Cirrus SR20 and Lancair Columbia 300 advanced general
aviation aircraft on display at Langley during a visit in 1999.*

systems technology developments have included graphical, integrated, intuitive pilot displays and advanced avionics system architecture for revolutionizing general aviation cockpit information retrieval, processing, and display. Flight-path guidance information displayed through flat panel displays in the cockpit provides a highway-in-the-sky presentation developed from a NASA concept that gives an intuitive three-dimensional (3-D) presentation of the flight path and replaces the conventional cockpit displays. Integrated graphical weather, terrain, and traffic data provide simplified situational awareness. The information rich environment created by these technologies allows the pilot to focus on critical decision-making information rather than on reducing data, which results in a significant impact on safety, reliability, and ease of use.

The first two advanced general aviation aircraft to make extensive use of the new Langley-inspired technology paid a courtesy visit to the Center on February 11, 1999. The Cirrus SR20, built by Cirrus Design Corporation, Duluth, Minnesota, and the Lancair Columbia 300, built by Lancair International, Inc., Redmond Bend, Oregon, both received flight certification in the fall of 1998. These pioneering four-to-six-seat airplanes incorporate technologies that contribute to ease of operation through single-lever power control—a concept that greatly simplifies the integrated control of the engine and propeller—and multifunction display of satellite navigation and airport information. The display technology also handles graphical display of real-time weather, terrain, and digital air-to-ground communications.

Applications

The flight systems area has proven to be one of the most difficult to penetrate with new technology. The obstacles to the implementation of new concepts are precipitated by the fact that any new concepts must not only be cost-effective but also seamlessly integrated into a complex air transportation system that demands acceptance and enthusiastic endorsement from pilots, air traffic controllers, airport operators, and the general public. For example, innovative approaches to improve en route and approach and landing flight operations must be compatible with existing and near-term infrastructure, and there must be agreement between pilots and air traffic controllers over roles and responsibilities for decision-making options. Because of these critical interactions, and factors that transcend technology, many of the promising results of Langley research in-flight systems have been slow to be implemented in current civil aircraft. Nonetheless, the national air transportation system has benefited tremendously from Langley's contributions to airborne wind-shear detection systems, advanced cockpit displays, avionics standards, and demonstrations of the potential improvements provided by new technologies.

LIGHTNING PROTECTION AND STANDARDS

Background

Thunderstorms and lightning are part of a global electric circuit. In compliance with nature's plan to maintain an electric potential between the Earth surface and the ionosphere, thunderstorms are a natural occurrence. The total number of thunderstorms occurring at any given time around the world is approximately 2,000. These thunderstorms average about 100 lightning strikes per second. To the flying public, lightning represents one of the most terrifying environmental phenomena. This apprehension to lightning is naturally founded on the frequently occurring property damage to ground-based objects and the human fatalities traditionally experienced during severe storms. The National Weather Service publication, *Storm Data*, recorded 3,239 deaths and 9,818 injuries from lightning strikes between 1959 and 1994. Only flash floods and river floods cause more weather-related deaths.

However, lightning strikes to aircraft have not recently been a major cause of aircraft accidents, though the potential of damage or upset to electronic systems that perform flight critical functions, to fuel systems, and to structures made of composite materials remains an important safety issue. Although commercial aircraft experience a direct lightning strike approximately once per year per aircraft, the damage is usually confined to burn marks on the aircraft skin and the trailing edges of wings or tail surfaces. The minimal damage experienced by most aircraft can be attributed to the widespread use of aluminum (an excellent

Typical lightning strikes; cloud to ground (left) and cloud to cloud (right). Photograph courtesy of NOAA.

electrical conductor) for the skins and primary structure, careful attention to ensure that electrical paths are not disrupted by gaps in the skin, and the use of mechanical and hydraulic flight control systems, which are relatively immune to the adverse effects of lightning. Initially, the lightning will attach to an aircraft extremity such as the nose or a wingtip. The aircraft then flies through the lightning flash, which reattaches itself to the fuselage at other locations while the airplane is in the electric "circuit" between the regions of opposite polarity. Most of the current will travel through the conductive exterior skin and structures of the aircraft and exit off some other extremity such as the tail. Lightning currents, therefore, do not usually enter critical systems within the aircraft, and personnel are protected from electrical shock hazards by the highly conductive aluminum skins and structures.

Nonetheless, certain aircraft components and systems are of special concern because of potential lightning effects. For example, some strikes have splintered the nonconductive plastic radar domes on the nose of some aircraft. Current flowing through the aircraft structure can also result in isolated arcing or sparking and heating. If this occurs in a fuel tank, explosion, fire, and catastrophic structural damage can result. Fuel vapor ignition has been identified as the cause of over 10 fatal lightning accidents in the past. In 1958, a Lockheed Constellation experienced fuel tank explosions after departing Milan, Italy, for Paris, France, and in 1963, a Pan American Boeing 707 exploded near Elkton, Maryland, with 82 fatalities. Several other Air Force and commercial transport airplanes experienced similar lightning-related accidents in succeeding years; and in September 1976, an Iranian Air Force Boeing 747 was destroyed near Madrid, Spain, with a loss of 17. In both accidents, ignition of fuel vapors caused explosions which in turn resulted in structural failure of the wing. Since those accidents, much has been learned about how lightning can affect aircraft, and protection design and verification methods have improved. Civil aircraft now undergo a rigorous set of lightning certification tests to verify the safety of designs so that accidents such as those just described are very rare today.

The expanding use of lightweight, performance-enhancing composite materials for aircraft structures and the use of low-voltage digital avionics for flight controls, engine control, cockpit displays, and systems management have resulted in new challenges to ensure adequate lightning protection in the design of new airframes and control systems in order to maintain today's excellent lightning safety record enjoyed by civil transport aircraft. For example, composite materials are relatively poor electrical conductors; advanced techniques such as metallization of exterior surfaces or fine metal wires interwoven into carbon fiber composite skins are required to provide adequate conductivity for lightning currents. Despite this protection, indirect lightning effects, including magnetic fields and potential differences that occur between different parts of the airframe during lightning current flow, may induce transient voltages in electrical and avionic systems. These effects may upset or damage electronic control and display systems that have not been lightning protected.

In addition to developing appropriate protection design and verification methods for the emerging advanced aircraft of the future, an ongoing need has also been to continue to update the characteristics of lightning that affect aircraft structures and systems. To minimize lightning strikes to airplanes, such fundamental information as how lightning strikes are initiated and how they interact with airplanes, electrical properties, and operational techniques represent key factors to continue to improve design practices and operational safety. In-flight experiments have shown that there are two types of aircraft lightning strikes. Probably the most frequent type is lightning triggered and initiated by an aircraft in a region with an intense electrostatic field created by cloud electric charges. The other type is the interception of a branch of a naturally occurring lightning leader by an aircraft.

Langley Research and Development Activities

In the summer of 1977, an unusually large number of thunderstorm-related commercial airliner accidents prompted the chairman of the National Transportation Safety Board (NTSB) to issue an urgent message to U.S. airline management, airline manufacturers, and researchers in government and academia that highlighted the seriousness of the problem and requested a concerted effort to find solutions and methods to avoid such environmental problems in the future. In particular, causal factors such as hail, turbulence, wind shear, and lightning were identified as key factors that should be addressed by a national organized research program to improve methods of detection of such phenomena and to define the operational methods for coping with them if they could not be avoided. The message carried extreme urgency and focused national attention on the hazards associated with severe storms.

At NASA Headquarters, Allen R. Tobiason and John H. Enders enthusiastically supported Langley's plans to attack the storm hazard problems. Within Langley, Joseph W. Stickle interfaced with headquarters, industry, and academia to lead the management of the overall effort. Langley researcher Norman L. Crabill defined a broad technical program that addressed each of the causal factors (lightning, wind shear, turbulence, and precipitation) in terms of prediction, detection, operational procedures, and design standards.

From 1978 to 1986, the Langley Research Center conducted the lightning element of the NASA Storm Hazards Program to improve the state of the art in storm hazards detection and avoidance; additional efforts were directed toward the protection of aircraft components against lightning-induced damage. In 1978, a commercially available airborne lightning locator was flown on a Langley DHC-6 Twin Otter aircraft to obtain preliminary information on lightning characteristics by flying on the periphery of thunderstorms. Project Manager Norman L. Crabill and Project Engineers R. Earl Dunham, Jr., and Bruce D. Fisher planned the flights, analyzed information from the data system, compared measurements with ground-based measurements of precipitation at NASA Wallops Flight Facility, and reported their findings at the 1980 Conference on Aircraft Safety and Operating Problems held at Langley. The results of the study showed no significant correlation of turbulence and lightning to the in-flight measurements, contrary to the initial claims for such systems.

Following the DHC-6 experiments, Crabill formulated and led a more comprehensive research program on storm hazards by using a specially instrumented and lightning-protected NASA F-106B aircraft. Prior to this program, the lightning environment included in FAA and European standards for aircraft lightning protection certification and most military aircraft qualifications was based upon the known aspects of the cloud-to-Earth lightning strikes; many measurements of these strikes had been made over the previous 50 years, mostly by researchers interested in lightning effects on electric power systems. Very little was

Langley DHC-6 Twin Otter Storm Hazards research aircraft used in 1978.

known of the characteristics of intracloud lightning strikes that aircraft were (and are) believed to encounter most frequently. This program subsequently became internationally recognized for its unique contributions to the knowledge base of the aircraft intracloud lightning environment and interaction technology.

In the F-106B program, Langley researchers intentionally attempted to encounter intracloud lightning strikes to quantify the electrical characteristics of the intracloud lightning environment, to determine aircraft lightning-triggering mechanisms, and to identify atmospheric conditions conducive to such strikes. Two basic questions were addressed: What are the mechanisms that influence lightning strike attachments to an aircraft? What are the electrical and physical effects of these in-flight strikes? The lightning electromagnetic effects quantification research program, formulated and led by NASA researcher Felix L. Pitts, was designed to provide data from in-flight measurements of direct-strike lightning characteristics to assess the lightning environment for aircraft electrical/electronic systems.

Langley's flight research programs, initially for the DHC-6 and later for the F-106B aircraft, were conducted with flights in Oklahoma and Virginia in cooperation with ground-based guidance and measurements by the National Oceanic Atmospheric Administration (NOAA) National Severe Storms Laboratory and the NASA Wallops Flight Facility.

F-106B (NASA 816) research aircraft during Storm Hazards Program in 1982.
Note paint spots applied to aircraft that denote lightning attachment points.

Throughout its research studies on lightning phenomena, Langley maintained close working relationships with industry, the FAA, academia, and unique commercial organizations with significant experiences in lightning protection and characterization. For example, a key participant in the Langley research activities was J. Anderson Plumer of Lightning Technologies, Inc. (LTI), specialists in eliminating lightning hazards to advanced systems through research, development, engineering, and testing services. In addition, coordination of research efforts and results was maintained with other lightning research activities conducted by the U.S. Air Force and the FAA.

Langley F-106B Research Aircraft

As Langley developed its research plan for lightning studies in the late 1970s, a high-priority item was the acquisition of a rugged, lightning-hardened aircraft capable of extended flights within severe thunderstorms. In January 1979, a two-seat NASA F-106B was transferred from the NASA Glenn (then Lewis) Research Center to Langley to serve as NASA 816 in the Storm Hazards Research Program conducted from 1979 to 1986. During the 1980–1986 thunderstorm seasons, the F-106B aircraft made 1,496 thunderstorm penetrations, during which an astounding 714 direct lightning strikes were experienced. The F-106B was selected because of its metal framed canopy, dual inlet to single-engine, and delta wing configuration, which minimized the potential for lightning effects on the crew and engines, and the number of extremities that would have to be instrumented to capture important lightning data.

The flight project was managed by Crabill, and the lead researcher was Bruce Fisher. In addition to his analysis and research roles, Fisher flew onboard the F-106B as the test engineer in the rear seat of the aircraft during thunderstorm penetrations and was in the aircraft for 216 of the 714 strikes obtained in the program. Harold K. Carney, Jr., the lead technician for electromagnetic measurements, also flew on numerous flights as test engineer. Project pilots included NASA pilots Perry Deal and Philip W. Brown and Air Force pilots Maj. Gerald L. Keyser, Jr., Maj. William R. Neely, Jr., Lt. Col. Michael R. Phillips, and Maj. Alfred J. Wunschel. The research program was designed to provide data from in-flight measurements of direct-strike lightning characteristics to assess the lightning threat to aircraft with digital systems and composite structures. The program also provided data for the correlation of the relative location and strength of the various severe storm hazards of precipitation, wind, turbulence, and lightning during the life cycle of severe storms.

Under the leadership of LTI, NASA 816 was protected against the hazardous effects of lightning by installing surge-protection devices and electromagnetic shielding of electrical

Damage to composite fin cap on F-106B. Note burn areas
around inspection panel and near trailing edge of cap.

power and avionics systems, improving protection of the fuel tanks, and using JP-5 fuel instead of the more volatile JP-4. A simulated lightning safety survey test was performed on the aircraft prior to each thunderstorm season. These on-ground tests were performed with the aircraft manned, the engine running, and all flight systems operating on aircraft power. The instrumentation system measured key electrical properties induced on the aircraft in response to an intentional current pulse of known amplitude and waveform that was generated by a high-voltage capacitor discharge apparatus attached to the nose boom. The current exited from the aircraft tail and was returned to the generator using symmetrical return wires. To further enhance hardening against the effects of sustained lightning attachment to the airframe, the aircraft exterior was stripped of paint in 1983 to minimize lightning attachment dwell times and melting damage. Electromagnetic sensors installed throughout the aircraft and a shielded recording system in the weapons bay recorded the electromagnetic waveforms from direct lightning strikes and nearby flashes. Several video, movie, and still cameras captured the lightning attachment and subsequent swept-stroke attachment patterns along the exterior of the aircraft. An X-band, color, digital weather radar displayed both airborne and ground-based images of the weather systems to the crew. An air sampling system was carried in the weapons bay of the aircraft to obtain atmospheric samples of air during the strikes, and a composite research fin cap was also used to evaluate the impact of lightning damage to composite materials. Storm penetrations were flown at altitudes from 5,000 to 50,000 ft for a variety of atmospheric conditions.

A specially developed lightning instrumentation system was developed in-house at Langley. Felix L. Pitts, Mitchel E. Thomas, Robert M. Thomas, Jr., and K. Peter Zaepfel conceived and developed a unique system with ultrawide bandwidth digital transient recorders housed in a sealed power isolated enclosure in the missile bay of the F-106B. For use in acquiring the fast lightning transients, they adapted and devised electromagnetic sensors based on those used for measurement of nuclear pulse radiation. To aid understanding of the lightning transients recorded on the F-106B, Rod Perala led a team at Electromagnetic Applications, Inc. (EMA), in mathematical modeling of the lightning strikes to the aircraft.

NASA Storm Hazards Program

The objectives of the Storm Hazards Program for Crabill and Fisher were focused on three factors relative to aircraft lightning strikes: electrical activity and aircraft initiated ("triggered") lightning, altitude and ambient temperature effects, and turbulence and precipitation effects. The lightning research community was especially interested in the manner in which lightning strikes occurred to aircraft. Two theories existed, including one which hypothesized that aircraft lightning strikes occurred because the aircraft was approached by a naturally occurring lightning leader. The second theory assumed that the aircraft itself could initiate a lightning flash when it enters an electric field associated with cloud electric charges. The research conducted by Langley with the F-106B, using onboard camera systems and ground-based radar, provided the first instrumented proof of aircraft-initiated lightning flashes originating at the aircraft. Most aircraft strikes were initiated by the F-106B at altitudes above 20,000 ft. The data also confirmed that intercepted lightning strikes could occur, with most of the intercepted strikes occurring at altitudes below 20,000 ft.

Rearward view showing Bruce Fisher in rear seat during lightning strike to F-106B.
Note plasma streamers exiting from wingtip of aircraft.

Data on lightning strike incidents as a function of altitude gathered before the NASA program indicated that most of the lightning strikes to operational civil and military aircraft (regardless of geographical location) occurred within 10°C of the freezing level (0°C). However, when the F-106B flight program began in 1980 and 1981, intentional flights at ambient temperatures within 10°C of the freezing level resulted in very few lightning strikes. In subsequent years, radar was used to provide the flight crew guidance to electrically active regions in the upper levels of thunderstorms, resulting in hundreds of high-altitude direct lightning strikes. In the NASA program, the ambient temperature values for lightning strikes ranged from 5°C to –65°C, and the peak strike rates occurred for ambient temperatures colder than –40°C. During one research flight through a thunderstorm anvil at 38,000 ft in 1984, the aircraft experienced 72 direct lightning strikes in 45 min of penetration time, with the rate of strikes reaching a value of 9 strikes/min. Lightning strikes were encountered at nearly all temperatures and altitudes in the Storm Hazards Program; therefore the indication is that there is no altitude or ambient temperature at which aircraft are immune to the possibility of experiencing lightning strikes in a thunderstorm.

The most successful piloting technique used during the NASA Severe Hazards Program in searching for lightning was to fly through the thunderstorm cells that were best defined visually and on the airborne weather radar. Frequently, heavy turbulence and precipitation were encountered during these penetrations. However, the lightning strikes rarely occurred in the heaviest turbulence and precipitation, and occasionally there was no lightning activity whatsoever. Most lightning strikes (approximately 80 percent) occurred in thunderstorm regions in which the crews characterized the turbulence and precipitation as negligible or light. During penetration of thunderstorms at low levels, lightning strikes were found to occur in areas of moderate or greater turbulence at the edge of and within large downdrafts. Conversely, lightning strikes experienced in the upper areas of thunderstorms and in the vicinity of decaying thunderstorms most frequently occurred under conditions of little turbulence or precipitation.

The objective of the lightning electromagnetics quantification research program was to statistically determine the electrical parameters of the intracloud lightning environment for aircraft. The key finding of this research was that lightning strikes to aircraft actually include multiple bursts of current pulses that are significantly shorter in time duration but more numerous than previously believed. The bursts are also more numerous than the more well-known strikes that occur in cloud to Earth flashes (that aircraft are also required to tolerate). This finding proved particularly important from the standpoint of devising protection of digital computers and other avionic systems against upsets which might occur in response to bursts of pulses that could be caused by lightning on new airframes and control systems. These findings are now reflected in lightning environment and test standards used to verify adequacy of protection for electrical and avionics systems against lightning hazards. They are also used to demonstrate compliance with regulations issued by airworthiness certifying authorities worldwide that require lightning strikes not adversely affect the aircraft systems performing critical and essential functions.

This remarkable 8-year research program peaked the interest of the international lightning community and rapidly disseminated its information via international symposia and industry and government technical committees responsible for updating environment and test standards applied for design and certification purposes. For example, the electromagnetics quantification research program provided focus for the U.S. civil and military lightning communities culminating in the National Interagency Coordinating Group (NICG) on Lightning and Static Electricity. The NICG consists of representatives from NASA, FAA, U.S. Air Force, U.S. Navy, and U.S. Army who coordinate research programs in these agencies and sponsor symposia and conferences. In recognition of the accomplishments of the electromagnetics quantification research program, the Flight Safety Foundation lauded the program for outstanding Contributions to Flight Safety in 1989, and peers at Langley chose the technical report on the activity as the outstanding paper of the Center in 1991 (the H. J. E. Reid Award).

In addition to its pioneering efforts to obtain critical data for the commercial and military operational fleets, the unique assets operated by the program were used for other national purposes. For example, in 1984, the NASA F-106B was used in a cooperative NASA and Air Force Weapons Laboratory test to compare the electromagnetic effects of lightning with those produced by nuclear blasts. Felix L. Pitts had generated cooperative interests with the Air Force early in the F-106B flight program; this led to the Air Force loaning Langley an advanced 10-channel recorder that had been developed by the Air Force for the measurement of electromagnetic pulse data. Langley utilized the advanced recorder in the F-106B flight tests, vastly expanding the capability to measure magnetic and electrical rates change as well as currents and voltages on electric wires inside the aircraft. In addition, the Air Force provided a researcher to fly in the back seat of the aircraft and operate the advanced equipment in July 1993, when 72 lightning strikes to the F-106B were obtained. In the subsequent electromagnetic pulse effort, the aircraft was subjected to the output of a nuclear electromagnetic pulse simulator at Kirtland Air Force Base, Albuquerque, New Mexico, while mounted on a special test stand and during flybys. Crabill and Plumer participated in the Air Force Weapons Laboratory review of these data.

NASA 816 during nuclear electromagnetic pulse simulation testing at Kirtland Air Force Base.
Photograph on left shows aircraft being hoisted to test platform and one on right shows aircraft in place for tests.

Following the Storm Hazards Program, the aircraft was used by Langley for flight evaluations of an advanced aerodynamic concept known as the vortex flap. In 1991, NASA 816 (the F-106B) was retired after 25 years of NASA research programs and transferred to the Virginia Air and Space Center in Hampton, Virginia, for public display.

Applications

Aircraft certification and flight safety authorities internationally require that aircraft structures and systems critical or essential to the safe flight of an aircraft must be protected from significant lightning-induced damage or system functional upset. These requirements are fulfilled through a certification plan that details the methods to be used to prove that the lightning protection designs are adequate and in accordance with applicable standards and regulations through verification testing.

Data gathered by the Storm Hazards Program provided vital information for the designers of future advanced aircraft systems. The lightning protection design and certification testing of future aircraft will reflect a more complete understanding of the in-flight lightning environment than was available prior to this program. The program also provided valuable guidelines on the probability of lightning occurrences at various altitudes and within various cloud conditions. The airborne data, in conjunction with ground-based data from the NASA Wallops Flight Facility, provided the first verification that aircraft frequently trigger their own lightning strikes in regions where there is no lightning activity until the airplane gets there. Additionally, atmospheric science benefited from an experiment designed by Langley's Joel S. Levine to capture samples of air directly struck by lightning. Analysis of the samples disclosed a significant amount of NO_2 in thunderstorms with electrical activity above approximately 30,000 ft; this disclosure impacted conventional wisdom regarding the relative amounts of NO_2 caused by natural and man-made sources.

This information has become increasingly critical for emerging modern aircraft that use low-voltage digital controls which might be susceptible to system upsets or advanced composite materials, which by themselves are significantly less conductive than aluminum. These aircraft use composites embedded with a layer of conductive fibers or screens designed to carry lightning currents. These designs are thoroughly tested before they are incorporated in an aircraft.

The growing popularity of kit-built composite aircraft and the growing desire of some kit manufacturers to manufacture and sell completed (and therefore FAA-certified) airplanes also raise some concerns over lightning protection. Because

Prototype of Glasair III LP manufactured by Stoddard-Hamilton Aircraft, Inc., undergoing direct-effect testing at LTI's laboratory.

owner-assembled aircraft kits are considered by the FAA to be "experimental," they are not subject to lightning protection regulations. Many owner-built aircraft are made of fiberglass or graphite-reinforced composites. Pilots of unprotected fiberglass or composite aircraft should not fly anywhere near a lightning storm or in other types of clouds because non-thunderstorm clouds may contain sufficient electric charge to produce lightning. In response to these concerns, Langley sponsored a Small Business Innovation Research (SBIR) project for the development of cost-effective lightning protection for kit-built aircraft. Conducted by Stoddard-Hamilton Aircraft, Inc., and Lightning Technologies, Inc., the program designed and tested lightning protection against severe in-flight strikes for Stoddard Hamilton's fiberglass composite Glasair III LP, a small high-performance, kit-built aircraft. The Glasair III LP was the world's first composite kit aircraft to achieve lightning protection to the level of FAA FAR 23.

The Langley lightning research and development activities have made a very significant contribution to improvement of the safety of modern aircraft in the lightning environment, and this is one reason that accidents caused by lightning strikes are very rare today. The Langley research followed other important research at the NASA Lewis Research Center (now Glenn), begun in the 1960s, to understand the causes of lightning-related fuel tank explosions. This small (as compared with other NASA aeronautics programs), but consistent, effort within NASA to understand the effects of one of the most dangerous flight environments has had an impact on flight safety that is far out of proportion to the resources that NASA has been able to devote to this technology area.

WIND SHEAR

Background

Since the beginning of manned flight, low-altitude encounters with atmospheric turbulence and gusts have been among the most challenging safety issues facing aircraft operators, air traffic controllers, and the aerospace engineering community. The prediction, detection, and avoidance of potentially hazardous wind conditions have been a high priority technical target internationally. Major wind-induced accidents caused by the inability of the pilots to maintain aircraft performance and control have historically plagued the entire spectrum of civil aircraft types, including large commercial transports, regional airliners, business jets, and small personal-owner general aviation vehicles.

In the 1970s and 1980s, an alarming number of fatal accidents in the United States and abroad were attributed to the phenomenon known as wind shear, defined as any rapid change in wind direction or velocity. Severe wind shear is a rapid change in wind direction or velocity and causes horizontal velocity changes of at least 15 m/sec over distances of 1 to 4 km, or vertical speed changes greater than 500 ft/min. About 540 fatalities and numerous injuries resulted from wind-shear crashes involving 27 civil aircraft between 1964 and 1994. Wind shear also caused numerous near accidents in which the aircraft recovered just before ground contact.

Research focused by industry, government agencies, academia, and airlines on this major threat to aviation safety in the 1980s resulted in a vastly improved fundamental knowledge of the atmospheric environment and the critical properties associated with wind shears. In particular, the experimental and analytical efforts of meteorologists, coupled with analyses of piloting strategies during wind-shear encounters, pilot training, and the development of ground-based and airborne sensing technology, paved the way for technical solutions to mitigate this serious problem. Prior to this concentrated research effort, a gust front, or a leading edge of rain-cooled air, was widely believed to be the main wind-shear threat presented by thunderstorms to aircraft in takeoff or landing. A gust front is formed along the leading edges of large domes of rain-cooled air that result from cold downdrafts from individual thunderstorm cells. At the leading edge of this gust front, a dynamic clash occurs between the cool outflowing air and the warmer thunderstorm inflowing air and produces the familiar wind shift, temperature drop, and gusty winds that precede a thunderstorm.

However, extensive studies of thunderstorm and related downburst phenomena in the vicinity of airports by the late meteorological researcher, T. Theodore Fujita of the University of Chicago, played a key role in reversing the incorrect implication of the gust front to aircraft accidents. Fujita, who developed the tornado severity scale that bears his name, had conducted extensive studies on airline crashes. A key causal factor in his analysis was the generation and effects of a rapidly descending vertical column of air formed when air at high altitudes quickly cools due to the evaporation of ice, rain, or snow. Fujita submitted that a concentrated, strong three-dimensional outflow associated with the ground impact of the downdraft was the real fatal hazard in aircraft encounters. Although not totally technically correct in details, a layman's interpretation of this physical phenomenon is the flow from a water-hose nozzle directed straight at a driveway, producing a spray of water in all

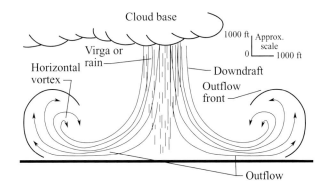

Cross-sectional view of microburst.

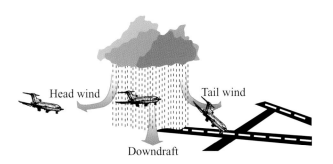

Aircraft landing in microburst first experiences headwinds followed by downdraft and tailwinds.

directions. In this simplified model, the impact pressure field causes the downflow component to decelerate as air approaches the surface, and the horizontal component of the wind to accelerate outward from the impact center. But Fujita's theory of a critical vertical "downdraft" in the mid-1970s was highly controversial at the time. Subsequently, photographic evidence of the phenomenon was obtained, and Fujita coined the name "microburst" for it. Fujita defined a microburst as a relatively small downburst whose outward, damaging winds extend no more than 4 km (2.2 nmi) over the surface. Radar meteorologists have redefined a microburst as a divergent low-level wind field with a velocity change of at least 15 knots over a distance between 1 and 4 km. The microburst exhibits severe, low-altitude wind-shear gradients that are experienced by a landing aircraft as rapid changes in the relative wind vector, sometimes to an extent that the performance capabilities of the airplane are exceeded, which results in ground impact. Roughly half of microbursts, as defined by radar meteorologists, are truly hazardous to aircraft.

Another characteristic feature of the microburst is air circulation in the form of a vortex ring surrounding the downdraft core. This vortex ring contains strong outflow winds that contribute to the larger hazards caused by horizontal shears and vertical winds over scales between 1 and 4 km. Most microbursts last for a few minutes, and generally less than 10 min. Microbursts can occur anywhere convective weather conditions (thunderstorms, rain showers, or virga) occur. Virga is rain that evaporates before it reaches the ground and is associated with a "dry" microburst. The terms "microburst" and "wind shear" are often used interchangeably because the vast majority of dangerous wind shears result from microbursts.

An aircraft flying through a microburst may experience extremely hazardous airspeed fluctuations. As the aircraft enters the edge of the downburst outdraft, it initially encounters an increased head wind. This head wind increases the lift of the aircraft and, therefore, the altitude of the aircraft. If the pilots are unaware that this speed increase is caused by wind shear, they are likely to react to correct the aircraft approach angle by reducing engine power. The aircraft then passes into the vertically descending microburst core, where it encounters an abrupt change from head winds to downflow winds, which results in a loss of lift and altitude. Immediately thereafter, the aircraft crosses into a region of tail winds. This

Photograph of vortex ring preceding downdraft core in microburst. Photograph ©1991 William Bunting.

wind change reduces the relative airspeed of the aircraft and further decreases lift, which causes the aircraft to lose more altitude. Because the aircraft is now flying on reduced power, it is vulnerable to sudden losses of airspeed and altitude. The pilots may be able to escape the microburst by adding power to the engines, but if the engine response time is not rapid or if the shear is strong enough, the aircraft may crash.

Obviously, technology that permits the detection and avoidance of severe wind-shear conditions is a key element in the national air transportation system. Working with industry, academia, and the FAA, Langley researchers provided key concepts and the validation of advanced airborne detection systems that have been implemented by airlines in the 1990s. As a result of these breakthrough efforts, wind-shear accidents have been virtually eliminated for large commercial transports.

Several excellent technical summaries that form the basis for the following brief discussion of Langley's contributions and technical leadership for this critical national program are available, especially those by Roland L. Bowles, P. Douglas Arbuckle, Michael S. Lewis, David A. Hinton, Fred H. Proctor, and Lane E. Wallace (see bibliography).

Langley Research and Development Activities

At Langley, initial interests in wind-shear studies were stimulated by a series of tragic accidents during the early 1980s. The national concern and technological challenges resulting from these accidents urgently demanded the identification of potential solutions that would eliminate future occurrences of such horrible events.

The first accident involved a Pan American Boeing 727 that attempted to depart the New Orleans International Airport on July 9, 1982, during a severe thunderstorm. Witnesses observed the aircraft climb after takeoff to an altitude of about 100 ft when it began to descend, striking some trees about 2,400 ft past the end of the runway, crashing into a residential area, and demolishing six houses. All 145 onboard the aircraft were killed, as well as 8 people in the residential area. The probable cause of the accident was identified as "The airplane's encounter during the liftoff and initial climb phase of flight with a microburst-induced wind shear which imposed a downdraft and a decreasing head wind, the effects of which the pilot would have had difficulty recognizing and reacting to in time for the airplane's descent to be arrested before its impact into trees. Contributing to the accident was the limited capability of current ground-based low-level wind-shear detection technology to provide definitive guides for controllers and pilots for use in avoiding low-level wind-shear encounters." Unfortunately, the Low Level Windshear Alert System (LLWAS) developed by the FAA in 1976 did not provide adequate warning in this particular accident. The early LLWASs were more "gust front" detectors than microburst detectors and had a sparse array of sensors. These sensors were only installed around the airport, not 1 or 2 miles away where needed. These LLWAS sensors were also installed before the physical characteristics of microbursts were common knowledge.

Following the accident, the FAA contracted with the National Academy of Sciences (NAS) to review the technological state of the art in wind-shear alerting systems and to define technical options that might be used to mitigate and reduce wind-shear induced accidents. The NAS participants in the study met at the Langley Research Center in 1984, and participation in the ensuing discussions stimulated Langley researcher Roland L. Bowles and others to analyze and brainstorm the wind-shear issue. Bowles and his peers in the FAA began to plan a joint technical program to address one of the major deficiencies cited in the NAS report—the need for accelerated research on airborne wind-shear detection systems—especially forward-looking systems that could provide adequate warning to the pilot before a wind shear was encountered.

Unfortunately, before Langley could assemble enough momentum to aggressively address airborne wind-shear detection, a second horrifying accident was thrust into the national spotlight. On August 2, 1985, a Delta Airlines Lockheed L-1011 approaching the Dallas-Fort Worth International Airport in a thunderstorm that included heavy rain and lightning encountered a microburst. The aircraft touched down in a field about 6,000 ft short of the runway, bounced, struck a car on a highway, collided with two water tanks, broke up, and burst into flames. The human toll was 137 fatalities. Subsequent analysis indicated that the pilot was able to traverse the downdraft winds, but the aircraft crashed as it tried to fly into the outflow winds that contained high velocity tail winds. The probable cause was stated as "The flight crew's decision to initiate and continue the approach into a cloud which they observed to contain visible lightning; the lack of specific guidelines, procedures, and training for avoiding and escaping from low-level wind shear; and the lack of definitive, real-time wind-shear hazard information. This resulted in the aircraft's encounter at low altitude with a microburst-induced, severe wind shear from a rapidly developing thunderstorm located on the final approach course." The ground-based LLWAS wind-shear warning system finally detected the microburst a full 2 min after the aircraft had crashed.

Immediately following the accident, national pressures on Congress to provide solutions to these traumatic accidents resulted in a fact-finding visit by Congressman George Brown of California to Langley for a briefing on wind-shear research. At the time, the most directly relevant NASA research was being conducted in the area of piloted simulation technology, involving cloud-scale modeling. Jeremiah F. Creedon, then Director for Flight Systems, briefed Brown on Langley's potential plans for a technical attack on the problem. An enthusiastic endorsement by Brown of the concepts and capabilities offered by Langley resulted from this briefing. Brown carried his impressions of the briefing back to Congress where he played a key role in pursuing support for wind-shear research. Subsequently, in 1986, the FAA announced a National Integrated Windshear Plan, which included Langley as the lead organization for airborne wind-shear detection research under a joint NASA and FAA Airborne Windshear Program. At Langley, wind-shear research was organized under the leadership of Roland L. Bowles. Bowles and his team quickly formulated analyses, simulations, laboratory tests, and flight tests that would help the FAA reach the objective of certifying predictive wind-shear detection systems for installation on all commercial aircraft. The program consisted of three main elements: hazard characterization, sensor technology, and flight management systems. This joint program was later expanded in 1990 to include the integration of both airborne and ground-based detection technology.

Hazard Characterization

One critical and fundamental element of Langley's Wind-Shear Program was a major effort aimed at understanding the detailed characteristics and relative hazard of microbursts. The use of Langley's supercomputer capability had already been instrumental in the development of a mesoscale numerical weather model by Langley contractor, Michael L. Kaplan, and others in the early 1980s. This sophisticated weather model became a useful research tool in understanding large severe storms events, and it also became the concept for the National Weather Service to develop a numerical weather model that became operational in the period. A more detailed model of wind-shear phenomena was developed by Fred H. Proctor and his associates. Known as the Terminal Area Simulation System (TASS), this three-dimensional, time-dependent model included representation of liquid and ice microphysics. The effects of condensation, evaporation, freezing, and sublimation in the atmosphere and their impact on atmospheric winds could be numerically simulated by this impressive tool to promote an understanding of microburst formation and structure. Using TASS, Proctor could actually simulate the time-dependent life cycle of a convective storm, including microbursts that might develop at subsequent times. Data sets generated from this model were eventually used by the FAA in its certification process for onboard wind-shear sensors. In 1993, Proctor and Bowles were awarded NASA Langley's prestigious award for the best technical paper, the H. J. E. Reid Award, for a case study of a Denver wind-shear incident using the TASS model.

Throughout the program, TASS was applied to numerous actual microburst cases and demonstrated the ability to produce simulation results that agreed closely with observations. The new capabilities provided by TASS were used in a multitude of analysis objectives: an understanding of microburst events, reconstructing missing information from actual observations, evaluating microburst sensor capabilities, and providing answers regarding flight management strategies during microburst encounters.

In addition to defining the detailed atmospheric characteristics produced by microbursts, the Langley researchers addressed the key issue of defining the relative hazard associated with microburst encounters. A brilliant approach to this problem was conceived and implemented by Bowles. He examined the overall performance capabilities of aircraft during a microburst encounter and subsequently derived a metric he named the "F-Factor," which quantifies the loss in aircraft performance capability that would be experienced during a specific wind shear. The nondimensional F-Factor is based on a consideration of the weight, thrust, and drag of the aircraft as well as the effects of local velocities in the wind shear on the specific excess thrust (thrust minus drag divided by weight) required to maintain steady flight conditions due to wind variations in a microburst. For example, if a representative aircraft was capable of a specific excess thrust value of 0.15 at a flight condition of interest, a wind shear with intensity greater than an F-Factor of 0.15 would exceed the maximum performance capability of the airplane. When encountering such a wind shear, the airplane would lose airspeed, altitude, or both, regardless of pilot inputs. The typical transport aircraft traveling at 150 knots and encountering a wind shear with an F-Factor of 0.15 over 1 nmi (24 sec) would lose 911 ft of altitude if recovery action was not taken. Refinements and the ultimate development of the F-Factor principle by Bowles, Michael S. Lewis, and David A. Hinton included a consideration of the length of time over which the aircraft is exposed to the wind shear to produce a refined definition of the F-Factor averaged over 1 km (about 15 sec of exposure at typical jet transport low-altitude airspeeds).

The breakthrough analysis and derivation of the F-Factor by Bowles is regarded by many as the key contribution of NASA in the taming of the wind-shear threat. As discussed in a later section, the F-Factor provided enabling analyses and assessments for advanced airborne wind-shear sensors and is now used as a FAA-mandated tool in the development and commercial sales of wind-shear sensors. In recognition of his outstanding contributions in wind-shear research, Roland Bowles was awarded an R&D 100 Award (1993), the Langley H. J. E. Reid Award (1993), and the AIAA Engineer of the Year Award (1994).

The scope of the Langley program to characterize wind-shear hazards also involved other aspects of operations in thunderstorms. For example, stimulated by concerns over the unknown effects of the extremely heavy rainfall that is typically experienced during wind-shear conditions, researcher R. Earl Dunham, Jr., led work to determine experimentally the impact of heavy rain on aerodynamic characteristics (especially lift) of representative transport airfoils. In this unique study, wind-tunnel tests were initially conducted in the Langley 14- by 22-Foot Subsonic Tunnel using water spray bars in the tunnel to determine if simulated rain particles would degrade the aerodynamic performance of representative subscale wing models. Subsequently, a "car wash" test section was constructed along the track of the Langley Aircraft Landing Dynamics Facility (ALDF), and a large-scale instrumented wing-flap model was propelled through simulated rain to obtain results more representative of actual aircraft conditions. Results of the wind-tunnel and ALDF testing showed significant degradation in the maximum lift, and a marked decrease in the stall angle of attack under extremely heavy rain conditions (greater than about 1,000 mm/hr). Results of the tests were then used by Dan D. Vicroy in a theoretical analysis of wind-shear encounters where it was determined that climb performance reductions equivalent to an F-Factor of about 0.01 would be experienced. A major conclusion of these activities, however, was that for the vast majority of wind-shear encounters, heavy rain was an insignificant effect. The extremely large rain rates needed to impact aircraft lift are extremely rare in nature.

Sensor Technology

While Langley researched the airborne detection technology, the FAA undertook an aircrew training program that focused on wind-shear recognition and procedures for recovering from its effects. The FAA also led the development of advanced ground-based wind-shear detection instruments, including the Terminal Doppler Weather Radar (TDWR) now being installed at major U.S. airports. Developed by the Raytheon Corporation, the TDWR can accurately measure wind velocities in terminal areas and generate real-time aircraft hazard displays that are updated every minute.

Langley's focus, however, was on the development of airborne systems capable of predicting the presence of wind shear in a forward-looking mode. In response to the terrible accidents of the early 1980s, the FAA in 1988 directed that all commercial aircraft have onboard wind-shear detection systems by the end of 1993. Three airlines—American, Northwest, and Continental—received exemptions until the end of 1995 in order to install and test emerging predictive wind-shear sensors rather than reactive systems that do not report the condition until an airplane already has encountered it. The reactive system processes data from standard aircraft instruments to determine the presence of wind shear. The reactive system, therefore, only advises a pilot of a wind-shear event, which allows an increase in engine power and possibly escape of the hazard; however, the airplane might not be capable of recovering from a severe wind shear at that point. Langley concentrated on a predictive system in the cockpit that would provide 10 to 40 sec of advance warning; thereby, the pilot would be able to determine the proper maneuver, add power for flight stability, or avoid the wind-shear area altogether. A Wind-Shear Program Office was established about the time that Langley realized that multiple sensors had to be flight-tested for assessments.

Langley TSRV research aircraft at Orlando during wind-shear flight research efforts.

Pushed by the 1995 implementation decision imposed by the FAA wind-shear implementation plan and augmented by technology application experts from the Research Triangle Institute, the Langley team initiated the development and assessments of three different types of microburst sensors. The one that ultimately became the first in airline service was the Doppler microwave radar, which sends a radio wave ahead of the aircraft to bounce off raindrops in the thunderstorm and return to the instrument. Computerized measurement of the Doppler shift (the difference in wavelength frequency between the outbound wave and the returning signal) provides an indication of wind-shear velocity. A second type of system known as Lidar, for Light Detection and Ranging, operates under the same Doppler shift principle but employs a laser beam instead of a radio wave. A third type, a passive infrared sensor, is based on the fact that a microburst, usually cooler than the surrounding air, can theoretically be detected by infrared measurement of the temperature differential ahead of the airplane.

Langley's task was essentially to build a technology base that would enable manufacturers to develop their own commercially viable, proprietary systems. The enormous job began with characterizing the wind-shear hazard and determining the warning time required. Extensive computational simulations by Langley's Fred H. Proctor, using his personal experience and the TASS computer models (which had been thoroughly validated by actual observations), documented the structure, strength, and evolution of microbursts. This work established the basic specifications for sensors and enabled development of algorithms for rejecting ground "clutter" that could confuse sensor signals. As would be expected, the Bowles F-Factor was a key factor in these analyses. All this knowledge gave manufacturers a broad knowledge base about how to extract wind-shear information from a sensor signal, how to process the data against hazard criteria, and how to alert flight crews to valid threats while rejecting "nuisance" indicators.

By 1991, 5 years into Langley's wind-shear sensor development program, the technology had advanced to the point where validation of the sensors required actual flight tests in wind-shear conditions. For that challenging job, Langley outfitted its unique Boeing 737 flying laboratory. Formally known as the Transport Systems Research Vehicle (TSRV), this particular 737 was the first production aircraft of the Boeing 737-100 jetliner series. This unique aircraft was extensively modified by Langley and equipped with a rear research cockpit in what would have been the forward section of the passenger cabin for studies of advanced flight displays and technology. Although it had been used for over 20 years in very significant aeronautical research at Langley, the wind-shear program was arguably the most important technical project for the TSRV. The aft flight deck was used as a command post to monitor ground radar uplinks and airborne sensors and to fly the airplane during maneuvers to intercept a microburst. In the rear cockpit, a moving-map display, with radar-derived microburst icons, was used as an efficient tool for setting up the straight-in approaches needed to allow radar and lidar scanning before entry. Before microburst entry, the forward deck took control and manually flew the microburst penetration.

Three types of forward-looking wind-shear sensors were evaluated during the flight tests: a modified doppler radar transmitter from Rockwell International, Collins Air Transport Division (Langley developed the research signal-processing algorithms and hardware for the

Laser beams used to align lidar and infrared detection systems on TSRV.

wind-shear application); a doppler lidar by Lockheed Corporation, Missiles and Space Division, United Technologies Optical Systems, Inc., and Lassen Research; and an infrared detector by Turbulence Prediction Systems. Emedio Bracalente, Langley, led the Airborne Radar Development Group.

Langley selected two field sites for the joint NASA and FAA flight test program: one at Orlando, Florida, and the other at Denver, Colorado. Both areas were noted for frequent microbursts in summertime, but it was anticipated that microbursts in the Orlando area would be predominantly "wet," whereas a major portion of the microbursts at Denver would be "dry." The flight test plan was challenging. The researchers had to anticipate when and where a microburst would form based on radar and other meteorological data because the life cycle of a microburst (and its parent thunderstorm) is shorter than the time it would take the aircraft to be boarded and airborne. When ground controllers predicted a potential wind shear, the Langley crew would scramble, take off, fly directly toward and into the microburst, observe and record the sensor findings, then validate them by cross-checking with ground radar data and with data from an airborne reactive system for measuring wind-shear velocities in situ. Orlando flights were supported by a TDWR operated by the Lincoln Laboratory at the Massachusetts Institute of Technology. At Denver, a research radar of similar capability was operated by the National Center for Atmospheric Research. For safety purposes, the

TSRV approaching thunderstorm for microburst studies.

TSRV was flown into wind shear at speeds higher than those of a normal jetliner approach and at altitudes greater than takeoff and landing levels (speeds of 240–260 mph and altitudes of 750–1,500 ft). Other safety factors employed during the deployment were to avoid flying into areas with radar reflectivity greater than 50 dBz (45 dBz in Denver), and F-Factors greater than 0.15. Over the summers of 1991 and 1992, the Langley team conducted 130 flights and experienced 75 wind-shear events. The airplane flew through heavy rains and dust clouds, near hail and frequent lightning, all in proximity to major airports without any safety incidents. The results of the test program demonstrated that Doppler radar systems offered the greatest promise for early introduction to airline service. The Langley forward-looking Doppler radar detected wind shear consistently and at longer ranges than other systems, and it was able to provide 20 to 40 sec warning of upcoming microbursts. Some of the predictive sensors showed good correlation with data from ground radars and the onboard reactive systems.

The personal professionalism, dedication, and individual contributions of the TSRV wind-shear flight test team were shining examples of this outstanding Langley contribution to aircraft of the 1990s. Michael S. Lewis led these flight efforts in his role as Deputy Program Manager, augmented by an enthusiastic team that included electronic technicians led by Artie D. Jessup; flight operations led by TSRV crew chief Michael Basnett; and research pilots Lee H. Person, Jr., and Kenneth R. Yenni.

Flight Management Systems

Yet another key element in the NASA and FAA Airborne Wind-Shear Program was directed at defining operational concepts to minimize or mitigate the hazards associated with microbursts. Research efforts included defining aircraft wind-shear recovery strategies, using ground-based radar information on the flight deck as an alternative for airborne weather radar, and determining the most effective crew information and procedures. David A. Hinton led numerical and piloted simulations to determine the pilot control strategy that would result in a minimum aircraft energy loss when a microburst was encountered. Hinton examined several methods of controlling aircraft energy, and all findings indicated that the factor that most strongly affected a microburst wind-shear recovery was the time the recovery was initiated. In the studies, the average recovery altitude for all strategies only varied by about 20 ft; however, the average recovery altitude varied by almost 300 ft when the initiation time of the recovery was advanced by 5 sec.

Hinton also led Langley's studies of the use of information provided by the FAA airport TDWR in the cockpit. Major challenges for this approach included the impact of time delays in view of the changing dynamics of microburst characteristics between updates from the TDWR (each minute) and correcting for the differences between the height of the ground-based radar beam and the altitude of the airplane. During flight tests of the Langley TSRV Boeing 737 aircraft in 1991 and 1992, uplinked TDWR data were used to locate microbursts and maneuver the TSRV to penetrate the event. However, the results of Hinton's study indicated that the ground-based TDWR information was more appropriate for microburst awareness and advisories rather than as a flight deck wind-shear hazard alerting system.

Langley conducted or sponsored several important studies aimed at issues regarding the most effective crew-alerting information and responses during wind-shear encounters. These detailed studies addressed issues such as how much advanced warning was required, should lateral maneuvers be attempted for escape, and should existing wind-shear pilot training be modified for forward-looking sensor systems. The scope of studies included numerical and piloted simulations using microburst models and candidate cockpit display formats. Another important issue identified by Langley involved the interpretation of valid forward-looking wind-shear system alerts as nuisance alerts. This concern involved the fact that pilots, having been alerted by the system, might conclude that the system had issued a false alarm if the microburst penetration was uneventful.

Following these research studies, the technology development effort of NASA for airborne wind-shear detection systems was essentially complete, but the Langley group continued working in a consulting capacity on the matter of FAA certification. No certification standards existed—they had to be invented and the Langley researchers now represented the most knowledgeable body in the world of wind-shear expertise. Langley worked with the FAA and industry to develop a set of standards for certification of wind-shear sensors. Collectively, the standards define the hazard, the cockpit interface and alerts to be given to flight crews, a suggested methodology for certification, and the requisite sensor performance levels. Langley research was the basis for most of the specifications. In addition to providing guidance for development of specifications, TASS simulations provided the microburst data sets required for certification testing. This set consists of a range of possible events (dry, wet, large scale, small diameter, multicore) that an aircraft may encounter.

A final wind-shear related Langley contribution occurred immediately after the NASA and FAA program ended. On July 2, 1994, a USAir DC-9-31 crashed following a missed approach at the Charlotte-Douglas International Airport. The accident resulted in 37 fatalities of the 57 onboard. As an altitude of 350 ft was reached during the go-around, the aircraft rapidly began to descend. The aircraft then collided with trees and a private residence and broke up. The accident investigation stated that the probable causes were (1) the decision of the flight crew to continue an approach into severe convective activity that was conducive to a microburst, (2) the failure of the flight crew to recognize a wind-shear situation in a timely manner, (3) the failure of the flight crew to establish and maintain the proper airplane attitude and thrust setting necessary to escape the wind shear, and (4) the lack of real-time adverse weather and wind-shear hazard information dissemination from air traffic control, all of these factors led to an encounter with and failure to escape from a microburst-induced wind shear that was produced by a rapidly developing thunderstorm located at the approach end of the runway. Contributing to the accident were (1) the lack of air traffic control procedures that would have required the controller to display and issue radar weather information to the pilots, (2) the failure of the Charlotte tower supervisor to properly advise and ensure that all controllers were aware of and reporting the reduction in visibility and the low-level wind-shear alerts that had occurred in multiple quadrants, (3) the inadequate remedial actions by USAir to ensure adherence to standard operating procedures, and (4) the inadequate software logic in the wind-shear warning system of the airplane that did not provide an alert upon entry into the wind shear.

In response to an NTSB request for assistance, a Langley team of Fred H. Proctor, Emedio Bracalente, and Steve Harrah, together with George Switzer and Charles Britt of Research Triangle Institute, used the TASS model to simulate the microburst and then used radar simulation to show what a wind-shear radar would have seen if onboard the aircraft. The Charlotte microburst was one of the smallest and most intense that the Langley team had ever seen (just under 1 km but with very high F-Factor); this was a worst-case situation because it gave the pilots no reaction time. The primary conclusion of the study was that the accident may have been avoided if the aircraft had been equipped with a wind-shear radar.

Applications

In addition to the usual practice of disseminating technical papers to effect technology transfer, NASA and the FAA jointly sponsored five well-attended national wind-shear conferences beginning in 1987 and ending in 1993. The Airborne Wind-Shear Program was based on one of the most effective methods of technology transfer—the participation of potential manufacturers, industry, and regulatory agencies to track the development and assessments of wind-shear detectors. Three major avionics manufacturers (Allied Signal, Westinghouse Electronic Systems Group, and Rockwell Collins Commercial Avionics) sent engineering teams to Langley to meet directly with the radar engineering personnel and follow the developmental effort of Langley step by step. The three companies each requested and were provided Langley wind-shear simulations, which they used extensively in developing their own commercial systems. Langley personnel and contractors also participated in several government-industry efforts to develop standards for forward-looking wind-shear detection systems.

On September 1, 1994, Allied Signal Bendix RDR-4B became the first predictive wind-shear system to gain FAA certification for airline operations. The RDR-4B forward-looking radar was the product of the decade-long FAA, NASA, industry, and academia research program spearheaded by Langley that developed the technology base to enable commercial manufacture of the Allied Signal and other wind-shear detection-prediction systems.

Many of Langley's technology concepts have been incorporated into industry's implementation of advanced wind-shear detection systems. For example, the F-Factor became a regulatory parameter. According to FAA regulations, wind-shear warnings must be given for F-Factors of 0.13 and greater. FAA regulations determine the combinations of altitude, airspeed, distance from wind shear, and F-Factor that result in an advisory, caution, or warning to the flight crew.

Three major U.S. airlines (United, Northwest, and Continental) subsequently selected the RDR-4B; collectively, they ordered more than 1,000 units. The technology is also being extended to foreign airlines, and among those who have purchased the RDR-4B are Swissair, Alitalia, Iberia, Gulf Air, and Kuwait Airways.

On November 30, 1994, Continental Airlines Flight 1637, a Boeing 737-300 jetliner, took off from Washington (D.C.) National Airport bound for Cleveland. It was a routine, regularly scheduled flight, but to aviation safety officials all over the world it was something more—it was a historic moment that marked the introduction to commercial airline service of an onboard cockpit instrument for detecting and predicting wind shear in a forward-looking mode.

In the mid- and late-1990s, avionics companies rapidly provided advanced wind-shear detection systems. By June, 1996, vendors such as Allied Signal/Bendix (now Honeywell), Rockwell Collins, and Westinghouse Electric produced certified forward-looking wind-shear radar systems. Over 2,000 orders had been placed for the systems from foreign and domestic carriers as well as the U.S. Air Force. These wind-shear detection systems issue microbursts warnings within a specific distance (e.g., 0.25 nmi above or below the flight path of the aircraft) and within a specific angular sector (e.g., –30°) of the aircraft heading. A warning icon is displayed on the radar display, and an aural warning is also issued by a voice synthesizer. Wind-shear alerts are typically inhibited during takeoff from the time the aircraft reaches 100 knots airspeed until it is 50 ft above ground level (AGL) to discourage avoidance maneuvers during this critical flight time. Similarly, alerts are inhibited during approach when the aircraft is below 50 ft AGL. Alerts are never given above a maximum altitude (e.g., 1,500 ft AGL).

It took almost a decade to bring the predictive wind-shear system from concept to commercial availability, but aviation experts say that was a remarkably brief period when the complexity of the phenomenon is considered. The program stands as a model of cooperative endeavor by a broad segment of the U.S. aviation community, including government agencies, aircraft manufacturers, sensor manufacturers, airlines, research organizations, and academia.

The contributions of the NASA Langley Research Center to this national success story stand out among the thousands of legendary technological accomplishments of the Center. Cited as "NASA at its best" by NASA's Aeronautics Advisory Committee, the NASA and FAA Airborne Wind-Shear Research Program was nominated in 1994 for the Nation's prestigious Robert J. Collier Trophy in recognition of the most significant aerospace accomplishment.

RUNWAY FRICTION AND TIRE TECHNOLOGY

Background

The technical challenge of ensuring satisfactory braking characteristics for aerospace vehicles, especially on wet or icy runways, has been a key element in a research program at the Langley Research Center. The contributions of this program have probably had more impact on the daily safety of the flying and nonflying public than many other Langley programs. Langley's leadership in this field is based on years of studies ranging from the fundamental tendencies of precipitation to affect hydroplaning and road/runway friction to the analysis and development of improved tire and landing gear designs. Recognized as international experts, Langley researchers are frequently requested by the civil aviation industry to provide analysis during new aircraft development programs, by international organizations to participate in cooperative studies to develop advanced instrumentation and friction measurement normalization, and by government agencies to assist in accident investigations for both aviation and ground vehicle mishaps. Thanks to the efforts of Langley researchers, their technical peers, and interorganizational cooperation, this critical technology has been transferred into products and services that have significantly enhanced the quality of life and safety of the U.S. public.

Langley Research and Development Activities

Langley's approach to accumulating its vast expertise and operational experiences in this area has included extensive hands-on research involving all aspects of surface friction characterization, precipitation runoff characteristics, the development of advanced instrumentation for friction measurements in all-weather conditions, landing gear dynamics, tire cornering characteristics, and tire wear. Throughout the program, extensive use has been made of the unique Langley Aircraft Landing Dynamics Facility (ALDF), which permits detailed studies of tire-runway interactions under actual and simulated environmental conditions. Perhaps the most important aspect of the program, however, has been the extremely active participation of the Langley staff during actual runway braking and friction-measuring studies at worldwide sites using actual aircraft operations and representative weather conditions.

Langley Aircraft Landing Dynamics Facility

The ALDF is a test track primarily used for landing gear research activities. The ALDF uses a high-pressure water-jet system to propel the test carriage along the 2,800-ft track. The propulsion system consists of an L-shaped vessel that holds 28,000 gallons of water pressurized up to 3,150 lb/in^2 by an air supply system. A timed quick-opening shutter valve is mounted on the end of the L-shaped vessel and releases a high-energy water jet, which catapults the carriage to the desired speed. The propulsion system produces a thrust in excess of 2,000,000 lb, which is capable of accelerating the 54-ton test carriage to 220 knots within 400 ft. This thrust creates a peak acceleration of approximately 20g. The carriage coasts through the 1,800-ft test section and decelerates to a velocity of 175 knots or less before it intercepts the five arresting cables that span the track at the end of the test section. The arresting system brings the test carriage to a stop in 600 ft or less. Essentially, any landing gear can be mounted on the test carriage, including those exhibiting new or novel concepts, and virtually any runway surface and weather condition can be duplicated on the track.

Runway Grooving

The process of bringing a relatively fast-moving aircraft to a stop following a landing on a wet runway involves the interactions of factors contributed by the environment, runway, aircraft, and the human pilot. For example, the water depth on the runway is determined by interactions between the rainfall rate, wind, and the slope and texture of the runway surface. In addition, the ability of a tire or pavement to drain water is affected by interactions of the tire ground speed, inflation pressure, and tread condition together with the microtexture and macrotexture of the runway surface. The resulting water depth and drainage capability in turn determine the tire-pavement friction coefficient available for stopping the aircraft. The efficiency of the friction coefficient is in turn affected by aircraft characteristics, such as aerodynamics, engine thrust, the brake system, and landing gear characteristics. Finally, piloting techniques and control inputs for braking and steering can also impact aircraft wet runway performance.

Launch of test sled at Langley Aircraft Landing Dynamics Facility.

*Thomas Yager (left) and Walter Horne inspect grooved concrete surface at NASA Wallops Flight
Facility in front of Convair 990 test aircraft. In 1968, these experiments evaluated
effectiveness of grooved runway surfaces for safer wet pavement landings.*

Langley researchers Walter B. Horne and Thomas J. Yager led Langley's program to improve the safety of aircraft landing operations on wet runways, beginning in the late 1950s. Their efforts started with the very fundamental consideration of the mechanics of water buildup on runways and the impact of runway surface configurations. The phenomenon of tire hydroplaning was identified as the key factor causing poor braking on wet runways. Hydroplaning occurs when water penetrates between a rolling tire and the pavement. This penetration results in the formation of water pressure, which raises a portion of the tire off the pavement. The pressure increases as the speed of the aircraft increases supporting more and more of the tire until, at the critical speed termed the "hydroplaning speed," the tire is supported only by water and loses all frictional contact with the pavement. Major factors that aggravate hydroplaning include the depth of water, a medium to high aircraft speed, poor pavement texture, and worn tire tread. In hydroplaning conditions, longer aircraft stopping distances are required, a potential loss of directional control may occur, the aircraft experiences a greater sensitivity to crosswinds, and the pilot must use a greater reliance on reverse thrust for stopping.

In 1962, Horne and Yager developed a method of cutting thin grooves across concrete runways; thus, channels were created through which excess water could be forced and the risk of tire hydroplaning was reduced. Grooving studies at the ALDF evaluated tire friction and wear performance for many different test pavement specimens. By 1966, track testing had been completed to identify the optimum groove arrangement, and an industry conference was held to review the test results and define a potential flight test program for actual aircraft evaluations. On the basis of these test track results at Langley, an optimum transverse groove arrangement was selected for installation on a specially constructed runway at the NASA Wallops Flight Facility in 1967. The grooves cut into the research runway surface at Wallops were 0.25-in. wide and 0.25-in. deep on 1-in. centers.

In 1968, with the assistance and support of the U.S. Air Force and the FAA, testing was initiated at Wallops to evaluate the effect of pavement grooving on aircraft braking performance for an F-4 fighter, a Convair 990 jet transport, and a Beech Queen Air twin-propeller aircraft. Impressive results from these tests were presented at a Langley Conference on Pavement Grooving and Traction Studies. By the time of the conference, pavement grooving had been installed on a few British and U.S. runways, as well as on some selected highway curves known for relatively high wet-pavement skidding accident rates. Results from these early evaluations were very positive.

The civil and military aviation sectors, however, desired additional full-scaled aircraft data to substantiate these initial promising studies. Therefore, new joint programs were conducted with the U.S. Air Force and the FAA from 1969 to 1972. A C-141, a Boeing 727, and a Douglas DC-9 were all instrumented by Langley to conduct braking performance tests for over 50 different grooved and ungrooved runway surfaces. Results from these tests at Wallops clearly indicated the benefits of grooving that improved wet tire traction. As a result of this additional testing, the application of grooving to both airport runways and public highways was accepted as a promising means for minimizing wet pavement accidents. By 1991, runways at 646 U.S. airports (including several Air Force bases) were transversely grooved, and every state in the United States has now grooved some of its main highways. The greatest use

*Langley's pioneering efforts on runway grooving have been extended
to national highways for enhanced safety in inclement weather.*

of highway grooving has occurred in California, where frequency of accidents on wet pavements has been reduced 98 percent on some highway sections. In addition, the grooved highways required less maintenance costs and last about 5 to 10 years longer than ungrooved highways. Other grooving applications to nontransportation scenarios have reduced injuries caused by wet surfaces on swimming pool decks, playgrounds, and work areas in refineries.

This relatively small NASA investment (about $1.4 million from 1962 to 1973) to develop and evaluate pavement grooving leveraged action by other organizations to improve the Nation's airport runways and public highways; this has significantly minimized wet pavement skidding accidents and improved the safety of aircraft and ground vehicle operations during wet weather. In recognition of this important safety spin-off from NASA's aeronautical program, in 1990 the U.S. Space Foundation inducted this Langley technology into the Space Technology Hall of Fame in Colorado Springs, Colorado.

Winter Runway Friction Measurement Program

Despite the advances in technology and operational procedures, safe winter operations remain a challenge for airport operators, air traffic controllers, airlines, and pilots who must coordinate their efforts under rapidly changing weather conditions. Complicating the winter weather picture is the fact that criteria for safe operations on a given runway snow condition differ from airport to airport because of differences in grooving, temperatures, and pavements. Runway water, ice, or snow was identified as a contributing factor in over 100 aircraft

Langley's Boeing 737 research aircraft during winter runway friction studies.

accidents between 1958 and 1993; many of these accidents involved fatalities. Inaccurate, incomplete, or confusing runway surface information has been a contributing factor in a number of accidents where airliners have slid off the end of the runway upon takeoff or landing or have been dangerously slow in reaching liftoff speed because of the slowing effect of snow, ice, or rain. To help reduce this type of accident, Langley partnered with Transport Canada and the FAA in a runway friction measurement program called the Joint Winter Runway Friction Measurement Program. Also participating were organizations and equipment manufacturers from Europe and several Scandinavian countries. The research effort included instrumented aircraft, friction-measuring ground vehicles, and an international test group. Langley researcher Thomas J. Yager served as the lead NASA participant in the program.

The research program was designed to meet several objectives. First, the researchers coordinated readings from different ground vehicle friction measurements to develop a consistent friction scale for similar potentially hazardous runway conditions. Second, the objective was to establish reliable correlation between ground vehicle friction measurements and the braking performance of aircraft. These two objectives provide airport operators a better way to evaluate runway friction and maintain acceptable operating conditions. Results also enhance safety for all ground operations and provide information to help relieve airport congestion during bad weather. Results also help industry develop improved tire designs, better chemical treatments for snow and ice control, more reliable ground vehicle friction-measuring systems, and runway surfaces that minimize bad weather effects.

In a related precursor study in 1994, about 80 engineers representing 43 organizations from 10 countries participated in controlled tire-runway friction studies that were conducted

*Langley's Boeing 757 aircraft during test run at joint runway friction testing
at Kenneth Ingle Sawyer Air Base at Gwinn, Michigan, February 1999.*

at the NASA Wallops Flight Facility. A better understanding of the factors that influence tire-runway friction performance was obtained from over 800 friction test runs and over 400 runway surface-texture measurements. Thirteen friction-measuring devices and 7 pavement-texture data collection techniques were operated on 11 different pavement surfaces.

In 1996, actual aircraft testing began in the Joint Winter Runway Friction Measurement Program with braking tests for instrumented aircraft and ground vehicles in the U.S. and Canada. Langley's Boeing 737 research aircraft and Canada's National Research Council (NRC) Falcon 20 aircraft completed a weeklong series of landing tests on ice-, snow-, and slush-covered runways at the Jack Garland Airport in North Bay, Ontario, Canada, about 200 miles north of Toronto. Surface conditions were artificially varied to expand the range of data collected. Many different runway friction-measuring ground vehicles—vans, trailers, and modified cars—took readings with continuous and fixed slip devices under similar runway conditions for comparison with each other and with the braking performance of the two instrumented aircraft. Subsequent winter test seasons have involved 9 aircraft and 18 different ground vehicles. Test aircraft include the Langley Boeing 737 and Boeing 757, the FAA Boeing 727, the NRC Falcon 20, a de Havilland Dash 8, a Dornier 328, Airbus A319 and A320 aircraft, and a Boeing 737-400.

Data collected in this program from 1996 to 1999 included nearly 400 instrument aircraft test runs and more than 10,000 ground vehicle runs. These tests were performed on a variety of runway conditions, from dry to various combinations of ice, snow, and slush. Researchers also took manual measurements to monitor conditions including ambient temperature, temperatures of pavement surface and snow, depth of cover material, and the density of cover material for snow or slush.

Langley Instrumented Tire Test Vehicle during friction measurements.

Using this substantial database, the Langley researchers and their peers have developed an International Runway Friction Index (IRFI) that standardizes friction reporting and minimizes piloting difficulties in making critical takeoff and landing decisions. The IRFI is anticipated to become a standard criterion used by airport operators to assess a runway under winter conditions. Safe takeoff and landing decisions will then be facilitated by use of the index. The index—probably in the form of a simple chart—will help pilots with "go/no-go" runway decisions based on readings taken by a ground friction-measuring vehicle on the same runway. The index will help airport operators determine if their runways are suitable for aircraft operations and when maintenance is required. A methodology standard that defines procedure and accuracy requirements is under review for approval by The American Society for Testing and Materials.

The research will also help industry develop improved tire designs, better chemical treatments for snow and ice, and runway surfaces that minimize bad weather effects. In nonaerospace applications, much of the equipment being used to monitor runways is being used to measure highway pavement friction performance. In areas with high accident rates, pavement textures can be modified, on the basis of friction measurements, to improve the safety of automobile travel.

Effects of Deicer Fluid on Aircraft Tire Friction

Cooperative NASA and FAA tests were conducted by Thomas J. Yager, Sandy M. Stubbs, Granville L. Webb, and William E. Howell at the Aircraft Landing Dynamics Facility in 1993 to determine the effects of deicer fluid on tire friction. A conventional transport aircraft main-gear tire was tested at speeds up to 160 knots on a nongrooved concrete test surface. Surface test conditions included dry, wet (water only), Type II deicer chemical-water mixture, and 100 percent Type II chemical. Test tire operational modes included antiskid controlled braking at zero yaw angle and yawed rolling at a yaw angle fixed at 6°. The results indicated that for the 3-to-1 mixture, the friction values were similar to the water-wet condition. The friction coefficient for 100 percent deicer was about 30 percent lower than the value for the water-wet condition. The 3-to-1 mixture is probably more representative than the 100-percent mixture of what might be found in normal aircraft operations. Therefore, the results suggested that, in practice, the deicer effects on friction will be similar to those of water. The information assisted in establishing a national database on the effects of aircraft Type II chemical deicer depositions on aircraft-tire–pavement friction performance. These data also help improve the safety of aircraft ground operations during winter runway conditions.

Tire and Landing Gear Studies

In addition to its extensive research on runway friction, Langley has conducted in-depth research on tires and landing gear. The scope of research includes tire cornering and durability characteristics, tire tread design, and landing gear dynamic behavior.

A major test program to measure the comparative dynamic response characteristics of radial-belted and bias-ply aircraft tires using radial-belted aircraft tires from an F-4 fighter was conducted by Pamela A. Davis. Both tire designs were tested in a free-vibration environment under combined vertical and lateral loads and under combined vertical and fore-and-aft loads. The free-vibration test data showed that the radial-belted tire was less stiff than the bias-ply tire under both loading conditions. The increase in elasticity of the radial-belted tire could adversely affect the operation of an antiskid braking system that was designed for the bias-ply tire. Damping of the bias-ply tire was greater than for the radial-belted tire under both test conditions, which suggested that this radial-belted tire should be a cooler-operating tire and should, thus, tend to have less wear during normal cornering and braking operations. Stiffness characteristics revealed by the tests have resulted in the reassessment by the manufacturer of the design of this radial-belted tire. Data from these tests helped to establish a national database for radial-belted aircraft tires that will be used to compare the response characteristics with those of bias-ply tires.

In another radial tire study, Langley joined with the Michelin Aircraft Tire Corporation in 1995 to define durability characteristics expected on new commercial aircraft tires. Various tire properties, including relaxation length and spring characteristics, are of great concern to the aerospace industry as the tire is the conduit between ground forces and the airplane structure. The project included testing at the Langley Aircraft Landing Dynamics Facility with the research test carriage in a quasi-static mode. Langley's Robert H. Daugherty led the joint investigation. The extremely high tire loads tested in the program required that concrete weights be placed on the drop carriage portion of the test carriage. A 6-month effort was required to design and fabricate a special test loading setup for the project. A 15-ft-long built-up runway was fabricated in the carriage hangar capable of withstanding 60 tons of vertical load combined with 40 tons of side load. A "frictionless platform," which allowed side loads to be induced into the test tire, was modified and installed as an integral part of the built-up runway. The breakaway tests define not only the friction values achieved by the tire, but also the spring characteristics of the tire as well as the movement of the center of pressure in the tire footprint. Eight breakaway and 8 unyawed relaxation tests were completed, as well as 35 yawed relaxation length tests. The test matrix contained vertical load and yaw angle combinations that encompassed the full range of tire conditions expected on the newest commercial transport aircraft. These data were used by Michelin in the design and certification of advanced radial tires for the Boeing 777 and will be used for other future commercial transports.

Michelin tire subjected to large side loads in joint testing at Langley in 1995.

WAKE-VORTEX HAZARD

Background

When an aircraft wing generates lift, it also produces horizontal, tornado-like vortices that create a potential wake-vortex hazard problem for other aircraft trailing. The powerful, high-velocity airflows contained in the wake behind the generating aircraft are long-lived, invisible, and a serious threat to aircraft encountering the system, especially small general aviation aircraft. Immediately behind the wake-generating aircraft is a region of wake turbulence known as the roll-up region, where the character of the wake that is shed from individual components (wingtips, flaps, landing gear, etc.) is changing rapidly with distance because of self-induced distortions. Farther away from the generating aircraft is an area of the wake known as the plateau region, where the vortices have merged and/or attained a nearly constant structure. Even farther downstream from the generating aircraft is a wake area known as the decay region, where substantial diffusion and decay of the vortices occur due to viscous and turbulence effects. Depending on the relative flight path of a trailing aircraft in the wake-vortex system, extreme excursions in rolling motion, rate of climb, or even structural load factors may be experienced during an encounter with the wake. If the encounter occurs at low altitudes, especially during the landing approach, loss of control and ground impact may occur. The severity of this wake-vortex hazard is mainly dependent on the size, geometry, and operating conditions of the generating and trailing aircraft; the distance between the two aircraft; the angle and altitude of the encounter; and local atmospheric conditions that influence the position, strength, merging, and decay of the vortices. In general, a pair of vortices drift downward with time behind the generating aircraft, and the strategy recommended to the pilot for avoiding vortex encounters is for the trailing aircraft to fly at altitudes equal to or above that of the flight path of the preceding aircraft. However, on many occasions (particularly near the ground), the vortices may persist at the generated altitude or even rise to a slightly higher altitude because of atmospheric conditions. If the vortices reach the ground, they typically move outward from the aircraft at a speed of about 2 to 3 knots in calm-wind conditions. However, if there is an ambient wind, then the net movement of the vortices is the sum of the ambient wind velocity and the no-wind motion of each vortex. A light crosswind can cause one vortex to remain nearly stationary over the runway, which will continue to pose a threat to the landing aircraft. Finally, operations from parallel runways with less than 2,500 ft separation require alertness for crosswinds that may push vortices onto the active runway. Because of these complex factors, the fundamental behavior of wake vortices and their avoidance have been especially challenging problems to the aviation community since the earliest days of flight.

Under visual flight rules (VFR) operations, the responsibility for aircraft separation distances may be given to the pilot during the approach phase. In this situation, the primary constraint on following distance is usually the time interval for the leading aircraft to clear the runway prior to the landing of the following aircraft. However, under instrument flight rules (IFR) conditions, air traffic control has direct responsibility for separation according to FAA-mandated standards that are a function of the weight classifications of the leading and trailing aircraft. A more complete discussion of the separation standards is included in a later section. An analysis of aviation accidents indicates that probable vortex-related

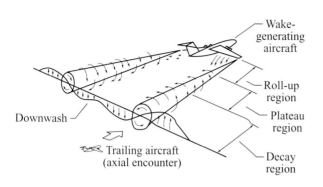

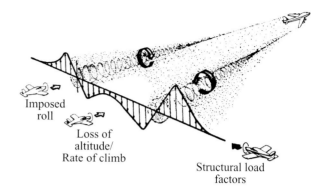

Sketch of wake characteristics behind generating aircraft.

Different vortex hazards created by relative flight paths of generating and trailing aircraft.

Sequence of photographs of Boeing 747 on landing approach as industrial smoke dramatically defines one of trailing vortices. Photo ©Bob Stoyles.

Wake-vortex separation requirements under instrument flight rules conditions aggravate airport capacity problem.

accidents constitute a relatively small percentage of all single aircraft accidents and that the vortex safety problem has been largely confined to general aviation aircraft (including business jets) operating under VFR conditions. In addition, the most frequent cause of vortex-related accidents involves an aircraft landing behind another aircraft on the same runway; the takeoff condition has been virtually free of vortex accidents. Perhaps the most important observation is that no accidents under IFR conditions have happened when full FAA separations were provided between aircraft. Prime reasons for the extremely small accident rate due to wake-vortex encounters are the IFR separation standards and the increasing awareness of the wake vortex problem on the part of operational personnel for both VFR and IFR conditions.

Although separations standards have proven to be effective from a safety point of view, they are frequently well in excess of the spacing required (due to weather conditions that rapidly decay or drift the wakes) and, as a result, significantly reduce airport operating capacities and impose costly delays affecting the airlines and the general public. With the projected accelerated growth in air traffic operating from essentially the same number of airports in the future, these penalties will become extremely large. Some quantitative measure

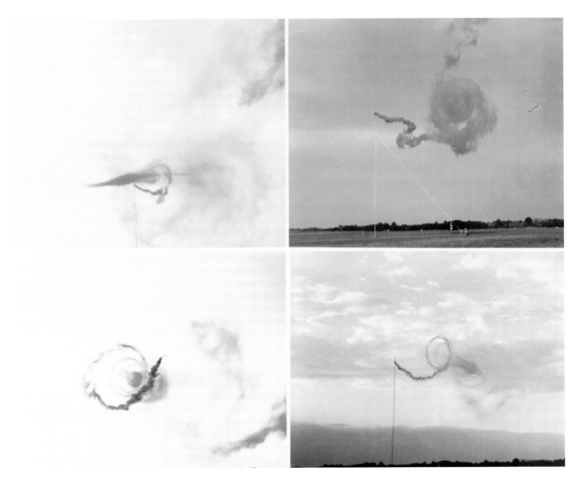

In 1970 NASA Marshall Space Flight Center conducted flyby studies of vortex-wake behavior with smoke ejected from tower entrained into vortex to permit visualization of character and persistence of vortex.

of the penalties imposed by wake-vortex separation distances can be obtained by considering an example case of a runway operating with a 3-nmi IFR radar spacing and a full capacity of 30 operations/hr. If the separation between aircraft using the runway is increased to 5 nmi, then capacity would be cut by a third. If the separation is increased to 7 nmi, capacity would be cut in half. Obviously, the operating costs to airlines and passengers are severely impacted.

Thus, strong incentives exist to remove wake-vortex turbulence as an impediment to air traffic operations at and around airports while retaining current levels of safety. Historically, two approaches have been used by researchers in attempts to mitigate the vortex problem. One approach has been to attempt to alter the aerodynamic vortex pattern shed by the generating aircraft so that its effects on other aircraft would be minimal. The second approach has been to develop and install wake-vortex detection and avoidance systems that would increase runway capacity by varying the separation distance to conform to the aircraft and the meteorological conditions present. A complete vortex separation system of this type must consider many factors, such as the detection or prediction of the presence and strength of the vortices at a given time; an evaluation of the threat on the basis of vortex strength, location, and trailing aircraft characteristics; and the determination of the proper hazard avoidance action.

Langley Research and Development Activities

The NASA Langley Research Center has actively pursued research to mitigate the wake-vortex hazard for over 45 years, beginning with flight tests in 1955 led by Christopher C. Kraft, Jr., to measure the wake-velocity characteristics of a P-51 aircraft. In 1968, Langley participated in a brief exploratory program to probe the vortices of an FAA Convair 880 transport using a T-33 aircraft. After the emergence of the first jumbo-sized transports, the FAA requested NASA's assistance in 1969 to determine the wake characteristics of large aircraft; this resulted in flight tests of a B-52 and C-5 aircraft by the Dryden Flight Research Center. Impressed with the potential wake hazard of these large aircraft, the FAA issued (January 1970) interim IFR separation standards with a minimum trailing distance of 10 miles for aircraft behind the C-5 or Boeing 747. After additional NASA and FAA flights of the C-5, Boeing flights of the 747 and 720, and flyby studies by the FAA, the FAA revised the separation standards to 5 mi behind aircraft with gross takeoff weights of over 300,000 lb. At the same time, Langley researchers Harry A. Verstynen, Jr., and R. Earl Dunham, Jr., participated in flight tests using a T-33 to measure the velocity profile of the wake of a C-5 aircraft. Perhaps the most interesting result of the study was the fact that, under the atmospheric conditions of the test site (Wright Patterson Air Force Base), the vortices often could be found above the flight path of the C-5. This early preview of the powerful influence of meteorological conditions on vortex behavior highlighted one of the most complex factors associated with the vortex hazard.

The focus of Langley's research in the early 1970s was to alter and minimize the aerodynamic wake-vortex characteristics of generating aircraft. In the 1980s, the studies were redirected to emphasize the fundamental character of wake-vortex phenomena and studies of the physics involved in the formulation of separation standards. The most recent focus in the

1990s has been the integration of advanced meteorological and vortex hazard technologies and sensors to permit the development of an integrated system for reduced separation for increased capacity. One of the most significant contributions by Langley researchers and their partners to the national air transportation system of the 1990s was joint activities with the FAA, which led to the quantification and development of separation standards and an emerging automated approach to spacing requirements.

NASA Wake-Vortex-Alleviation Program

In the summer of 1972, faced with what was a growing concern over the potential impact of large aircraft on the safety of small aircraft operations and the explosive growth of air traffic, the FAA requested NASA's help to develop technology and design information that might be used to alter the aerodynamic characteristics of the vortex pattern of generating aircraft so that the intensity of wake-vortex encounters might be minimized. At the same time, the FAA (with some help from NASA) focused on the development and installation of wake-vortex detection and avoidance sensors and systems at airports. NASA responded to the FAA's request, and research activities began immediately at the Langley Research Center, the Ames Research Center, and the Dryden Flight Research Center. The coordinated research program performed at the centers investigated the effectiveness of a myriad of aerodynamic schemes such as spoilers, vortex generators, wingtip vortex-attenuating devices, steady and pulsed mass injection, oscillating control inputs, and span load variations. The effectiveness of the schemes was assessed by measurements on trailing aircraft configurations and visualized with various flow visualization techniques. Tests were completed in several unique NASA facilities and several contractor water channels, as well as actual aircraft flight tests. A complete discussion of these extensive studies far exceeds the intended scope of this publication. Thus, the included information is restricted to only highlights of the program, and the reader is referred to the bibliography for sources of more detailed information.

At Langley, Joseph W. Stickle led the Center's Wake-Vortex-Alleviation Program, with several teams conducting the effort by using various ground-based facilities and aircraft flight tests. In addition to a broad experimental research program, analytical studies of vortex viscous effects and interactions were conducted by industry and academia under Langley contracts. Noteworthy contributions in the analytical effort were contributed by Alan J. Bilanin and Coleman duP. Donaldson of Aeronautical Research Associates of Princeton, Inc.

Facilities

An important initial task of Langley's research program on wake-vortex alleviation was to assess the many devices and concepts that had been proposed to aerodynamically alter vortex formation and decay. In accomplishing this objective, Langley had to develop facility test capabilities that could permit studies of the characteristics of the wake-vortex system from the point of generation to locations far downstream, representing in scale dimensions the downstream distances of interest for trailing aircraft. The testing problems, measurement techniques, and scaling of Reynolds number and viscosity effects were predominant issues in the program. Langley's ground-based facilities included the Langley 14- by 22-Foot Tunnel (formerly the Langley V/STOL Tunnel and the Langley 4- by 7-Meter Tunnel) and the Langley Vortex Research Facility (VRF), which was a new facility derived from an inactive

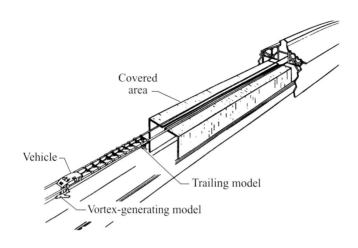

Covered area

Vehicle

Trailing model

Vortex-generating model

Sketch of Langley Vortex Research Facility.

Model of Boeing 747 during wake-vortex testing in Langley 14- by 22-Foot Tunnel with traversing rig mounted downstream to permit measurements of trailing wake.

NACA towing basin. The 1,800-ft long, water-filled towing basin had been modified with a new overhead carriage system to propel models, whereas observations and measurements of the wake characteristics of the passing model were made at a fixed observation position. In conjunction with complementary facility tests at Ames and the Tracor Hydronautics Ship Model Basin at Laurel, Maryland, these Langley facilities carried the load of Langley's ground tests. Researchers at Ames and Langley agreed to use similar 0.03-scale models of the Boeing 747 for common representation of a generating aircraft, and trailing aircraft models used in the studies ranged from simple wing models to representative business jet aircraft. Other configurations of interest including the Lockheed L-1011 and the Douglas DC-10 were also tested.

In the 14- by 22-Foot Tunnel, the test setup consisted of a generating transport model mounted to a static force test sting-strut apparatus in the tunnel test section, and the trailing model was mounted on a special strut-traverse mechanism that could be mounted at various distances downstream in the tunnel test section or farther downstream in the tunnel diffuser section. In this approach, the model could be remotely moved about 6 ft laterally and vertically to permitting researchers to probe the strength of the trailing vortices shed by the generating model. With the use of flow visualization techniques, such as smoke and neutrally buoyant hydrogen soap bubbles, positioning the model into specific areas of the wake-vortex pattern behind the generating model was possible. The magnitude of rolling moment imposed on the trailing model by the generating model was measured with a strain-gauge balance and analyzed for various generator configurations.

The Langley Vortex Research Facility was a unique approach to wake-vortex research in which the impact of the wake shed by a moving aircraft model was measured on a moving trailing model and observed and measured (by laser velocimetry) at a fixed observation point in the ambient air of the facility as time progressed following the passage of the model. James C. Patterson, Jr., conceived and led the development and operational research for the facility. A gasoline-powered automobile carriage was mounted on an overhead track with the vortex-generating model blade-mounted beneath the carriage. The trailing model was also attached to the carriage through a series of trailers, which resulted in the trailing model being located at a scale distance of about 1 mile downstream of the generating model. After the carriage was launched, the automotive drive system accelerated to a velocity of about 100 fps, which was held constant by cruise control throughout the length of the covered test area. At the test position, inside the covered area, smoke produced by vaporized kerosene was deployed and entrained by the wake for flow visualization. High-speed motion-picture cameras were used to film the motion of vortices produced by the generating model, and the aerodynamic forces experienced by the model were recorded.

Highlights of Wake-Vortex-Alleviation Research

The scope of Langley's Wake-Vortex-Alleviation Research Program included ground-based subscale model tests, theoretical studies, and full-scale aircraft flight tests to identify concepts and techniques that would reduce the rolling motion imparted to a smaller trailing aircraft. The investigation of a particular concept usually began with a preliminary evaluation through flow visualization of the wake-vortex pattern, with and without the vortex-alleviation concept. If the initial flow visualization indicated a change in the vortex

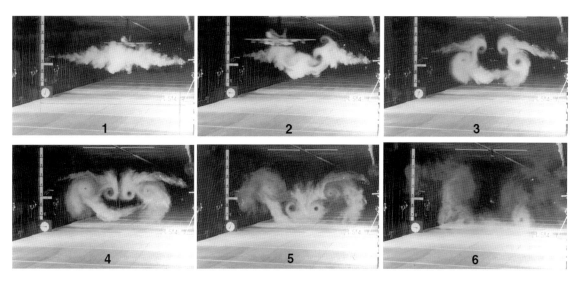

Flow visualization of wake of Boeing 747 model with inboard wing flaps deflected in Langley Vortex Research Facility. Time sequence shows model entering test area and vortices shed by the flaps and wingtips rotating around each other. As wingtip vortices approach the ground they are displaced laterally.

structure, a quantitative assessment of the effectiveness was undertaken, either through detailed velocity measurements or through measurements of the vortex-induced rolling moment imposed on a trailing-wing model. Many in the international research community believed it would be impossible to alter the wake, whereas others believed that the task could be easily accomplished.

During the course of the program, several concepts were identified that altered the wake and reduced the upset on a trailing aircraft. For example, the injection of turbulence into the vortex field was found to alter the vortex structure and cause premature aging and dissipation of the trailing vortices. Turbulence from jet engines also changed the vortex structure, as did an alteration of the span-load distribution. The combined effects of turbulence injection and span-load alteration through the use of wing spoilers were also found to be effective in altering the wake. Even oscillating inputs to the wing control surfaces proved effective.

Langley researchers were constantly challenged by the complexity of the wake flow field for representative transports. Many concepts that appeared to affect the wake properties in the immediate roll-up area behind the generating aircraft were found to have little impact on the magnitude of roll upset at downstream distances representative of the location of trailing aircraft. Furthermore, it was found that numerous interacting vortices were shed by the typical transport in the landing configuration. For example, in addition to the vortices expected at the wingtips, strong vortices were also shed at the edges of wing trailing-edge flaps, and aft fuselage. As a result of these types of interactive vortex effects, some wingtip vortex control concepts that were known to provide beneficial effects for cruise drag (such as winglets) had little or no effect on the wake vortex hazard when the aircraft was in the flaps-down, landing approach configuration.

As previously mentioned, the program was closely coordinated such that common concepts were cross tested in different facilities for correlation and verification of effectiveness;

however, certain researchers focused on particular concepts in their studies. An excellent summary of the results of both successful and unsuccessful vortex alleviation concepts by the Langley staff is given in NASA SP-409, Wake Vortex Minimization (see bibliography).

Research in the VRF was led by James C. Patterson, Jr., with assistance from by Frank L. Jordan, Jr. Both researchers had worked under the supervision of Richard T. Whitcomb in the Langley 8-Foot Transonic Pressure Tunnel, and were familiar with Whitcomb's interest in controlling the wingtip vortex with drag-reduction wingtip concepts, such as winglets. Patterson and Jordan investigated a wide range of alleviation concepts in the VRF, which included the potential of utilizing the high-energy wake produced by the large jet engines incorporated on wide-body transports for vortex alleviation. Interest in this concept was stimulated by earlier work that indicated forcing a mass of air forward into a vortex would interrupt the vortex axial flow (which provides the energy that normally sustains the vortex long after its generation). Because the jet exhaust wake of large engines is a source of high energy, it was hypothesized that when this energy was directed into the vortex, the wake hazard might be mitigated. After considerable research on engine location effects, thrust reversers, and differential engine thrust, it was determined that operating the outboard engines at maximum

Laser beams used to measure air velocities at specific points in wake for Boeing 747 model in VRF.

thrust while operating the inboard engine thrust reversers at idle thrust resulted in a significant reduction in the roll upset of the trailing aircraft. Although considered not practical from an operational viewpoint, these positive results provided additional incentive for further research.

Langley's early flight test activity in the aircraft wake-vortex minimization program was led by Joseph W. Stickle, Earl C. Hastings, Jr., and James C. Patterson, Jr. In one Langley flight project led by Hastings, Robert E. Shanks, and test pilot Robert A. Champine, a vortex-attenuating device referred to as a "spline" was developed from ground-based testing and assessed during flight tests of a C-54 propeller-driven transport. Early research leading to the spline concept had been conducted by Patterson in the VRF with a wing panel. It was proposed that an unfavorable or positive pressure gradient applied just downstream of the wingtip might force the vortex to dissipate. In the initial testing, this mechanism was verified by the brute-force approach of utilizing a decelerating parachute at each wingtip. As a more practical application of the idea, the spline concept was tested and found to produce the same vortex-attenuating effect as the decelerating chute. The spline configuration was envisioned to be retracted during cruise flight and deployed only for landing, when the vortex hazard was greatest. After extensive parameter variations in the VRF and in-flight assessments with the C-54 as a generating aircraft and a Piper PA-28 general aviation aircraft as a probe aircraft, the researchers concluded that the spline device was effective in reducing the strength of the trailing vortex. When the PA-28 approached behind the basic C-54 (no splines), the PA-28

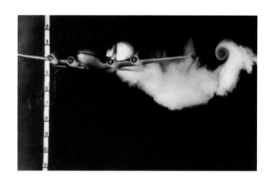
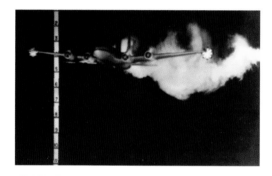

Langley's evaluation of spline device on C-54. Top photographs show VRF results for basic (left) and modified model, showing diffuse wake with spline. Lower photographs show installation of splines on full-scale aircraft.

could not approach closer than about 3 nmi before full aileron deflection was required to prevent a severe roll off. For the C-54 with splines, however, the PA-28 could be easily flown to a separation distance of less than 1 nmi. The vortex attenuation achieved in flight was greater than that obtained in the VRF, and the researchers anticipated that the installation of stowable spline devices on commercial jet aircraft would avoid the obvious penalties in climb capability in the landing phase of flight and increased approach noise due to increased power settings.

R. Earl Dunham, Jr., conducted cooperative studies with Vernon J. Rossow at the Ames Research Center on the effect of trailing-edge-flap settings on wake alleviation. These far-ranging tests included wind-tunnel studies at Ames and Langley, water tow experiments, and full-scale flight tests of a Boeing 747 at the Dryden Flight Research Center. The motivation for this project was to distribute the lift on the wing so that the interactions of wake vortices would lead to a very diffused wake. This approach was attractive because of the potential ease of application and minimal retrofit costs. The results of these extensive investigations demonstrated that variations in span-load distribution using flap deflections could produce significant reductions in the wake-vortex hazard. For example, an approximately 50-percent reduction in both the wake rolling moment imposed on a trailing aircraft and aircraft separation requirement was achieved in ground-based and flight experiments by deflecting the inboard trailing-edge flaps more than the outboard flaps.

*NASA conducting flight assessments of wake-alleviation concepts
at Dryden with NASA Boeing 747, T-37, and Learjet aircraft.*

Langley's Delwin R. Croom led research activities in the Langley 14- by 22-Foot Tunnel. Yet another concept that significantly modified the wake of representative jet transport configurations was developed by Croom and the intercenter NASA team. The focus of Croom's studies was the use of wing spoilers, commonly used by jet transports (for speed brakes and to decrease aerodynamic lift after landing), as a possible method of vortex attenuation, because the deflection of spoilers will inject turbulence into the wake as well as alter the span-load distribution. Croom had been inspired by earlier investigations conducted at Ames in 1970 that combined wind-tunnel and flight investigations of the effects of wingtip-mounted spoilers on the wake characteristics of a Convair 990 transport. The Ames experiment, however, ended with reports from pilots of a Learjet probe aircraft citing no differences in wake behavior between the modified and unmodified transport. In 1971, Langley initiated more detailed semispan wing studies in the VRF to determine the proper location for a spoiler to cause the largest alteration to the trailing vortex. Testing then shifted to the 14- by 22-Foot Tunnel and the Tracor Hydronautics Ship Model Basin, with emphasis on the impact of deflecting various combinations of the wing spoilers available on the Boeing 747 configuration. Exploratory testing by Croom in the 14- by 22-Foot Tunnel, which began in March 1975, defined an effective spoiler configuration, which had a spoiler deflection of about 30°. The effectiveness of the spoiler concept was verified in the VRF and the Hydronautics facility. With these promising results, a flight program using a NASA Boeing 747 aircraft was initiated at Dryden. In the flight program, NASA T-37 and Learjet aircraft were used to penetrate the trailing vortex.

Tests without the wing spoilers of the Boeing 747 deployed produced violent roll upset problems for the T-37 aircraft at a distance of approximately 3 miles. In one instance, the wake of the 747 caused the T-37 to perform two unplanned snap rolls and develop a roll rate of 200 deg/sec, despite trailing the jetliner by more than 3 miles. Tests showed the rotational velocity of the 747 wake vortex could exceed 240 km/hr and persist for a distance of 30 km. With two spoilers on the outer wing panels deflected, the T-37 could fly within a distance of 3 miles and not experience the upset problem. Although initial flight results tended to verify the effectiveness of the spoiler concept, additional flight tests indicated that the effectiveness was sometimes not repeatable (probably because of atmospheric conditions) at low altitudes. Later, flight tests of a Lockheed L-1011 at Dryden indicated considerably less effectiveness of the spoiler concept. Finally, additional concerns over unacceptable buffet characteristics produced by the spoilers shelved further research on the concept.

At the conclusion of the NASA Wake-Vortex-Alleviation Program, Langley and its intercenter partners had conducted extensive ground-based and flight research for a myriad of alleviation concepts. These concepts included altered span loading, turbulence ingestion, mass ingestion, oscillating controls, and combinations of these approaches. Actual flight evaluations indicated that several aerodynamic attenuation concepts were effective and these concepts would probably be operationally practical. However, in addition to issues such as effects on buffet and aircraft controllability and costs of retrofit, a significant obstacle to the implementation of this technology remained unconquered: the tremendous impact of variations in meteorological conditions on wake persistence and decay characteristics. Because of these appropriate concerns, none of the promising wake-alleviation concepts identified by the NASA research was incorporated into civil aircraft of the 1990s.

Nonetheless, an immense increase in knowledge of the nature and sensitivity of aircraft aerodynamic wake characteristics was obtained and served as the fundamental building block for future advanced approaches to the operational prediction, detection, and avoidance of the wake hazard. For an excellent summary of experiences and the outlook for wake alleviation concepts, the reader is referred to the excellent paper by Vernon J. Rossow in the bibliography.

Vortex Characterization

As the funding and momentum of the NASA Wake-Vortex-Alleviation Program were dramatically reduced in the 1980s, the focus of wake-vortex research turned away from aerodynamic alleviation concepts. Instead, Langley researchers directed their efforts toward more fundamental studies of the impact of atmospheric conditions on wake-vortex formation and decay.

During the 1980s, George C. Greene, Dale R. Satran, G. Thomas Holbrook, and others from Langley began to reassess the impact of meteorological conditions on wake characteristics. Critical changes in vortex position, strength, and decay were analytically and experimentally determined as a result of atmospheric density stratification caused by temperature gradient effects and temperature inversions. Dramatic demonstrations of the impact of stratification in the VRF, together with earlier FAA-sponsored observations of vortex-wake descent and decay characteristics, and the experiences of the Wake-Vortex-Alleviation Program during flight tests at Dryden, provided new insight and sensitivity to the powerful influences of real atmospheric effects on the wake-vortex hazard problem.

Typical meandering of trailing vortices due to local atmospheric effects.

Aircraft Separation Standards

Before 1970, radar operating limits and, to a lesser extent, runway occupancy restrictions dictated aircraft separation standards—no regulatory aircraft separations were imposed because of wake vortices. Separation requirements for IFR conditions were established in 1970 after NASA, the FAA, industry, and others conducted flight tests to determine the wake-vortex characteristics of existing jet aircraft. Until March 1976, separation distances of 5 nmi were required for "nonheavy" aircraft (less than 300,000 lb) trailing heavy aircraft (greater than or equal to 300,000 lb), and separations of 3 nmi for all other conditions. In 1976, the distances were increased, with the maximum being 6 nmi for a "small" aircraft (less than 12,500 lb) trailing a heavy aircraft.

As the 1980s closed, new concerns arose regarding the wake-vortex characteristics of certain new transports and the spacing requirements for them. In particular, a series of wake-related accidents and incidents involving the Boeing 757 during landing approaches resulted in a concern over the wake characteristics of this particular transport. In one accident on December 18, 1992, a Cessna Citation crashed while on a VFR approach at the Billings Logan International Airport, Billings, Montana. The two crew members and six passengers were killed. Witnesses reported that the airplane suddenly and rapidly rolled left and then contacted the ground while in a near-vertical dive. Recorded ATC radar data showed that, at the point of upset, the Citation was about 2.8 nmi behind a Boeing 757 and on a flight path that was about 300 ft below the flight path of the 757. Then, on December 15, 1993, an Israel Aircraft Industries Westwind, operating at night, crashed while on a VFR approach to the John Wayne Airport, Santa Ana, California. The two crew members and three passengers were killed. Once again, witnesses reported that the airplane rolled abruptly and that the onset of the event was sudden. The Westwind was about 2.1 nmi behind a Boeing 757 and on a flight path that was about 400 ft below the flight path of the 757. An additional accident, involving a Cessna 182 during VFR conditions, resulted in loss of the aircraft but no fatalities. Additionally, significant but recoverable losses of control occurred for a McDonnell Douglas MD-88 and a Boeing 737 (both required immediate and aggressive flight control deflections by their flight crews) trailing Boeing 757 aircraft.

Although all the wake accidents had occurred during visual conditions, when pilots are responsible for wake turbulence avoidance, the NTSB sent an urgent recommendation to the FAA to increase the controller-imposed IFR landing separation distances behind the Boeing 757 and similar weight aircraft to 4 nmi from 3 nmi for the 737, MD-80, and DC-9; to 5 nmi from 3 nmi for aircraft such as the Westwind or Citation; and to 6 nmi from 4 nmi for small airplanes. By June 1994, the FAA had accepted some of the NTSB recommendations, and separation standards were modified August 1994. Meanwhile, the aviation community initiated several exercises to determine if the wake of the Boeing 757 was more hazardous than other transports.

Tower flyby tests of the Boeing 757 and 767 had been conducted at the NOAA vortex facility in Idaho Falls, Idaho, during 1990. The NOAA results proved to be controversial because they showed, for a peculiar set of weather conditions that lasted about 0.5 hour, the vortex velocity of the 757 was approximately 50 percent higher than that of the 767 at similar vortex ages (younger than 60 sec) measured in less favorable weather conditions.

Generating aircraft	Separation distance for trailing aircraft, nmi		
	Small	**Large**	**Heavy**
Small	2.5	2.5	2.5
Large	4	2.5	2.5
757	5	4	4
Heavy	6	5	4

Current FAA standards for aircraft separation during IFR conditions. Note 2.5-nmi separation increased to 3 nmi when airport has >50 sec runway occupancy time.

However, the results also showed that overall the wake of the 757 decayed faster than that of the 767; in fact, the wake behaved as would be expected for an aircraft of the size and weight of the 757. However, the single unusual measurement was widely quoted as showing that the 757 should be treated as a heavy category aircraft like the Boeing 747 and 767. Another factor cited as relevant to the 757 accidents was the approach speed of the aircraft (125 knots) is relatively slow, in part because of its relatively low wing sweep and large wing area. As a result, business jets (such as those involved in the accidents) approach at higher speeds with inadvertently close separation.

At the request of the FAA, Langley's Roland L. Bowles, George C. Greene, and others participated in the analysis and deliberations over the Boeing 757 wake characteristics. A wake turbulence government and industry team, composed of representatives from the FAA, NASA, air carriers, pilots, air traffic controllers, and manufacturers, provided the FAA with recommendations on how to best separate aircraft to prevent wake turbulence incidents and accidents. A key analysis providing support to the reclassifications of weight was performed by Bowles and George Washington University (GWU) graduate student Chris Tatnall. Following hotly debated analyses and discussion among various agencies, industry, and the airlines, the FAA implemented new aircraft separation standards on August 17, 1996, for all aircraft operating in the United States under IFR conditions. Separation standards for small aircraft traveling behind a Boeing 757 increased from 4 to 5 nmi, and 57 types of aircraft, including several business jets and some smaller commercial aircraft, were moved from the large to small aircraft category. Specifically, the small category was changed to less than 41,000 lb (previously less than 12,500 lb); the large category, to 41,000 lb to 255,000 lb (previously 12,500 lb to 300,000 lb); and the heavy category, to 255,000 lb or more (previously 300,000 lb or more).

Controversy over the new standards existed, however, with objections to the increased distances. Opponents of the new regulations pointed out that all reported wake turbulence incidents or accidents had occurred in VFR conditions. There had been no reports of wake turbulence upset accidents (757 related or otherwise) from aircraft operating in IFR conditions; therefore, controversy still exists as to whether the modifications to IFR separation standards will prevent VFR accidents such as the Billings and Santa Ana crashes.

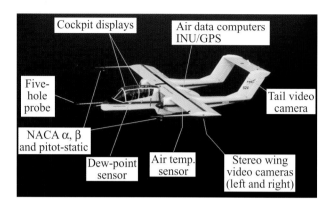

*Special instrumentation carried by Langley OV-10 research
aircraft for wake characterization research flights.*

As the separation issues spawned by the 757 controversy became a high-level concern, Langley researchers were stimulated to examine the more general subject of the development of a more scientific approach to determining separation standards. Extensive studies were required to provide the tools and understanding necessary to provide confidence if the separation standards were to be reduced for improved airport capacity. Efforts in the NASA Terminal Area Productivity Project within the NASA Advanced Subsonic Transport Program provided the impetus and funds for these contributions. Key capabilities in achieving the goals set for the program were the definition of valid wake models, analytical tools to examine the severity of encounters, and the development of a high-fidelity simulation model that could be used to develop wake vortex encounter hazard criteria. Langley's R. Earl Dunham, Jr., Eric C. Stewart, Dan D. Vicroy, Robert A. Stuever, and George C. Greene contributed significant leadership during ground- and flight-testing activities that provided the foundation for the development of simulations (both piloted and unpiloted) for wake-vortex encounter analysis. In addition to this analytical work, a successful first-ever feasibility study was conducted by Jay M. Brandon, Frank L. Jordan, Jr., Catherine W. Buttrill, and Robert A. Stuever to determine if free-flying models in the Langley 30- by 60-Foot (Full-Scale) Tunnel could be used in the analysis of the vortex hazard.

In 1995 and 1997, Langley conducted flight tests of a modified North American Rockwell OV-10 research aircraft behind a C-130 at the NASA Wallops Flight Facility to generate a quantitative, detailed set of data on wake characteristics for use in the validation of simulators and wake prediction methods. A unique feature of this research was that atmospheric data were obtained along with the wake measurements. The OV-10, which was equipped with special instrumentation for atmospheric measurements, first probed the atmosphere and completed a "weather profile" run before joining with the C-130 and probing the wake of the C-130. About 230 wake penetrations at different atmospheric conditions were accomplished; this provided valuable data for wake characterization research.

Analytical studies of separation effects on upset parameters were conducted by Stewart and Stuever, as well as further improvements in the state of the art for piloted simulator studies of hazard criteria. The ultimate objective of this effort was to permit the definition of hazardous and nonhazardous levels of vortex encounters for various aircraft types and atmospheric conditions and pave the way for a predictive element that might be used in a real-time ATC system. Unfortunately, funding for the study was eliminated before the final objective could be accomplished.

During the 1990s, the Langley staff continued to participate in supporting national issues and safety investigations involving wake-vortex phenomena. After USAir Flight 427 (a Boeing 737) plunged from the sky near Pittsburgh on September 8, 1994, killing 127 passengers and 5 crew members, the NTSB frantically accelerated its efforts to determine what might have triggered the 6,000-ft nose dive. A bump (a sudden airspeed increase detected by the plane's flight-data recorder) indicated that the 737 had encountered wake turbulence created by a Delta 727 that preceded Flight 427 into the Pittsburgh International Airport. Flight 427 trailed the 727 by 4.1 nmi, well within the FAA regulation that requires two planes of such weights to maintain a separation of 3 nmi. As part of the investigation to determine the potential impact of such an encounter, the NTSB requested that Langley conduct flights of its specially instrumented OV-10 and 737 research aircraft trailing an FAA 727 generating aircraft. Following the longest aviation accident investigation in safety board history (4 years), the results of this cooperative activity helped investigators conclude that the vortex encounter might have been the initiating mechanism resulting in a hardover failure of the rudder actuator, which was determined to be the primary cause of the accident.

Aircraft Vortex Spacing System Program

In the 1990s, the NASA Terminal Area Productivity (TAP) Program directed its resources toward the extremely challenging objective of providing the same levels of airport capacity during instrument operations that are presently experienced during visual airport operations. Within the elements of the TAP Program, the Langley Research Center was tasked to perform the research and development required to devise an automated wake vortex spacing system, known as the Aircraft Vortex Spacing System (AVOSS). The AVOSS concept would use available and emerging knowledge of aircraft wake generation, atmospheric modification of the wakes, wake encounter dynamics, and operational factors to provide dynamic spacing criteria for use by Air Traffic Control (ATC). When considering ambient weather conditions, the wake separation distances between aircraft could possibly be relaxed during appropriate periods of airport operations. With an appropriate interface to planned ATC automation, spacing could be tailored to specific generating/trailing aircraft types rather than the existing broad weight categories of aircraft. The fundamental architecture for the AVOSS system was first proposed by Roland L. Bowles of Langley, who had played a key role in the initiation and highly successful completion of the Langley Wind-Shear Program. The lead researcher and project manager for AVOSS was David A. Hinton, assisted by Leonard Credeur and an extraordinary team that included Fred H. Proctor and others that had made many contributions.

The development of the AVOSS concept built on past wake-vortex research conducted by NASA, the FAA, the Volpe National Transportation Systems Center, and industry. Advances in computational fluid dynamics modeling, weather sensors, ATC automation, and aircraft vortex behavior predictions had advanced to the point that encouraged the implementation of a practical AVOSS concept. The most critical single element in the development of the system was the accurate representation of vortex behavior in the airport area, especially the effects of meteorological characteristics. The AVOSS differed substantially from previous efforts to characterize wake vortex systems in that the atmospheric conditions from the surface to the top of the instrument approach path were measured and used rather than only surface winds. This analysis is significant in situations where temperature inversions or wind gradients along the approach path may require greater spacing intervals than would be predicted by surface winds alone. Because metering of aircraft to meet airport acceptance rates occurs during the vectoring and descent process as aircraft enter the initial approach area, the AVOSS system was required to provide a predictive capability of 30 to 50 min in advance of the actual approach to take full advantage of reduced wake constraints.

The general AVOSS structure designed by Langley includes a meteorological subsystem that provides current and expected atmospheric states to a predictor subsystem. The predictor subsystem utilizes the atmospheric data, airport configuration, and aircraft specifications to predict the separation time required for a matrix of aircraft. A sensor subsystem monitors actual wake-vortex position and strength to provide feedback to the predictor subsystem and to provide a warning. The AVOSS as demonstrated did not interact with ATC but actually ran in a "shadow mode."

David A. Hinton's conceptual design for AVOSS included a broad perspective of the research required in the areas of analytical studies, wind-tunnel testing, field evaluations, and flight tests. In the area of numeric wake vortex modeling, Fred H. Proctor's Terminal Area Simulation System (TASS), which had proven highly effective in the successfully completed NASA-FAA windshear program, was modified to model the effects of various atmospheric conditions of the behavior of aircraft vortices. Crucial to the validation of TASS, prediction algorithm development, and full system testing and demonstration was a field

MIT Lincoln Laboratory continuous wave lidar at Memphis for wake measurements in 1994.

effort sponsored by Langley and conducted by the MIT Lincoln Laboratory. This effort provided comprehensive field capability to gather meteorological, aircraft, and wake data at major airports. The Lincoln effort established a facility at the Memphis International Airport and in 1994 provided the most comprehensive wake-vortex and weather data obtained to date with approximately 600 aircraft wakes studied. Data collection was also performed in 1995. During these field measurements, the Langley OV-10 aircraft participated by collecting atmospheric wind, temperature, and humidity data along the approach path to answer questions concerning the variability of critical atmospheric parameters.

The AVOSS concept was originally conceived to use two factors, singly or in combination, for reducing aircraft spacing. These factors would be wake-vortex motion out of a predefined approach corridor and wake decay below a strength that is operationally significant. Initial predictions indicated that AVOSS technology has the potential to reduce takeoff delays as well as increase single-runway throughput by 10 percent or more during conditions requiring instrument approaches.

An ambitious goal of demonstrating the AVOSS concept at the Dallas-Fort Worth International Airport (DFW) was set for 2000, and a proof-of-concept prototype of AVOSS was installed there in 1997. MIT Lincoln Laboratory and Langley set up an extensive suite of meteorological sensors using two sodar (sound detection and ranging) systems and a Doppler radar profiler (to measure winds aloft), an instrumented 150-ft tower, and shorter towers to estimate the required atmospheric profiles. In addition, algorithms were developed for using the two FAA Terminal Doppler Weather Radars (TDWR) in Dallas-Fort Worth as high-resolution wind profilers and to combine the wind data from the various sensors into a single wind profile.

One key instrumentation capability developed under the Langley leadership of Ben C. Barker, Jr., was a pulsed coherent lidar system. The pulsed coherent lidar system was designed by Coherent Technologies, Inc. (CTI), under a NASA Small Business Innovation Research (SBIR) contract to provide the necessary confirmation that actual wake-vortex behavior agreed with predictions. The transceiver uses a solid-state, eye-safe laser beam that is expanded through a telescope and directed to a hemispherical scanner that scans the beam across the approach path. Light reflected from microscopic particles in the air, and shifted in frequency due to the swirling particle motion in the vortex, is detected by the lidar transceiver. These return signals are then analyzed to detect, track, and measure strength of the wake vortices.

The milestone demonstration of AVOSS at Dallas-Fort Worth International Airport occurred July 18–20, 2000. As implemented for the demonstration, the system provided spacing values to separate aircraft from wake-vortex encounters by defining a corridor of protected airspace, predicting wake motion and decay at numerous locations along the approach path for all aircraft, providing a safe separation criteria for the entire approach, and monitoring safety with a wake-vortex sensor. AVOSS did not render any go- or go-around decisions nor did it actually alter real spacing. AVOSS produced recommended reductions in spacing, measured actual wakes to compare with the predictions, and then developed statistics to determine the effectiveness and safety of the reduced spacing. This system ran in real time with automated weather observations, data quality assessments, and auto-

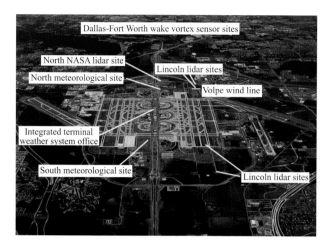

*Locations of AVOSS components at
Dallas-Fort Worth International Airport.*

*Langley pilot Philip Brown flies Thrush Commander over
smoke injection system for visualization of wake of aircraft.*

mated comparison of predicted and measured wake behavior. Although the data were not provided to Air Traffic Control during the demonstration, a large audience of airport, airline, and government officials were able to watch AVOSS predictions and confirm lidar measurements in real time.

Key members of the weather subteam included MIT Lincoln Laboratory, North Carolina State University, Langley, and the National Oceanic and Atmospheric Administration (NOAA); the prediction subsystem team was composed of Langley, NorthWest Research Associates, Inc., and the Naval Post-Graduate School; and the wake detection subsystem team was Langley, the Research Triangle Institute, MIT Lincoln Laboratory, and the Volpe National Transportation Systems Center.

Based on results of the DFW experiments, the increase in calculated daily throughput averaged 6 percent and ranged from 1 to 13 percent. At DFW, a capacity increase of 6 percent means 6 additional planes that would normally face delays would be allowed to land each hour. The average throughput gain translates to a 15- to 40-percent reduction in delay when applied to realistic capacity ratios at major airports.

In May 2001, the AVOSS project won the Administrator's Award at NASA's Turning Goals Into Reality Conference, and the Air Transport Association named AVOSS to its top 10 list of air traffic control improvements.

Other Wake-Vortex Activities

Another Langley aircraft wake research activity of the late 1970s and early 1980s involved the potential alteration of the wake of agricultural aircraft used in aerial applications for improved efficiency (more uniform distribution patterns) and reduced drift of potentially harmful insecticides and herbicides. As part of a larger NASA Aerial Applications Program that began in 1976, these aerodynamic studies included ground testing in the Langley 30- by 60-Foot Tunnel and the Vortex Research Facility (VRF), as well as cooperative flight tests of an Ayres Thrush Commander agricultural aircraft. In the 30- by 60-Foot Tunnel, Frank L. Jordan, Jr., and H. Clyde McLemore conducted extensive aerodynamic evaluations of the full-scale Thrush Commander aircraft with various dispersal systems installed. In addition to identifying performance-enhancing airframe modifications, such as wing-fuselage fillets, the characteristics of droplets spread by liquid spray rigs (using water spray) were also determined in the wind tunnel. In the VRF, the ability to simulate the aerial dispersal of materials from small-scale models and the development of numerical methods to predict particle trajectories were demonstrated. Exploratory tests of various wake control concepts, including wingtip winglets, were also conducted.

In 1984, pilot Philip W. Brown and researchers Dana J. Morris, Cynthia C. Croom, and Bruce J. Holmes conducted flight tests of the Thrush Commander aircraft at the NASA Wallops Flight Facility to collect experimental data on the wake characteristics of the aircraft and the impact of aircraft modifications on particle deposition patterns during representative aerial spraying operations. The researchers developed theoretical methods simultaneously with the experimental efforts to simulate the dispersal of particles, including the complex interaction of the dispersed particles with the aircraft wake. The results of the study indicated good agreement between the experimental results and the theoretical predictions, and the ability to change the wake characteristics to produce desirable effects on deposition and drift characteristics were demonstrated. The success of the study provided fundamental information for aerial application operators, and the theoretical method known as AGDISP has been provided to designers and other pertinent users such as the U.S. Forestry Service.

At the same time that researchers were attempting to modify the wake-vortex characteristics of aircraft to provide solutions to safety and airport capacity issues, others were attempting to control and harness the energy expended in the formation of wingtip vortices in an effort to improve aircraft performance. The pioneering efforts of Langley's Richard T. Whitcomb and his conceptual development and maturation of wingtip-mounted winglets is the most outstanding example of an application of performance-enhancing control of wingtip vortices. Whitcomb's approach, however, stimulated additional efforts to reduce aircraft-induced drag through the use of wingtip devices. James C. Patterson, Jr., worked for Whitcomb in both wake alleviation research as well as drag-reduction efforts. Patterson led efforts on research on two wingtip vortex control concepts for drag reduction. In the first concept, Patterson and Whitcomb explored the potential of using wingtip-mounted jet engines to modify the formation of the wingtip vortex in a manner beneficial to reducing induced drag. The scope of the studies included tests of powered semispan models in the Langley 8-Foot Transonic Pressure Tunnel and other facilities. Although significant reductions in drag were measured in these experimental studies, real-world concerns involving aircraft controllability and other issues have limited the application of this concept to date.

Another performance-enhancing concept explored in ground testing and limited flight testing by Patterson was the use of wingtip turbines for reduced cruise drag or power extraction. In this concept, multiblade turbines mounted at each wingtip are either fixed in the swirling wingtip vortex for induced drag reduction or allowed to freewheel and rotate (driven by the wingtip vortex) for the generation of electrical power for aircraft systems. Patterson's research on the tip turbines included tests in several Langley wind tunnels and limited flight tests using Langley's PA-28R research aircraft.

To complete this brief survey on Langley contributions to wake-vortex technology, it should be pointed out that Langley researchers have participated on numerous occasions with the DOD on many high-priority classified activities requiring expertise in the field.

Applications

As indicated by the foregoing discussion, the Langley Research Center has expended considerable effort and made valuable contributions to the Nation's knowledge and approach to the wake-vortex hazard. The results of the early Wake-Vortex-Alleviation Program, although frustrating to the researchers who had hoped for an aerodynamic solution to the problem, nonetheless serve as a foundation of knowledge for potential airframe modifications to mitigate the problem. In addition to providing clarification and data for the civil applications, the work resulted in activities in support of the military, such as analysis and improvement of C-17 paratroop capabilities. The vortex characterization research focused the attention of the research community on the impact of atmospheric conditions on the prediction and control of vortices. Combined meteorological and wake-vortex data sets from Memphis and DFW deployments are in use internationally, including Canada, Germany, and France. Langley's research on spacing requirements provided analysis to support reclassification of weight categories. Finally, the development of an integrated aircraft spacing concept such as AVOSS has developed weather profiling, wake lidars, and wake prediction to a point where a wake system implementation is feasible and demonstrated the potential of technology to provide solutions to the current and impending capacity issues at major U.S. airports.

As the new millennium begins, the Nation faces a rapidly growing issue of airport capacity, and the FAA must ultimately provide options for solutions. NASA's research has provided fundamental technology and stimulated interest by airport management, the Air Transport Association (ATA), and the FAA in developing wake systems for delay reduction. Aircraft manufacturers like Boeing and Airbus are also beginning to design new aircraft with wake characteristics in mind.

CRASHWORTHINESS

Background

The technical discipline known as crash dynamics focuses on technologies to improve the structural crashworthiness of aircraft and the potential survivability of occupants. The scope of interests includes the measurement and understanding of structural and passenger loads experienced during crashes, studies of the energy-absorbing characteristics of new aircraft materials and assembled components such as subfloors and seats, the development and validation of analytical design methods, and the impact of crashes on special aircraft equipment such as emergency locator transmitters. A key goal in this area of research is to provide enhanced survivability with little or no increase in aircraft weight or cost.

Crash dynamics first evolved as a world-wide technical discipline in the 1940s. In the 1950s and early 1960s, a series of full-scale crash tests of transport aircraft with instrumented dummies by the National Advisory Committee for Aeronautics (NACA) and the Federal Aviation Administration (FAA) provided valuable information on crash/fire characteristics. The NACA tests were performed by accelerating an airplane along a guide rail and crashing it into an earthen mound. Later, NACA studies on the dynamic response of seat structures to impact loads resulted in a key Civil Aeronautics Administration update of static seat-strength requirements. Other organizations, such as the U.S. Army, also conducted extensive pioneering crash research, which culminated in a Crash Survival Design Guide published in 1967 by the Army. In the 1970s, the NASA Langley Research Center converted its existing Lunar Landing Research Facility to a unique crash dynamics testing facility, which has been continuously used since that time for numerous key research projects focused on full-scale aircraft and components. Langley has also led the development of sophisticated analytical methods to analyze and predict structural and human tolerance data.

The emergence of new materials for aircraft structures, especially advanced composites, has resulted in new challenges for the analysis tools, technologies, and design methodologies used in the field of crash dynamics. The application of composite materials to aircraft structures offers potentially significant reductions in weight and improved corrosion resistance when compared with metal aircraft structures. However, the different physical characteristics of composites, and their failure characteristics in high-energy impacts, have required significant modifications to existing design methods and, in some cases, existing criteria for crashworthiness. In view of the emphasis on the weight-savings potential of composites, meeting the crashworthiness criteria with minimal impact on weight has become even more critical for modern aircraft.

The Langley Research Center has been an international leader in crash dynamics technology, using its close working relationships with industry, other government agencies such as the FAA and the National Transportation Safety Board (NTSB), Department of Defense (DOD), and academia to aggressively pursue technological advances in this critical area. The main area of contributions by Langley for civil aircraft of the 1990s has centered on general aviation aircraft; however, structural crash test investigations of commercial transports have also been conducted, and extensive research programs (not reported herein) have resulted in contributions to U.S. Army rotorcraft and the design of the U.S. Air Force F-111 crew escape capsule.

Langley Research and Development Activities

Langley researchers have conducted and maintained a broad spectrum of research programs directed at crash dynamics technology. Historically, projects have included studies of aircraft structural integrity during ditching at sea as well as detailed studies of the effects of ground impact for various types of soil/concrete materials. Most of Langley's contributions to crashworthiness characteristics of modern aircraft have resulted from the ground impact studies; however, a brief review of Langley's ditching studies is presented for completeness.

Ditching

NASA, and its predecessor, NACA, have been cognizant of the challenges of ditching an aircraft since the early days of World War II, when ditching at sea was a major problem. About 60 different airplane configurations were subsequently investigated with subscale models in the water-filled towing tanks of the Langley Research Center. One of the most spectacular Langley ditching investigations occurred in late 1944, when a modified full-scale B-24 bomber was intentionally ditched in the James River near Newport News, Virginia, in order to obtain instrumented data for correlation with subscale model testing in the Langley towing tanks. This particular aircraft included a reinforced bottom in response to a U.S. Army Air Corps request to investigate structural strengthening for potential improved ditching characteristics for the B-24. The aircraft was landed by an expert Army pilot in the James under ideal conditions and smooth water. The landing was fairly smooth and the crew was unharmed, but very severe damage occurred to the airplane, even though the bottom was very much stronger than that of a normal B-24. Water pressures as high as 60 psi were recorded. This early experiment provided evidence that airplanes are never designed to have fuselages that are undamaged in a ditching event. As a matter of fact, the undamaged shape of a typical aircraft is not very good for a water landing.

Water-impact accidents of commercial transports have varied greatly in severity and fatalities to occupants, largely dependent on sea state, ditching procedures, and certain aircraft characteristics including floor structure and wing location. No ditching investigations were conducted by Langley for a number of years following World War II because of the similarity of most transport airplanes at that time with respect to ditching behavior. Ditching tests of a subscale model of the Boeing 707 were conducted at Langley in 1955 to produce information for the first generation of swept-wing jet transports. Then, in the 1970s, the emergence of a new family of large jet airplanes, such as the jumbo jets and the C-5 military transport, renewed ditching investigations. The results of the subsequent Langley tests showed that as the size of the aircraft increased, the ditching behavior became less violent. This result was, in part, due to the large size of the aircraft relative to typical waves.

The damage that is expected in a ditching event will be severe, and it is extremely difficult to accomplish an optimal design for minimal ditching impact. However, the Langley testing provided extremely valuable guidelines for airline operators and the military regarding recommendations for forced ditching maneuvers, including the preferred landing attitude, flap settings, and aircraft orientation relative to wave crests during water impact. The critical nature of the design of the floor structure was also highlighted.

Although Langley's contributions in ditching research have proven very significant and widely recognized, an even more impressive array of contributions to aircraft technologies has resulted from research studies of aircraft during land crashes.

Langley Impact Dynamics Research Facility

Full-scale aircraft and component crash testing is performed by NASA and its industry, DOD, FAA, and academia partners at the Langley Impact Dynamics Research Facility (IDRF). This facility is the former Lunar Landing Research Facility, which Langley modified following the Apollo Program for free-flight crash testing under controlled test conditions. The basic gantry structure is 240-ft high and 400-ft long, supported by three sets of inclined legs spread 265 ft apart at the ground. An 8-in-thick reinforced concrete impact surface is centered under the facility gantry and is approximately 396-ft long and 29-ft wide. A movable bridge with a pullback winch for raising the test specimen spans the top and traverses the length of the gantry. In a typical test, the aircraft is suspended from the top of the gantry by two swing cables and is drawn back above the impact surface by a pullback cable. An umbilical cable used for data acquisition is also suspended from the top of the gantry and connected to the top of the aircraft. When the aircraft is released from the pullback cable, it

Aircraft suspended from Langley Impact Dynamics Research Facility in preparation for crash test.

Postcrash photograph of dummies used in IDRF testing.

swings as a pendulum into the impact surface. The swing cables are separated from the aircraft by pyrotechnics just prior to impact, which frees the aircraft from restraint. The umbilical cable remains attached to the aircraft for data acquisition, but pyrotechnics also separates it before it comes taut during skid out. The flight-path angle is adjusted from 0° to 60° by changing the length of the swing cable. The initial height of the aircraft above the impact surface at release determines the impact velocity, which can be varied from 0 to 60 mph. For some tests, the flight-path velocity has been increased to about 100 mph by using wing-mounted rockets to accelerate the aircraft on its downward swing. After the aircraft is released with the rockets ignited, the rockets continue to burn during the downward acceleration trajectory, but they are expended by the time of impact. Data acquisition from full-scale crash tests is accomplished with extensive photographic coverage and onboard strain gauges and accelerometers. Instrumented anthropomorphic dummies are onboard the aircraft for full-scale tests.

Since 1974, numerous types of aircraft have been successfully crash tested, including helicopters, high- and low-wing single- and twin-engine general aviation aircraft, and aircraft fuselage sections. Test scenarios have included vertical drop tests to simulate aircraft cabin sink rates experienced in a crash, as well as swing tests conducted using various impact surfaces, including dirt and concrete.

General Aviation Crashworthiness Studies

In 1972, Langley embarked on a cooperative effort with the FAA and industry to develop the technology required for improved crashworthiness and occupant survivability in general aviation aircraft. The research included extensive analytical and experimental work as well as structural concept development; this research was directed at enabling future general aviation aircraft designs to have enhanced survivability under specified crash conditions and little or no increase in weight at acceptable cost. The program was divided into three areas. The first area, environmental technology, consisted of acquiring and evaluating the field crash data to support and validate studies conducted under controlled full-scale crash testing. The goal of this area was to define a crash envelope within which the impact parameters allow human tolerable acceleration levels. The second area, airframe design, was to assess and apply existing analytical methods to predict structural collapse and develop and validate new analytical techniques. The average acceleration time histories (crash pulses) in the cabin area for each principal direction were calculated for each crash test. Airframe design also included the validation of new load-limiting concepts for use in aircraft subfloor designs. The third element, component design technology, consisted of exploring new and innovative load-limiting concepts to improve the performance of the seat and occupant restraint systems by providing for controlled seat collapse while maintaining seat/occupant integrity.

Early in the Langley research program, critical quantitative information began to be contributed by full-scale tests. The test parameters included in the Langley full-scale crash tests could not possibly encompass all crash scenarios, but the data obtained were found to adequately represent some of the more serious but potentially survivable general aviation airplane crash situations. The data were used in a number of applications to make reasonable estimates of the critical accelerations and survivability issues for postcrash analysis.

Langley researchers who led research efforts on crash tests for the general aviation program included Victor L. Vaughn, Jr., Emelio Alfaro-Bau, Claude B. Castle, Susan M. Williams, and Edwin L. Fasanella. The objectives of the studies were to determine the dynamic responses of the aircraft structure, seats, and occupants during simulated crashes; to determine the effect of flight parameters at impact (i.e., flight speed, flight-path angle, pitch angle, and roll angle) on the magnitude and pattern of structural damage; to determine the failure modes of the seats and occupant restraint systems; and to determine the loads imposed upon the occupants.

This information proved invaluable to crash investigation assessments and technology development. An example of this application involved an accident that occurred on August 30, 1978, when a twin-engine Piper Navajo Chieftain aircraft, carrying a pilot and nine passengers, crash-landed in the desert shortly after taking off from the Las Vegas airport. All 10 persons on board were killed. A comparative study of this crash and a Langley controlled-crash test was made to compare damage modes and estimates of acceleration levels in the actual accident and to assess the validity of Langley's full-scale crash simulation.

Typical crash sequence for twin-engine aircraft.

The Langley crash test utilized the velocity augmentation method, wherein the aircraft reached a flight path velocity of about 93 mph at impact. The aircraft pitch angle was 12° with nose down and the wing was rolled about 5° at impact. Although the aircraft tested was a Piper Navajo, which was slightly smaller (6 to 8 passengers versus 10), the similarity of the damage and failure distortions of the seats enabled the investigators to estimate that the peak pelvic accelerations of passengers were probably in excess of 60*g* normal to the aircraft longitudinal axis, 40*g* longitudinal, and 10*g* transverse. The Langley data were also extremely valued for studies of human tolerance characteristics, especially the development of prediction criteria for spinal injury and the correlation of such injuries with various formulations for impulse-momentum relationships during crashes.

Aircraft Subfloor and Seat Technology

The development of structural concepts to limit the loads transmitted to the occupants of the aircraft is an ongoing element of the Langley program in determining crash loads and identifying structural failure mechanisms during aircraft crashes. The objective of the research is to mitigate the loads transmitted by the structure, either by modifying the structural assembly, changing the geometry of the elements, or adding specific load-limiting devices to help dissipate the kinetic energy during a crash. The focal point of these efforts has been the development of crashworthy subfloor systems. These subfloor systems provide a high-strength structural floor platform to retain the seats (and resist overturning) and a crushable subfloor zone to absorb energy, distribute the loads evenly across the fuselage, and limit vertical loads by "stroking." In the general aviation program, several subfloor concepts were defined that showed a significant reduction in cabin decelerations over a representative unmodified subfloor. Laboratory and full-scale crash tests provided substantiating data to validate the effectiveness of these concepts. In the design of load-limiting seats, Langley research highlighted the critical importance of available stroke in determining the load-attenuating characteristics of different configurations. Vertical stroking of general aviation seats was found to be more critical than horizontal stroking from the allowable human tolerance standpoint. This finding was especially significant because little crushable structure in the vertical direction is normally available in most subfloor structures of single-engine general aviation airplanes. Langley developed energy-absorbing seats that utilized seat linkages and wire roller trolley assemblies that were especially effective in attenuating the vertical loads transmitted to the seat to a human tolerable value.

Analytical Methods

The extensive experimental crash tests and analyses conducted in the Langley program were complemented by the development and applications of computer-based analytical studies that model the complex, nonlinear responses of aircraft subfloor sections to crash loads. A nonlinear, finite-element, structural dynamics program known as DYCAST was developed by Grumman Aerospace Corporation (now Northrop Grumman) under contract to Langley and the FAA to accurately analyze load-limiting subfloors. Static crush tests of simplified components that characterize the nonlinear load-deflection behavior of the crushable elements of the subfloor are used in the model to predict dynamic behavior. Utilization of this computer program was successful for certain configurations and these efforts also showed the validity of using statically determined crush data for dynamic analyses. However, the results also indicated that the analyst must have some assurance that the static deformation behavior will approximate the dynamic deformation behavior.

Analytical efforts were also directed toward developing methodology for the design of load-limiting seats. The DYCAST code was applied to numerous studies of the dynamics of seat configurations, including the characteristics of wire-bending load limiters, shoulder harnesses, lap belts, seat back stiffeners, and pelvis stiffness properties. The computer model proved very useful for detailed modeling of load-limiting seats with a hybrid finite-element approach. This approach builds on a database of static crush characteristics of component seat structures to help predict mathematically the dynamic behavior of the seat occupant restraint system response. The analyst can start with a simple seat and occupant and provide increasing sophistication of the representation as needed for the specific task.

In 1992, Huey D. Carden published the results of a key analytical study made to (1) provide comparative information on various crash pulse shapes that potentially could be used to test seats under conditions included in Federal Regulations Part 23 for dynamic testing of general aviation seats, (2) show the effects that crash pulse shape could have on the seat stroke requirements necessary to maintain a specified limit loading on the seat/occupant during crash pulse loadings, (3) compare results from certain analytical model pulses with approximations of actual crash pulses, and (4) compare analytical seat results with experimental aircraft crash data. Carden's study derived structural and seat/occupant displacement equations in terms of the maximum deceleration, velocity change, limit seat pan load, and pulse time for five potentially useful pulse shapes; from these, analytical seat stroke data were obtained for conditions as specified in Federal Regulations Part 23 S 23.562(b)(1) for dynamic testing of general aviation seats.

Emergency Locator Tests

Since the early 1970s, general aviation aircraft have been required to carry an Emergency Locator Transmitter (ELT) to help identify the location of crashed aircraft by automatically activating a transmitting distress signal in the event of a crash. Unfortunately, early systems displayed a high rate of false activation and failures to activate as desired in a crash situation. Langley assisted the FAA and industry through a special committee of the Radio Technical Commission for Aeronautics (RTCA) by studying the ELT problems to help identify solutions.

Langley replicated and demonstrated the ELT problems by mounting a sampling of ELT devices in full-scale crash test aircraft and in a test apparatus used for dynamic seat tests. Evaluation of the test results indicated that one of the key factors in failure was the vibration sensitivity of the ELT switches and sensors. Testing showed that the critical resonant frequencies of most commercial crash sensors fell within the range of structural vibrations that existed on general aviation aircraft. However, the frequency range of crash pulses that needed to be detected was on the lower end of the frequency spectrum. Thus, the sensors were too responsive to the local structural vibrations during aircraft operations, causing unwarranted activation in some cases and nonresponsive action in other cases. Langley conceived and demonstrated improvements by redesigning a typical ELT device to have a much lower resonant frequency and superior response characteristics for crash alerts.

Composite Structures

During the general aviation crash dynamics program at Langley, the efforts in the area of subfloor designs for crash dynamics were directed toward metal aircraft. The aggressive emergence of composite materials for aircraft structures, however, introduced new issues regarding the energy-absorbing properties of composite materials and their crashworthy characteristics. For example, because composites typically are brittle and did not necessarily exhibit plasticity prior to failure, changes may be required in the geometry and designs for many composite aircraft structural elements to protect occupants in the event of a crash and to provide efficient energy-absorbing mechanisms. Therefore, new concepts of subfloor

Lear Fan test specimen prepared for crash test.

Test aircraft suspended for crash test in Langley and Terry Engineering investigation of improved crashworthiness. Note soil spread over impact surface for soft soil test.

structures need to be formulated and tested to verify the behavior of properties of composite designs.

One particular characteristic of composite aircraft structures that should be a concern to the designer is the intersections of longitudinal subfloor beams and lateral bulkheads which form efficient load paths or hard points which transfer high loads to the seat and occupant and often prevent desirable energy-absorbing failure modes from occurring during a crash. In 1989, Lisa E. Jones and Huey D. Carden conducted experiments to determine the energy-absorbing characteristics and performance of typical DuPont Kevlar and graphite-epoxy aircraft subfloor intersections. Various concepts for the attachment of laminated longitudinal floor beams and lateral bulkheads were incorporated into specimens for static testing. Quasi-static testing was performed with a testing machine that crushed the specimens to 25 percent of their original heights at a travel rate of about 2 in/min. This detailed study of failure modes and the differences observed between Kevlar and the graphite-epoxy specimens provided fundamental information for the design of more efficient composite subfloors.

In 1993, Huey Carden and Sotiris Kellas of Lockheed Engineering & Sciences Company collaborated in a study of an energy-absorbing beam design for composite aircraft subfloors. The tests were one element of a broader full-scale aircraft crash test program using a Lear Fan composite aircraft. The composite fuselage of the Lear Fan with its original subfloor structure had four aluminum spars that supported the seat rails, whereas the remainder of the structure was constructed of graphite composite. Static tests of the subfloor section showed that the original structure was too strong to provide reasonable occupant loads at crash speeds of about 30 ft/sec as recommended by Part 23 of the Federal Aviation Regulations for aircraft seat tests. The objective of the Langley study was to design and test a composite subfloor structure that would provide the desired cushioning (less than 20g on an occupant) as a potential retrofit to the original aluminum spar design. A sandwich spar construction based on a sine-wave beam was chosen for evaluation and found to have excellent energy-absorbing characteristics. The design objective of obtaining sustained crushing loads of the spar for potential limiting loads of around 20g was obtained.

In 1995, Lisa Jones and Huey Carden reported on crash tests of a Lear Fan aircraft with composite wing, fuselage, and empennage (but with aluminum subfloor) at the Langley IDRF. The test was conducted to determine composite aircraft structural behavior for crash loading conditions and to provide a baseline for similar aircraft crash tests of the modified subfloor. Langley had obtained two nonflying Lear Fan test airplane structures, and one aircraft was tested in essentially an "as received" condition to provide a baseline. Avionics, seats, engines, propellers, tails, and landing gear were not included in the test. The scope of testing included three different energy-absorbing seats as well as a bulkhead airbag experiment. The results of the crash test showed that the accelerations on the floor of the composite aircraft were much higher than those for comparable all-metallic aircraft, that the subfloor structure did not crush but failed in a brittle manner, and that very little energy was absorbed. Although the structural design was not considered the optimum composite design for crashworthiness, postcrash integrity and cabin volume were maintained.

Although not covered by the fixed-wing aircraft focus of the present document, it is important to note that the Langley staff has conducted extensive crashworthy research on rotary wing aircraft in partnership with the U.S. Army. The program has been particularly productive regarding the characteristics of composite materials and structures. U.S. Army helicopters are designed to dissipate prescribed levels of crash impact kinetic energy without compromising the integrity of the fuselage. Because of the complexity of the energy-absorption process, it is imperative for designers of energy-absorbing structures to develop an in-depth understanding of how and why composite structures absorb energy. Karen E. Jackson and Edwin L. Fasanella were key leaders in this research.

In the late 1990s, Langley's Lisa Jones and James E. Terry of Terry Engineering led a cooperative NASA SBIR project to design and test an improved crashworthiness small composite airframe representative of general aviation applications. The study was motivated by the fact that the NTSB had studied a large number of general aviation accidents in detail and concluded that fatalities could have been reduced by 20 percent if the occupants had worn shoulder harnesses and 88 percent of the seriously injured occupants would have had less serious injuries if shoulder harnesses had been worn. Also, it was estimated that energy-absorbing seats could have reduced the severity of injuries by 34 percent and reduced fatalities by about 2 percent.

This project had also noted that previous drop tests of both high-wing and low-wing single-engine general aviation configurations by Langley showed very different responses during impact with soil (representative of off-runway conditions) compared with impact on hard surfaces. In particular, the results showed that traditional single-engine aircraft tended to dig nose first into the soil on impact, producing twice the deceleration experienced during similar crashes on concrete. As a result of the high deceleration loads, the fuselage structure normally failed catastrophically with a complete loss of cabin integrity and survivable volume. The objective of the Langley and Terry Engineering study was to expand the survival envelope and reduce the severity of injuries and survivable accidents. Particular emphasis was placed on design of an engine mount and forward fuselage whose failure mode would preclude "digging in," a fuselage floor that would minimize loads, and air bags and load limiters designed to expand the survivability envelope. Simulated crashes at the Langley IDRF began in 1996 and included impact flight angles of –30° and an impact velocity of about 82 ft/sec on concrete and soft soil. A soil bed approximately 3-ft deep was placed on a concrete surface for the soft soil tests. Results of the IDRF drop tests indicated that improved survivability was possible (compared with prior Langley tests of conventional airplanes) for symmetrical impact at approximately stall speed, even for a relatively severe impact angle onto both hard and soft soil surfaces. The airframe weight penalty for this improved survivability was approximately 50 lb, with airbags adding another 12 lb and load-limiting shoulder harnesses adding an additional 1 lb.

Controlled Impact Demonstration Program

The original NASA, FAA, and industry joint general aviation crash program was concluded in 1982 following a decade of extremely productive research. At the conclusion of the program, national interests in crash research became focused on commercial transport aircraft, stimulated by the introduction of wide-body jumbo jets with large passenger complements, which represented a potential for a substantial loss of life or injuries in a single accident. In 1980, Langley and the FAA began a research program to quantitatively assess transport aircraft crashes. As part of this program, an intentional survivable, full-scale crash test of a transport aircraft was planned. The agencies subsequently conducted the Controlled Impact Dynamics (CID) Program that involved a controlled crash of an out-of-service, mid-1960 four-engine Boeing 720 research aircraft at the NASA Dryden Flight Research Center. Although the 720 was considered obsolete, its structural design and construction were still representative of narrow-body transport aircraft in use at that time. Two major objectives were included in the tests: (1) to test an antimisting kerosene fuel in an FAA program to reduce the severity of aircraft crash fires and (2) to study structural crashworthiness. Langley's responsibilities were to build the data acquisition system, collect and analyze the data from the 350 transducers onboard, conduct crashworthiness experiments, provide onboard film coverage, and perform finite-element modeling assisted by the Boeing Commercial Airplane Company. Dryden developed the flight research program, the remotely piloted aircraft technique, and remotely piloted the aircraft to the impact site.

Prior to the flight test program, Langley had conducted a series of three Boeing 707 transport fuselage section drop tests at the Impact Dynamics Research Facility. These tests provided data to qualify instrumentation and test the impact tolerance of data acquisition hardware in preparation for the CID. Analytical correlation with the predictions from the DYCAST code had also been completed. The FAA had conducted an additional drop test of a complete Boeing 707 aircraft that also had provided valuable crush and damage information for the Langley analytical studies.

During the preparations for the crash flight at Dryden, 14 flights of the Boeing 720 aircraft with crews were flown, with Dryden providing superlative efforts to develop the remote piloting techniques necessary for the 720 to fly as a drone aircraft. The 14 flights had 9 take-offs, 13 landings, and approximately 69 approaches to about 150 ft above the prepared crash site under remote control. On the final flight (15) with no crew onboard on December 1, 1984, all fuel tanks were filled with the special antimisting fuel, and all engines ran from start-up to impact (flight time was 9 min). The aircraft was to have a sink rate of 17 ft/sec and a longitudinal velocity of approximately 150 knots. After the primary impact, the airplane fuselage was to slide between a corridor of wing openers designed to cut the wing tanks and ensure spillage of the special fuel. The structural crashworthy experiment would be completed before the airplane contacted the wing openers. In the actual impact, however, the approach to crash was not controlled as precisely as desired and the outboard engine of the left wing contacted the ground first as a result of a 13° roll and yaw attitude. The controlled impact was spectacular, with a large fireball enveloping and burning the 720 aircraft. From the standpoint of the antimisting fuel, the test was a major setback; but for Langley, the data collected on crashworthiness was deemed successful and extremely significant. Ninety-seven percent of the channels were active at impact, and the interior photography was also very successful. One hundred percent of the cameras functioned. The film contained unique information on the development of fire and smoke in the interior of the aircraft. From a human tolerance point of view, the CID test was the simulation of a survivable crash.

Edwin L. Fasanella and Martha P. Robinson of Langley and E. Widmayer of Boeing led the acquisition and analysis of data from the CID structural objectives. Their use of DYCAST

Impact of Boeing 720 during NASA and FAA Controlled Impact Dynamics Program in 1984.

in a series of progressively more difficult modeling tasks was extremely successful. Following the modeling of isolated aircraft frames and fuselage section vertical drop tests, modifications to DYCAST were made in predictions correlated with the results of the CID crash. Predictions of crush and acceleration levels agreed well with the flight data; this indicated the validity of the building-block analysis approach of using results from detailed models of the substructure to form hybrid elements for inputs to more complex structures (thereby limiting the size of the model) and provided a useful prediction to the crash assessments.

Further analyses of transport aircraft crash characteristics were contributed by Edwin L. Fasanella, Karen E. Jackson, Yvonne T. Jones, and Gary Frings of Langley and Tong Vu of the FAA during a 30-ft/sec vertical drop test of a fuselage section of a Boeing 737 aircraft conducted in October 1999, at the FAA Technical Center in Atlantic City, New Jersey. This test was performed to evaluate the structural integrity of a conformable auxiliary fuel tank mounted beneath the floor and to determine its effect on the impact response of the airframe structure and the occupants. The test data were used to compare with those from a finite-element simulation of the fuselage structure and to gain a better understanding of the impact physics through analytical-experimental correlation. To perform this simulation, a full-scale three-dimensional finite-element model of the fuselage section was developed. The

Instrumented dummies in Boeing 720 for CID test.

emphasis of the simulation was to predict the structural deformation and floor-level acceleration responses obtained from the drop test of the Boeing 737 fuselage section with the auxiliary fuel tank.

Applications

Crash safety systems, devices, and concepts that have been and continue to be the focus of research at the Langley IDRF are capable of moving accidents categorized as "potentially survivable" (having serious injury and fatalities) into the "survivable" category (minor or no injury). The database, analytical methods, and design guidelines provided by the extensive Langley studies have been incorporated into design considerations for virtually all general aviation aircraft.

A striking example of the application of this technology is the experience of the Jungle Aviation and Radio Service (JAARS) Organization, a mission service group that supports mission aviation aircraft that operate all over the world. Langley had conducted tests on an energy-absorbing seat being qualified for JAARS in support of efforts to retrofit many of the mission aviation aircraft with the improved seat concept. Personnel from JAARS subsequently shared feedback relative to two real-world crash events. The information regarded two mission aviation aircraft that were involved in accidents in different parts of the world. Investigators were able to determine that the attitude and impact parameters were quite similar for the two accidents. In one accident the aircraft had been retrofitted in all positions with the energy-absorbing seats and restraint systems that had been tested at the IDRF. All the crew and passengers of this aircraft walked away with just minor scrapes and bruises. In the other accident, the aircraft was equipped with standard seating, and the occupants suffered serious back injuries and fatalities.

APPENDIX—SUMMARY OF LANGLEY CONTRIBUTIONS TO CIVIL AIRCRAFT OF THE 1990s

Contributions in Aerodynamics

The Langley Research Center has been a world leader in aerodynamics technology for over eight decades. Langley was among the first organizations worldwide to employ wind tunnels for research and development, develop and refine analytical and computational methods, develop advanced instrumentation systems and measurement techniques to define the fundamental character and physical flow properties associated with critical aerodynamic phenomena, and evaluate and validate aerodynamic theory with aircraft flight tests. Many of Langley's contributions to the U.S. industry and the state of the art in aerodynamics are legendary, including such concepts as advanced airfoils and the engine cowl. The scope of this research has encompassed all critical facets of aircraft design, including flow physics, similitude and scaling, high-lift systems, airfoils and wing design, cruise performance, stability and control, propulsion integration, computational design and analysis methods, and the impact of environmental factors such as rain and icing on aerodynamic behavior.

Langley's relationship with the U.S. aircraft industry in the field of aerodynamics has been extremely close and productive. Initially, the unique expertise and wind-tunnel facilities of the NACA and the Langley Memorial Aeronautical Laboratory represented the sole source of information for national interests. A close bond existed between working-level aerodynamicists; frequent consultations and cooperative studies between Langley and industry were commonplace. Technology transfer requirements for effective and timely dissemination of results to industry were accomplished by frequent national aerodynamic conferences and symposia, as well as briefings conducted at industry and Langley sites.

With the growth of the U.S. aviation industry, companies rapidly expanded their aerodynamics personnel and constructed their own wind-tunnel facilities and laboratories for proprietary requirements. Meanwhile, as a NASA Center, Langley continued its liaison with industry, but pursued leading-edge problems identified by the accelerated advances in aeronautical sciences. For example, advanced cryogenic wind tunnels, which provide more accurate simulation of full-scale flight conditions, were built and calibrated with recent aircraft experiences to provide the U.S. industry with powerful tools for future development programs.

In the 1990s the mission of Langley's wind tunnels in support of civil aviation was to study fundamental aerodynamic flow physics issues, calibration of new facilities with flight data and design tools, and the development of advanced testing techniques. These wind tunnels, in conjunction with powerful computer-based prediction and analysis methods and a world-class staff of experts, ably support the civil industry's requirements for advanced aircraft. The examples presented herein are limited to those that resulted in civil industry applications for specific aircraft that were operational in the 1990s.

Winglets

Developed by Langley in the 1970s, winglets provide enhanced performance for civil aircraft, especially those constrained by wingspan limitations. Winglets were implemented worldwide for large commercial transports, business jets, and small personal-owner aircraft of the 1990s.

Supercritical Airfoil

Langley researchers developed the supercritical airfoil concept in the late 1960s as a means of reducing cruise drag for advanced commercial transports and business jets. The concept provides for trade-offs between cruise speed and cruise efficiency by permitting the use of thicker airfoils for wings with increased aspect ratio. The civil aircraft industry has modified and refined the concept for specific applications.

Low- and Medium-Speed Airfoils

In the 1970s Langley conducted extensive experimental and computational research to develop advanced airfoils for propeller and jet-powered general aviation aircraft. Applications of this family of airfoils to aircraft of the 1990s included natural laminar flow airfoils.

Area Rule

The development of the area rule by Langley provided a breakthrough analysis capability for understanding and solving critical aerodynamic phenomena, such as engine-pylon-wing interference effects for commercial transports and business jets at high subsonic speeds.

Flow Control Concepts

Innovative flow control concepts, such as microvortex generators, were conceived and matured by Langley research to the point that applications for enhanced cruise and low-speed performance occurred within the business jets and general aviation communities in the 1990s.

Computational Methods

World-class computational methods developed and validated by Langley have been widely distributed within the U.S. civil aircraft industry, where they have been integrated into proprietary computer codes and design methodology. The contributions range from mathematical modeling (gridding) of complex aircraft configurations to the development of rapid flow solvers and visualization techniques to enhance the interpretation of results for a variety of applications.

Wind-Tunnel–Flight Correlation

With the high Reynolds number capability provided by the National Transonic Facility (NTF), Langley has provided the results of wind-tunnel tests at flight Reynolds numbers to directly guide industry assessments in wind-tunnel–flight correlation studies and flight prediction methods.

Advanced Instrumentation

Langley contributions include the development of advanced measurement and instrumentation systems used by industry in the aerodynamic design and analysis of civil aircraft of the 1990s. The concepts developed include multiport, rapid-scanning pressure systems, pressure-sensitive paints, laser-velocimeter systems, and other critical systems that have been matured and transferred to the aircraft industry and commercial companies. The applications by industry have included ground-based activities as well as in-flight studies.

Contributions in Flight Dynamics

Langley conducts generic and applied research on stability, control, and flying qualities of civil aircraft. The investigations have included scale-model wind-tunnel tests, wind-tunnel tests of full-scale general aviation aircraft, piloted simulator studies of the handling qualities of aircraft for various environmental conditions, and flight tests of subscale models and full-scale research aircraft to assess flight characteristics. Langley's contributions to the U.S. civil aircraft industry in flight dynamics have largely focused on personal-owner general aviation aircraft.

Langley's operation of unique facilities, such as piloted simulators and the Nation's only operational vertical spin tunnel, has been a key factor in the interactions with the civil aviation community. The challenge of ensuring satisfactory spin and spin recovery characteristics for personal-owner general aviation aircraft was a major thrust for research at Langley in the 1970s and 1980s. Because of the complex aerodynamic interactions and piloting procedures involved in spin technology, the U.S. industry conducted extensive cooperative studies with Langley researchers and consulted with Langley personnel on numerous occasions during the development of specific small general aviation aircraft. The contributions made by Langley regarding design guidelines for the geometric layout of aircraft, the general approach to be utilized in spin investigations, and the implementation of emergency spin recovery devices for flight tests greatly enhanced the safety and success of several specific aircraft programs.

The following examples of Langley's flight dynamics contributions to civil aircraft of the 1990s resulted in application of the research results and concepts to specific aircraft.

Deep-Stall Recovery

Following a fatal accident of a British commercial transport prototype, Langley provided an early identification of the physical causes of potentially catastrophic unrecoverable "deep-stall" characteristics for T-tail aircraft. Followed by extensive wind-tunnel and piloted simulator studies, Langley provided an approach for the analysis and prevention of this phenomenon that was routinely used by designers of T-tail aircraft of the 1990s.

Spin Technology

The results of an extensive research program by Langley during the late 1970s and 1980s on the stall and spin characteristics of light general aviation aircraft have been incorporated in the design methodology and analysis techniques used by many aircraft companies. The technology contributed by the ground-based and research aircraft spin studies included guidelines for the design of tail surfaces for satisfactory spin recovery, the use of radio-controlled models for prediction of spin characteristics, and the design and implementation of emergency spin recovery parachute systems. The Langley 20-Foot Vertical Spin Tunnel has also provided industry with contractual mechanisms to conduct spin research on specific configurations.

Wing Modifications for Spin Resistance

As part of its stall and spin program for general aviation, Langley conceived and demonstrated the effectiveness of a discontinuous leading-edge-droop wing modification that significantly enhances the inherent spin resistance for general aviation aircraft. Wind-tunnel tests and flight tests of research aircraft documented the effectiveness of the concept. As a result of cooperative research on this concept with NASA, the Federal Aviation Administration (FAA) modified its existing certification requirements to include provisions for spin resistant aircraft. Advanced general aviation aircraft emerging in the late 1990s have incorporated the concept.

Contributions in Structures and Materials

Langley augments the technical leadership and expertise in structures and materials of its research staff with unique, specialized facilities and laboratories designed for applications to national challenges in structures and materials. The scope of the Langley research program includes the fundamental development and applications of advanced materials and polymers, the development and validation of computational methods and analysis, technologies associated with aeroelasticity, landing loads and landing gear technology, crashworthiness and impact dynamics, aging aircraft technology, and structural component failure analysis.

Langley's research contributions to major NASA civil aircraft programs, such as the Aircraft Energy Efficiency (ACEE) Program, have resulted in widespread applications of advanced structures and materials concepts to the civil aircraft fleet of the 1990s. In particular, the development of composites for aircraft applications has been a major product of Langley's research. Advanced aluminums and other metallic materials have been conceived and matured as well as advanced manufacturing techniques. Unique facilities, such as the Langley Aircraft Landing Dynamics Facility, the Langley Impact Dynamics Research Facility, and the Langley 16-ft Foot Transonic Dynamics Tunnel, have provided data and test opportunities for the civil aircraft industry.

Composites Technology

Langley's aggressive research efforts in composites have covered all critical technical aspects and challenges required for transfer of the technology to the civil aircraft sector. For example, Langley's pioneering contributions to the development of high-performance polymers and matrix composite materials resulted in numerous licensing agreements with industry and guidance for industrial applications of high-performance polymers. Langley and industry activities in the ACEE Program provided design, fabrication, and full-scale aircraft flight test verification of composite secondary structures for commercial transports. The joint activities led to the introduction of secondary composite structures and limited primary structures on aircraft of the 1990s. Research at Langley on structural design criteria for composites, including damage tolerance, has been adopted as industry standards for assessing composite structural designs. Langley's leadership in the design and fabrication of advanced composite structures, especially stitched composites, has rapidly accelerated the introduction of revolutionary composite material and economically feasible fabrication techniques for civil aircraft. Langley's leadership and participation in the Advanced General Aviation Technology Experiments (AGATE) Program has led to a new, more economically feasible approach to the certification procedure for composite general aviation aircraft.

Fatigue and Fracture Mechanics

Extensive research by Langley in the critical areas of structural fatigue and fracture mechanics has been adopted by industry and the Department of Defense (DOD) for engineering standard practice and design handbooks.

Aging Aircraft Technology

Stimulated by the tragic in-flight structural failure of the upper fuselage skin and structure of an Aloha Airlines transport in Hawaii in 1988 and a subsequent request from the FAA for increased research in the area, Langley augmented its efforts in research on the structural integrity of aging aircraft. In a national cooperative program with the DOD, industry, and the FAA, Langley has contributed methodology and instrumentation that has significantly enhanced the prediction, detection, and repair of structural failures in aging aircraft components. For example, Langley developed and validated a new method—now used as an industry standard—to predict crack growth from multirivet sites. Langley also developed an analysis procedure for complex fuselage structural components, that was used by industry in the design of recent commercial transports. Contributions also include a thermal-bond inspection system for large airframe structures, a self-nulling eddy current probe for detecting structural corrosion, and an ultrasonic system for detecting disbonds and corrosion. Concepts developed in this area by Langley were rapidly embraced by commercial vendors, and were applied to aircraft beginning in the mid-1990s.

Advanced Metallic Materials

Langley's contribution to advanced metals include the development of aluminum and titanium materials, as well as forming and joining technologies for these materials. Contributions include corrosion protection for titanium alloys, development of standard test methods to determine stress-corrosion cracking properties of advanced metallic alloys, brazing methods and weld bonding for joining of aluminum and titanium panels, and the development of techniques for superplastic forming of complex components. Light metallic alloy fabrication technology developed by Langley was used by commercial vendors for aluminum alloys for major commercial transports of the 1990s.

Computational Methods

The development of computational structural methods by Langley has led to numerous codes that have been incorporated into industry's proprietary analysis methods. A particularly noteworthy contribution was Langley's management of the NASA Structural Analysis (NASTRAN) Program, which spawned an entire industry in the field of structural analysis.

Aeroelasticity and Flutter

The combination of a unique national facility and decades of research on aeroelastic phenomenon and flutter have resulted in an internationally recognized leadership position for Langley. Langley has cooperatively conducted extensive flutter tests of commercial and business jet aircraft since the early 1960s in the Transonic Dynamics Tunnel. By validating flutter prediction methodology, identifying potentially catastrophic characteristics prior to flight, and reducing risk and the extent of flights required for flutter-free flight demonstrations, Langley contributions have significantly enhanced the safety and reduced the developmental costs of civil aircraft.

Contributions in Flight Systems

Cooperative research programs between Langley, industry, and the FAA in flight systems have been directed at pilot, airplane, and air transportation system interfaces since the early 1970s. Research and development of innovative concepts typically progressed through ground-based analytical and piloted simulator studies; the development and systems verification of advanced avionics, sensors, and other flight systems; flight assessments and development in Langley's unique Boeing 737 research aircraft; and extensive demonstrations to potential users of the technology. Applications to aircraft of the 1990s have been extensive, including virtually all classes of civil aviation.

Contributions to flight systems by Langley have been particularly focused on safety problems, including the detection and accommodation of potentially deadly wind-shear conditions, wake-vortex hazards, and the rapid assessment of the health of aircraft systems.

Digital Flight Controls

Research at Langley in the 1950s with analog fly-by-wire control systems and the use of advanced digital computers in the NASA Apollo Program led to major Langley contributions in digital fly-by-wire technology. Partnering with the Dryden Flight Research Center, Langley conducted development efforts that led to the first flight demonstration of this technology on a modified F-8 research aircraft. Used widely in U.S. military aircraft since the 1980s, fly-by-wire controls were first implemented in U.S. commercial transports in the mid-1990s.

Glass Cockpit Technology

In the early 1970s, Langley began studying the advantages of displaying flight management information to flight crews by using cathode-ray tube (CRT) systems in commercial transports. Using the unique Boeing 737 Transport Systems Research Vehicle (TSRV) and ground-based simulators, researchers impressed industry and airline decision makers with the potential benefits of the advanced systems, which helped to promote the widespread applications of glass cockpit technology in virtually all modern commercial transports and business jets.

Flight Management Systems

Concepts developed by Langley for improved flight management by pilots in the complex air transportation system included the first piloted simulations and flight tests of time-dependent (four-dimensional) navigation methods, algorithms for computing air-traffic constrained fuel-conservative flight paths, and data-link communications with Air Traffic Control. Langley also played a critical role in the mid-1970s during the demonstration and ultimate acceptance of the U.S. Microwave Landing System by the international community. Much of Langley's technology in flight management is used in current commercial transports.

Crew-Aiding Systems

Research conducted at Langley led to civil applications of subsystem monitoring concepts that assist flight crews and help prevent accidents. Contributions include an engine monitoring and control system, a fault monitoring and diagnosis aid, and updates of electronic approach plates. (An approach plate is a flight-planning document for a specific airport that gives details such as minimum heights, safe headings, and weather minimums and includes a horizontal map and often a vertical profile for the approach to each instrument runway.) Langley also developed a precision landing-flare control algorithm, and demonstrated the accuracy and impact of this concept on runway occupancy time. The algorithm was studied and modified by industry for commercial transports in the 1990s.

Digital Data Bus

In the mid-1980s, Langley teamed with Boeing to develop, flight test, and demonstrate the practical use of an innovative concept that used a global data bus as an interface between electronic flight systems onboard transport aircraft. As a result of flight demonstrations using the Langley Boeing 737 TSRV aircraft, the system was adopted as an industry standard for transport aircraft.

Reliability Tools

Langley researchers developed extremely effective reliability estimation methods for advanced controls and aircraft systems. In addition, fault-tolerant architecture for advanced aircraft avionics systems was developed. Industry also adopted results from pioneering Langley research in the application of formal methods, which utilized mathematical logic for the design verification of advanced digital aircraft systems.

Demonstrations of GPS Accuracy

Highly successful demonstrations of the accuracy of the Global Positioning System (GPS) by Langley and industry flight demonstrations with the Langley Boeing 737 research aircraft provided significantly increased confidence in the potential use of GPS for automatic landings and guidance under adverse weather conditions. Flight testing in a cooperative Langley-industry flight evaluation of differential GPS (DGPS) in 1993 demonstrated remarkable accuracy, and several automatic landings were made. Data from these demonstrations stimulated the avionics community during the late 1990s.

Contributions in Noise Reduction

In recognition of the impact and challenge of existing and future environmental noise regulations to the aviation industry, Langley participated in the development of noise-reduction technology research and development in close cooperation with industry, airport and airline operators, and the FAA beginning in the early 1960s. Initially, Langley's efforts were part of a national Aircraft Noise Abatement Program, directed by the Department of Transportation. However, Langley and other NASA centers and their industry contractors conducted other focused efforts, such as the NASA Acoustically Treated Nacelle Program. Widely disseminated results from Langley studies on noise reduction since that time have included the identification of noise-generation mechanisms, noise-absorption concepts, the development of analytical tools for noise predictions of propeller- and jet-powered aircraft (also rotorcraft), community noise acceptance levels, reduction of structurally borne interior noise, impact of modifications of aircraft flight path operational procedures, and measurement and predictions of noise levels contributed by nonpropulsive airframe components.

In addition to analytical studies of complex noise generation and interaction phenomena, Langley uses specialized ground-based laboratories, powered model wind-tunnel tests, measurements from aircraft flight tests, and other acoustic measurement devices to mature and validate noise reduction technology.

Engine Liner Technology

The advent of jet-powered commercial transports resulted in intensified research to reduce noise levels at airports and surrounding communities. As part of extensive cooperative and contractual studies with the Boeing Company and McDonnell Douglas Corporation, Langley led the development of acoustic duct liners for jet propulsion systems that were adopted and implemented in the civil transport fleet.

Noise Prediction Codes

Langley researchers developed and validated a noise prediction code known as the Aircraft Noise Prediction Program (ANOPP) that is widely used by the aircraft and engine industries to predict operational noise levels of aircraft configurations and the impact of modifications to operational procedures.

Community Noise Impact

With volunteer evaluation subjects and laboratory equipment that simulates the critical characteristics of aircraft noise-generation mechanisms, Langley has provided industry and regulatory agencies with fundamental data on acceptability and annoyance levels for a variety of noise-generating mechanisms, such as sonic booms. In addition, analytical research on the impact of modifications to operational procedures has been verified by flight test measurements.

Interior Noise

The transmission of noise generated by external sources, such as jet engines and propellers, into the cabin of civil aircraft has been studied analytically and experimentally by using actual aircraft structures and noise-canceling technology. Results of the studies have been disseminated to the civil industry and implemented on several general aviation aircraft.

Contributions in Operating Problems

Many of Langley's most valuable contributions to civil aviation involve the development and maturation of concepts to alleviate or eliminate major operating problems for civil aircraft. Most of the topics directly study the safety of the aircrew and passengers, especially during adverse weather conditions. Langley researchers successfully met the difficult technical and hazard challenges embodied by research in this area, with the result that aircrews and the flying public greatly benefited by their contributions.

Operational problems typically involve full-scale aircraft and atmospheric conditions that cannot be simulated easily in subscale or analytical studies. Thus, research efforts in this area involved aircraft flight testing with its particular safety and operational constraints. Experiments with Langley's research aircraft, including the Boeing 737 and F-106B, provided unprecedented data to designers and operators of the U.S. civil aircraft fleet in the 1990s. Working in close collaboration with industry, the FAA, and the National Transportation Safety Board (NTSB), Langley researchers also provided contributions by participation in accident investigations involving specific operational problems. In addition, participation in standards-setting activities provided additional contributions and influence by the Langley staff.

The following contributions toward the alleviation of operating problems for aircraft of the 1990s are particularly significant.

Airborne Wind-Shear Detection

A Langley, FAA, and industry team conceived, developed, and demonstrated airborne wind-shear detection systems designed to provide flight crews with sufficient warning and strategy for the avoidance of deadly wind-shear accidents. The scope of activity in this very significant accomplishment included mathematical modeling of atmospheric wind-shear phenomena; identification, development, and evaluation of candidate airborne detection systems; refinement of radar characteristics for low-altitude operations in clutter; the development and demonstration of a standard-setting hazard criteria known as the F-Factor; and extensive demonstrations and evaluations by industry, the FAA, and airline flight crews. In addition, Langley staff participated in standards-setting and other regulatory studies in wind-shear technology. The highly successful research of the 1990s by Langley in this area led to the commercialization of airborne detection systems and implementation in most of the civil transport fleet.

Wake-Vortex Hazard

Langley researchers have contributed extensive information, data, and potential operational solutions to the hazardous conditions created by the powerful trailing vortices of large commercial transports during approach and landing. Beginning in the early 1970s, ground-based and flight studies on the physical characteristics of the trailing vortex phenomenon, and the impact of aircraft modifications on those characteristics, contributed to the fundamental understanding and characterization of the wake-vortex hazard. Efforts in the 1980s were directed at defining and modeling vortex behavior in various atmospheric conditions. In the 1990s, Langley researchers conducted a focused program to define technology approaches to an integrated system for avoidance of vortex encounters by trailing aircraft. The avoidance system was demonstrated to airport managers and the FAA in the late 1990s.

Lightning Protection

Langley addressed the potential threats posed by lightning to advanced digital systems and composite aircraft with laboratory simulations and flight studies of the Langley F-106B research aircraft in the 1980s. During intentional flights into severe storms and lightning-prone atmospheric conditions, unprecedented data on the occurrence of lightning strikes, the mechanisms involved in such encounters, and the magnitude and characteristics of currents induced in the aircraft were obtained for analysis. Coupled with theoretical analysis, the experimental data provided the basis for modifications to aircraft design standards for lightning protection. Studies of the conductive properties of composite structures and approaches to minimize lightning damage also provided extremely valuable design information for all segments of civil aviation.

Runway Friction

Langley research on aircraft tire braking and traction characteristics during adverse weather conditions provided tire manufacturers, the aircraft industry, the FAA, and DOD with fundamental information on tire hydroplaning and potential solutions to the problem. Runway grooving concepts were conceived and extensively evaluated for many aircraft during adverse weather landings. The highly successful results of the Langley program were incorporated in most of the Nation's airport runways, as well as major highways. Langley's leadership and participation in international studies on runway characteristics during adverse conditions are internationally recognized for their valuable contributions; and Langley researchers have participated in numerous accident investigations and other international advisory activities.

Crashworthiness

Since the early 1970s, Langley has investigated making aircraft crashes more survivable. The staffs of the Langley Impact Dynamics Research Facility and supporting laboratories have conducted extensive research on failure mechanisms and loads generated in typical crashes of general aviation and rotorcraft vehicles. Unprecedented experimental data generated by crash tests of full size general aviation and rotor aircraft have been augmented by the development and validation of analytical methods for the prediction of crash loads and the effect of energy-absorbing concepts. Extensive cooperative testing with industry and other government agencies have led to new concepts, such as energy-absorbing seats and regulatory standards within the industry. Pioneering contributions on impact characteristics of advanced composite materials, cabin floors, and engine support components have been incorporated in design technology across the industry.

BIBLIOGRAPHY

Aerodynamics

Anon.: *Advanced Technology Airfoil Research, Vol. II.* NASA CP-2046, 1979.

Anon.: *Supercritical Wing Technology—A Report on Flight Evaluations.* NASA SP-301, 1972.

Ethell, Jeffrey L.: *Fuel Economy in Aviation.* NASA SP-462, 1983.

Flechner, Stuart G.; and Jacobs, Peter F.: Experimental Results of Winglets on First, Second, and Third Generation Jet Transports. *CTOL Transport Technology—1978.* NASA CP-2036, Pt. 1, 1978, pp. 553–569.

Flechner, Stuart G.; and Jacobs, Peter F.: *Experimental Results of Winglets on First, Second, and Third Generation Jet Transports.* NASA TM-72674, 1978.

Hallion, Richard P.: *On the Frontier—Flight Research at Dryden, 1946–1981.* NASA SP-4303, 1984.

Harris, Charles D.: *NASA Supercritical Airfoils—A Matrix of Family-Related Airfoils.* NASA TP-2969, 1990.

Hodge, Kenneth E.: *Proceedings of the F-8 Digital Fly-by-Wire and Supercritical Wing First Flight's 20th Anniversary Celebration.* NASA CP-3256, Vols. I and II, 1996.

Holmes, Bruce J.: *Flight Evaluation of an Advanced Technology Light Twin-Engine Airplane (ATLIT).* NASA CR-2832, 1977.

Kutney, John T.; and Piszkin, Stanley P.: Reduction of Drag Rise of the Convair 990 Airplane. *J. Aircr.,* vol. 1, no. 1, Jan.–Feb. 1964, pp. 8–12. (Also available as AIAA Paper 63-276.)

Langhans, Richard A.; and Flechner, Stuart G.: *Wind-Tunnel Investigation at Mach Numbers From 0.25 to 1.01 of a Transport Configuration Designed to Cruise at Near-Sonic Speeds.* NASA TM X-2622, 1972.

Lin, J. C.: Control of Turbulent Boundary-Layer Separation Using Micro-Vortex Generators. AIAA Paper 99-3404, 1999.

Lynch, F. T.: Commercial Transports—Aerodynamic Design for Cruise Performance Efficiency. *Progress in Astronautics and Aeronautics,* D. Nixon, ed., Vol. 81, AIAA, 1982, pp. 81–147.

McGhee, Robert J.; and Beasley, William D.: *Low-Speed Aerodynamic Characteristics of a 17-Percent-Thick Airfoil Section Designed for General Aviation Applications.* NASA TN D-7428, 1973.

Porter, Donald J.: *The Cessna Citations.* TAB Books, 1993.

Potsdam, M. A.; Intemann, G. A.; Frink, N. T.; Campbell, R. L.; and Smith, L. A.: Wing/Pylon Fillet Design Using Unstructured Mesh Euler Solvers. AIAA Paper 93-3500, 1993.

Reynolds, P. T.; Gertsen, W. M.; and Voorhees, C. G.: Gates Learjet Model 28/29, the First "Longhorn" Learjet. AIAA Paper 78-1445, 1978.

Somers, Dan M.: Subsonic Natural-Laminar-Flow Airfoils. *Natural Laminar Flow and Laminar Flow Control,* R. W. Barnwell and M. Y. Hussaini, eds., Springer-Verlag, 1992, pp. 143–176.

Somers, Dan M.: *Design and Experimental Results for a Natural-Laminar-Flow Airfoil for General Aviation Application.* NASA TP-1861, 1981.

Staff, Douglas Aircraft Co.: *DC-10 Winglet Flight Evaluation.* NASA CR-3704, 1983.

Szurovy, Geza: *Learjets.* Motorbooks International. 1996.

Whitcomb, Richard T.: Interview with Author, August 16, 2000. (Unpublished)

Whitcomb, Richard T.: Research on Methods for Reducing the Aerodynamic Drag at Transonic Speeds. The Inaugural ICASE/LaRC Eastman Jacobs Lecture presented at the Langley Research Center, November 14, 1994. (Unpublished)

Whitcomb, Richard T.: *A Design Approach and Selected Wind-Tunnel Results at High Subsonic Speeds for Wing-Tip Mounted Winglets.* NASA TN D-8260, 1976.

Whitcomb, Richard T.; and Sevier, John R., Jr.: *A Supersonic Area Rule and an Application to the Design of a Wing-Body Combination With High Lift-Drag Ratios.* NASA TR R-72, 1960. (Supersedes NACA RM L53H31a.)

Whitcomb, Richard T.: *A Fuselage Addition To Increase Drag-Rise Mach Number of Subsonic Airplanes at Lifting Conditions.* NACA TN 4290, 1958.

Whitcomb, Richard T.: *Special Bodies Added on a Wing To Reduce Shock-Induced Boundary-Layer Separation at High Subsonic Speeds.* NACA TN 4293, 1958.

Whitcomb, Richard T.: *A Study of the Zero-Lift Drag-Rise Characteristics of Wing-Body Combinations Near the Speed of Sound.* NACA Rep. 1273, 1956. (Supersedes NACA RM L52H08.)

Williams, B.: Advanced Technology Transport Configuration Development. AIAA Paper 72-756, Aug. 1972.

Aeroelasticity

Abbott, Frank T., Jr.; Kelly, H. Neale; and Hampton, Kenneth D.: *Investigation of Propeller-Power-Plant Autoprecession Boundaries for a Dynamic-Aeroelastic Model of a Four-Engine Turboprop Transport Airplane.* NASA TN D-1806, 1963.

Bahatia, K. G.; Nagaraja, K. S.; and Ruhlin, C. L.: Winglet Effects on the Flutter of Twin-Engine-Transport Type Wing. AIAA Paper 84-0905, 1984.

Bennett, Robert M.; Kelly, H. Neale; and Gurley, John D.: *Investigation of 1/8-Size Dynamic-Aeroelastic Model of the Lockheed Electra Airplane in the Langley Transonic Dynamics Tunnel.* NASA TM SX-456, FAA, 1960.

Bland, Samuel R.; and Bennett, Robert M.: *Wind-Tunnel Measurement of Propeller Whirl-Flutter Speeds and Static-Stability Derivatives and Comparison With Theory.* NASA TN D-1807, 1963.

Cole, Stanley R.; and Garcia, Jerry L.: Past, Present, and Future Capabilities of the Transonic Dynamics Tunnel From an Aeroelasticity Perspective. AIAA Paper 2000-1767, 2000.

Corliss, James M.; and Cole, Stanley R.: Heavy Gas Conversion of the NASA Langley Transonic Dynamics Tunnel. AIAA Paper 98-2710, June 1998.

Doggett, Robert V., Jr.; and Farmer, Moses G.: *Preliminary Study of Effects of Winglets on Wing Flutter.* NASA TM X-3433, 1976.

Farmer, M. G.: *Flutter Studies To Determine Nacelle Aerodynamic Effects on a Fan-Jet Transport Model for Two Mount Systems and Two Wind Tunnels.* NASA TN D-6003, 1970.

Farmer, Moses G.; and Florance, James R.: Boeing 777 Flutter Model Test Conducted in TDT. *Research and Technology Highlights—1993.* NASA TM-4575, 1993, pp. 25–26.

Garrison, Peter: The Hammer. *Air & Space Magazine,* Feb./Mar. 2001.

Keller, Donald F.: Flutter Study of Simple Business-Jet Wing Conducted in TDT. *Research and Technology Highlights—1993.* NASA TM-4575, 1993, p. 19.

Rauch, Frank J.; and Clark, William B.: Results of Test Conducted on Gulfstream G-V Wing Conducted on a 1/10th Scale Flutter Model. Rep. GV-GER-614, Gulfstream Aerospace, Mar. 1993.

Reed, Wilmer H., III; and Bland, Samuel R.: *An Analytical Treatment of Aircraft Propeller Precession Instability.* NASA TN D-659, 1961.

Ricketts, Rodney H.: *Experimental Aeroelasticity—History, Status and Future in Brief.* NASA TM-102651, 1990. (Also available as AIAA Paper 90-0978.)

Rivera, Jose A., Jr.; and Florance, James R.: Contributions of Transonic Dynamics Tunnel Testing to Airplane Flutter Clearance. AIAA Paper 2000-1768, 2000.

Ruhlin, C. L.; Rauch, F. J.; and Waters, C.: *Transport Flutter Study of a Wind Tunnel Model of a Supercritical Wing With/Without Winglet.* NASA TM-83279, 1982.

Flight Dynamics

Bennett, George: *Flight Test of a Stall Sensor and Evaluation of Its Application to an Aircraft Stall Deterrent System Using the NASA RC General Aviation Simulator.* NASA CR-146324, 1976.

Bowman, James S., Jr.: *Summary of Spin Technology as Related to Light General-Aviation Airplanes.* NASA TN D-6575, 1971.

Chambers, Joseph R.; and Stough, H. Paul, III: Summary of NASA Stall/Spin Research for General Aviation Configurations. AIAA Paper 86-2597, 1986.

Chevalier, Howard L.: *Summary of Theoretical Considerations and Wind-Tunnel Tests of an Aerodynamic Spoiler for Stall Proofing a General Aviation Airplane.* NASA CR-165100, 1982.

Feistel, T. W.; Anderson, S. B.; and Kroeger, R. A.: A Method for Localizing Wing Flow Separation at Stall To Alleviate Spin Entry Tendencies. AIAA Paper 78-1476, 1978.

Fink, Marvin P.; and Freeman, Delma C., Jr.: *Full-Scale Wind-Tunnel Investigation of Static Longitudinal and Lateral Characteristics of a Light Twin-Engine Airplane.* NASA TN D-4983, 1969.

Holcomb, M. L.: The Beach Model 77 "Skipper" Spin Program. AIAA Paper 79-1835, 1979.

Holcomb, M. L.; and Tumlinson, R. R.: Evaluation of a Radio-Control Model for Spin Simulation. SAE Paper 770482, 1977.

Lina, L. J.; and Moul, M. T.: A Simulator Study of T-Tail Aircraft in Deep Stall Conditions. AIAA Paper 65-781, 1965.

Montgomery, R. C.; and Moul, M. T.: Analysis of Deep-Stall Characteristics of T-Tailed Aircraft Configurations and Some Recovery Procedures. AIAA Paper 66-13, 1966.

Ray, E. J.; and Taylor, R. T.: A Systematic Study of the Factors Contributing to Post-Stall Longitudinal Stability of T-Tail Transport Configurations. AIAA Paper 65-737, 1965.

Satran, Dale R.: *Wind-Tunnel Investigation of the Flight Characteristics of a Canard General-Aviation Airplane Configuration.* NASA TP-2623, 1986.

Shevell, Richard S.; and Schaufele, Roger D.: Aerodynamic Design Features of the DC-9. *J. Aircr.,* vol. 3, no. 6, Nov.–Dec. 1966, pp. 515–523. (Also available as AIAA Paper No. 65-738).

Staff of Langley Research Center: *Exploratory Study of the Effects of Wing-Leading-Edge Modifications on the Stall/Spin Behavior of a Light General Aviation Airplane.* NASA TP-1589, 1979.

Stough, H. Paul; and DiCarlo, Daniel J.: Spin Resistance Development for Small Airplanes—A Retrospective. SAE Paper 2000-01-1691, 2000.

Stough, H. Paul, III; DiCarlo, Daniel J.; and Patton, James M., Jr.: Evaluation of Airplane Spin Resistance Using Proposed Criteria for Light General Aviation Airplanes. AIAA Paper 87-2562-CP, 1987.

Taylor, Robert T.; and Ray, Edward J.: Deep-Stall Aerodynamic Characteristics of T-Tail Aircraft. *Conference on Aircraft Operating Problems.* NASA SP-83, 1965, pp. 113–121.

Yip, L. P.: *Wind-Tunnel Investigation of a Full-Scale Canard-Configured General Aviation Airplane.* NASA TP-2382, 1985.

Yip, Long P.; Ross, Holly M.; and Robelen, Donald B.: Model Flight Tests of a Spin-Resistant Trainer Configuration. *J. Aircr.,* vol. 29, no. 5, Sept.–Oct. 1992, pp. 799–805.

Operating Problems

Anon.: Safety Issues Related to Wake Vortex Encounters During Visual Approach to Landing. *Flight Safety Digest,* Flight Safety Foundation, June 1994.

Anon.: *Wake Vortex Minimization.* NASA SP-409, 1976.

Arbuckle, P. D.; Lewis, M. S.; and Hinton, D. A.: Airborne Systems Technology Application to the Windshear Threat. *20th Congress of the International Council of the Aeronautical Sciences,* 1996, pp. 1640–1650. (Also available as ICAS paper 96-5.7.1.)

Bowles, Roland L.: Windshear Detection and Avoidance—Airborne Systems Survey. *Proceedings of the 29th IEEE Conference on Decision and Control,* Vol. 2, 1990, pp.708–736.

Brandon, Jay M.; Jordan, Frank L., Jr.; Buttrill, Catherine W.; and Stuever, Robert A.: *Application of Wind Tunnel Free-Flight Technique for Wake Vortex Encounters.* NASA TP-3672, 1997.

Caracena, Fernando; Holle, Ronald L.; and Doswell, Charles A., III: *Microbursts—A Handbook for Visual Identification.* National Severe Storms Lab., 1990.

Carden, Huey D.: *Evaluation of Emergency-Locator-Transmitter Performance in Real and Simulated Crash Tests.* NASA TM-81960, 1981.

Carden, Huey D.; and Hayduk, Robert J.: Aircraft Subfloor Response to Crash Loadings. SAE Paper 810614, Apr. 1981.

Dunham, R. E., Jr.; Stuever, Robert A.; and Vicroy, Dan D.: The Challenges of Simulating Wake Vortex Encounters and Assessing Separation Criteria. AIAA Paper 93-3568, 1993.

Fasanella, Edwin L.; Widmayer, E.; and Robinson, Martha P.: Structural Analysis of the Controlled Impact Demonstration of a Jet Transport Airplane. *J. Aircr.,* vol. 24, no. 4, Apr. 1987, pp. 274–280.

Fisher, Bruce D.: Effects of Lightning on Operations of Aerospace Vehicles. Presented at the AGARD Flight Mechanics Panel Symposium on Flight in Adverse Environmental Conditions (Gol, Norway). May 8–11, 1989, paper 20.

Fisher, Bruce D.; and Plumer, J. Anderson: Managing Risk From Lightning Strikes to Aircraft. *Human Factors and Risk Management in Advanced Technology: 40th Annual International Air Safety Seminar Proceedings,* Flight Safety Foundation, 1987, pp. 353–375.

Fisher, Lloyd J.: Factors Affecting Ditching of New Transport Airplanes. *NASA Aircraft Safety and Operating Problems,* Vol. 1, NASA SP-270, 1971, pp. 1–10.

Hastings, Earl C., Jr.; Shanks, Robert E.; Champine, Robert A.; Copeland, W. Latham; and Young, Douglas C.: *Preliminary Results of Flight Tests of Vortex Attenuating Splines.* NASA TM X-71928, 1974.

Hinton, D. A.: An Aircraft Vortex Spacing System (AVOSS) for Dynamical Wake Vortex Spacing Criteria. Presented at 78th Fluid Dynamics Panel Symposium (Trondheim, Norway), May 20–23, 1996.

Horne, W. B.; Phillips, W. P.; Sparks, H. C.; and Yager, T. J.: *A Comparison of Aircraft and Ground Vehicle Stopping Performance on Dry, Wet, Flooded, Slush-, Snow-, and Ice-Covered Runways.* NASA TN D 6098, 1970.

Jones, Lisa E.; and Carden, Huey D.: *Overview of Structural Behavior and Occupant Responses From a Crash Test of a Composite Airplane.* NASA TM-111954, 1995. (Also available as SAE Paper 951168.)

Joyner, Upshur T.; Phillips, W. Pelham; and Yager, Thomas J.: Recent Studies on Effects of Runway Grooving on Airplane Operations. AIAA Paper 69-773, 1969.

Lewis, M. S.; Robinson, P. A.; Hinton, D. A.; and Bowles, R. L.: *The Relationship of an Integral Wind Shear Hazard to Aircraft Performance Limitations.* NASA TM-109080, 1994.

Patterson, J. C., Jr.; and Jordan, F. L., Jr.: *A Static Air Flow Visualization Method To Obtain a Time History of the Lift-Induced Vortex and Circulation.* NASA TM X-72769, 1975.

Pitts, Felix L.; Lee, Larry D.; Perala, Rodney A.; and Rudolph, Terence H.: *New Methods and Results for Quantification of Lightning-Aircraft Electrodynamics.* NASA TP-2737, 1987.

Pitts, Felix L.; and Thomas, Mitchel E.: In-Flight Direct-Strike Lightning Research. *1980 Aircraft Safety and Operating Problems.* Joseph W. Stickle, compiler, NASA CP-2170, Pt. 1, 1981, pp. 359–372.

Proctor, F. H.; Bracalente, E. M.; Harrah, S. D.; Switzer, G. F.; and Britt, C. L., Jr.: Simulation of the 1994 Charlotte Microburst With Look-Ahead Windshear Radar. *27th Conference on Radar Meteorology,* American Meteorol. Soc., 1995, pp. 530–532.

Proctor, Fred H.: The NASA-Langley Wake Vortex Modelling Effort in Support of an Operational Aircraft Spacing System. AIAA Paper 98-0589, 1998.

Proctor, Fred H.; Hinton, David A.; and Bowles, Roland L.: A Windshear Hazard Index. *Ninth Conference on Aviation, Range and Aerospace Meteorology,* American Meteorol. Soc., 2000, pp. 482–487.

Pryzby, J. E.; and Plumer, J. A.: *Lightning Protection Guidelines and Test Data for Adhesively Bonded Aircraft Structures.* NASA CR-3762, 1984.

Stewart, Eric C.: A Piloted Simulation Study of Wake Turbulence on Final Approach. AIAA Paper 98-4339, 1998.

Stough, H. P., III; Greene, George C.; Stewart, Eric C.; Stuever, Robert A., Jordan, Frank L., Jr.; Rivers, Robert A.; and Vicroy, Dan D.: NASA Wake Vortex Research. AIAA Paper 93-4004, 1993.

Stuever, Robert A.; and Stewart, Eric C.: The Role of Simulation in Determining Safe Aircraft Landing Separation Criteria. Presented at the FAA International Wake Vortex Symposium (Washington, D.C.), Oct. 29–31, 1991.

Switzer, G. F.; Proctor, F. H.; Hinton, D. A.; and Aanstoos, J. V.: *Windshear Database for Forward-Looking Systems Certification.* NASA TM-109012, 1993.

Tatnall, C. R.: A Proposed Methodology for Determining Wake-Vortex Imposed Aircraft Separation Constraints. M.S. Thesis, George Washington University, Aug. 1995.

Terry, James E.: Design and Test of an Improved Crashworthiness Small Composite Airframe. SAE Paper 2000-01-1673, 2000.

Thompson, William C.: *Model Ditching Investigation of the Boeing 707 Jet Transport.* NACA RM SL55K08, Civil Aeronautics Administration, 1955.

Thomson, Robert G.; Carden, Huey D.; and Hayduk, Robert J.: *Survey of NASA Research on Crash Dynamics.* NASA TP-2298, 1984.

Vaughan, Victor L., Jr.; and Alfaro-Bou, Emilio: *Impact Dynamics Research Facility for Full-Scale Aircraft Crash Testing.* NASA TN D-8179, 1976.

Wallace, Lane E.: Airborne Trailblazer: *Two Decades With NASA Langley's 737 Flying Laboratory.* NASA SP-4216, 1994.

Yager, T. J.; and White, E. J.: Recent Progress Toward Predicting Aircraft Ground Handling Performance. *1980 Aircraft Safety and Operating Problems,* Joseph W. Stickle, compiler, NASA CP-2170, Pt. 2, 1981, pp. 583–611.

Yager, Thomas J.; and White, Ellis J.: *Recent Progress Towards Predicting Aircraft Ground Handling Performance.* NASA TM-81952, 1981.

Flight Systems

Abbott, Terence S.: *A Simulation Evaluation of the Engine Monitoring and Control System Display.* NASA TP-2960, 1990.

Bortolussi, Michael R.: *An Investigation of General Aviation Problems and Issues: An Integration of Pilot-Cockpit Interface Research.* NASA/CR-97-113005, 1997.

Knox, Charles E.; and Scanlon, Charles H.: *Flight Tests With a Data Link Used for Air Traffic Control Information Exchange.* NASA TP-3135, 1991.

Lambregts, Anthony A.; and Creedon, Jeremiah F.: Development and Flight Evaluation of Automatic Flare Laws With Improved Touchdown Dispersion. AIAA Paper 80-1757, 1980.

Morello, Samuel A.: Recent Flight Test Results Using an Electronic Display Format on the NASA B-737. *Guidance and Control Design Considerations for Low-Altitude and Terminal-Area Flight,* AGARD-CP-240, Apr. 1978, pp. 16-1–16-10. (Available from DTIC as AD-A057177.)

Morello, Samuel A.; Knox, Charles E.; and Steinmetz, George G.: *Flight-Test Evaluation of Two Electronic Display Formats for Approach to Landing Under Instrument Conditions.* NASA TP-1085, 1977.

Person, Lee H., Jr.; and Steinmetz, George G.: The Integration of Control and Display Concepts for Improved Pilot Situational Awareness. Presented at the Flight Safety Foundation 34th International Air Safety Seminar, Nov. 9–12, 1981.

Person, Lee H., Jr.; and Yenni, Kenneth R.: Flying NASA's Terminal Configured Vehicle Against the Microwave Landing System. Paper presented to the Society of Experimental Test Pilots, 1978. (Unpublished)

Reeder, John P.; Schmitz, Robert A.; and Clark, Leonard V.: *Operational Benefits From the Terminal Configured Vehicle.* NASA TM-80046, 1979.

Reeder, John P.; Taylor, Robert T.; and Walsh, Thomas M.: *New Design and Operating Techniques and Requirements for Improved Aircraft Terminal Area Operations.* NASA TM X-72006, 1974. (Also available as SAE Paper 740454.)

Stough, H. Paul, III; Shafer, Daniel B.; Schaffner, Philip R.; and Martzaklis, Konstantinos S.: Reducing Aviation Weather-Related Accidents Through High-Fidelity Weather Information Distribution and Presentation. ICAS Paper 2000-6.5.1, 2000.

Wallace, Lane E.: Airborne Trailblazer: *Two Decades With NASA Langley's 737 Flying Laboratory.* NASA SP-4216, 1994.

Walsh, Thomas M.; Morello, Samuel A.; and Reeder, John P.: Review of Operational Aspects of Initial Experiments Utilizing the U.S. MLS. *Aircraft Safety and Operating Problems,* NASA SP-416, 1976, pp. 3–19.

Structures and Materials

Anon.: *Risk to the Public From Carbon Fibers Released in Civil Aircraft Accidents.* NASA SP-448, 1980.

Bell, Vernon L.: *The Potential for Damage From the Accidental Release of Conductive Carbon Fibers From Burning Composites.* NASA TM-80213, 1980.

Buffum, Harvey E.; and Thompson, Vere S.: Transition From Glass to Graphite in Manufacture of Composite Aircraft Structure. *CTOL Transport Technology—1978,* NASA CP-2036, Pt. 1, 1978, pp. 331–347.

Davis, John G., Jr.: Overview of the ACT Program. *Ninth DOD/NASA/FAA Conference on Fibrous Composites in Structural Design,* Vol. 2, Joseph R. Soderquist, Lawrence M. Neri, and Herman L. Bohon, compilers, NASA CR-198722, 1992, pp. 577–599.

Davis, John G., Jr.; Starnes, James H., Jr.; and Johnston, Norman J.: Advanced Composites Research and Development for Transport Aircraft. *17th ICAS Congress,* Vol. 1, 1990, pp. XLV–LIV.

Dexter, H. Benson: *Long-Term Environmental Effects and Flight Service Evaluation of Composite Materials.* NASA TM-89067, 1987.

Dexter, H. Benson; Harris, Charles E.; and Johnston, Norman J.: Recent Progress in NASA Langley Research Center Textile Reinforced Composites Program. *Second NASA Advanced Composites Technology Conference,* John G. Davis, Jr., and Herman L. Bohon, compilers, NASA CP-3154, 1992, pp. 295–323.

Dow, Marvin B.: *The ACEE Program and Basic Composites Research at Langley Research Center (1975–1986)—Summary and Bibliography.* NASA RP-1177, 1987.

Dow, Marvin B.; and Dexter, H. Benson: *Development of Stitched, Braided and Woven Composite Structures in the ACT Program and at Langley Research Center.* NASA TP-97-206234, 1997.

Ethell, Jeffrey L.: *Fuel Economy in Aviation.* NASA SP-462, 1983.

Harris, Charles E.; and Heyman, Joseph S.: An Overview of NASA Research Related to the Aging Commercial Transport Fleet. AIAA Paper 91-0952, 1991.

Harris, Charles E.; and Poe, Clarence C., Jr.: Role of Mechanics of Textile Preform Composites in the NASA Advanced Composites Technology Program. *Mechanics of Textile Composites Conference,* Clarence C. Poe, Jr., and Charles E. Harris, eds., NASA CP-3311, Pt. 1, 1995, pp. 1–4.

Harris, Charles E.; Starnes, James H., Jr.; and Shuart, Mark J.: *An Assessment of the State-of-the-Art in the Design and Manufacturing of Large Composite Structures for Aerospace Vehicles.* NASA TM-2001-210844, 2001.

Pride, Richard A.: *Large-Scale Carbon Fiber Tests.* NASA TM-80218, 1980.

Pride, Richard A.: Environmental Effects on Composites for Aircraft. *CTOL Transport Technology—1978,* NASA CP-2036, Pt. 1, 1978, pp. 239–258.

Stauffer, Warren A.; and James, Arthur M.: Development of Advanced Composite Structures. *CTOL Transport Technology—1978,* NASA CP-2036, Pt. 1, 1978, pp. 259–279.

Stone, M.: Key Issues in Application of Composites to Transport Aircraft. *CTOL Transport Technology—1978,* NASA CP-2036, Pt. 1, 1978, pp. 281–310.

INDEX

C

D

E

H

I

J

K

M

N

O

P

S

T

U

V

W

Y

Z

NASA HISTORY SERIES

Reference Works, NASA SP-4000

Grimwood, James M. *Project Mercury: A Chronology.* (NASA SP-4001, 1963.)

Grimwood, James M.; and Barton C. Hacker, with Peter J. Vorzimmer. *Project Gemini Technology and Operations: A Chronology.* (NASA SP-4002, 1969).

Link, Mae Mills. *Space Medicine in Project Mercury.* (NASA SP-4003, 1965).

Astronautics and Aeronautics, 1963: Chronology of Science, Technology, and Policy. (NASA SP-4004, 1964).

Astronautics and Aeronautics, 1964: Chronology of Science, Technology, and Policy. (NASA SP-4005, 1965).

Astronautics and Aeronautics, 1965: Chronology of Science, Technology, and Policy. (NASA SP-4006, 1966).

Astronautics and Aeronautics, 1966: Chronology of Science, Technology, and Policy. (NASA SP-4007, 1967).

Astronautics and Aeronautics, 1967: Chronology of Science, Technology, and Policy. (NASA SP-4008, 1968).

Ertel, Ivan D.; and Mary Louise Morse. *The Apollo Spacecraft: A Chronology, Volume I, Through November 7, 1962.* (NASA SP-4009, 1969).

Morse, Mary Louise; and Jean Kernahan Bay. *The Apollo Spacecraft: A Chronology, Volume II, November 8, 1962–January 20, 1966.* (NASA SP-4009, 1973).

Ertel, Ivan D.; and Roland W. Newkirk, with Courtney G. Brooks. *The Apollo Spacecraft: A Chronology, Volume III, January 21, 1966–July 13, 1974.* (NASA SP-4009, 1978).

Astronautics and Aeronautics, 1968: Chronology of Science, Technology, and Policy. (NASA SP-4010, 1969).

Newkirk, Roland W.; and Ivan D. Ertel, with Courtney G. Brooks. *Skylab: A Chronology.* (NASA SP-4011, 1977).

Van Nimmen, Jane; and Leonard C. Bruno, with Robert L. Rosholt. *NASA Historical Data Book, Volume I: NASA Resources, 1958–1968.* (NASA SP-4012, 1976, *rep. ed.* 1988).

Ezell, Linda Neuman, *NASA Historical Data Book, Volume II: Programs and Projects, 1958–1968.* (NASA SP-4012, 1988).

Ezell, Linda Neuman. *NASA Historical Data Book, Volume III: Programs and Projects, 1969–1978.* (NASA SP-4012, 1988).

Gawdiak, Ihor Y., with Helen Fedor. Compilers. *NASA Historical Data Book, Volume IV: NASA Resources, 1969–1978.* (NASA SP-4012, 1994).

Rumerman, Judy A. Compiler. *NASA Historical Data Book, 1979–1988: Volume V, NASA Launch Systems, Space Transportation, Human Spaceflight, and Space Science.* (NASA SP-4012, 1999).

Rumerman, Judy A. Compiler. *NASA Historical Data Book, Volume VI: NASA Space Applications, Aeronautics and Space Research and Technology, Tracking and Data Acquisition/Space Operations, Commercial Programs, and Resources, 1979–1988.* (NASA SP-2000-4012, 2000).

Astronautics and Aeronautics, 1969: Chronology of Science, Technology, and Policy. (NASA SP-4014, 1970).

Astronautics and Aeronautics, 1970: Chronology of Science, Technology, and Policy. (NASA SP-4015, 1972).

Astronautics and Aeronautics, 1971: Chronology of Science, Technology, and Policy. (NASA SP-4016, 1972).

Astronautics and Aeronautics, 1972: Chronology of Science, Technology, and Policy. (NASA SP-4017, 1974).

Astronautics and Aeronautics, 1973: Chronology of Science, Technology, and Policy. (NASA SP-4018, 1975).

Astronautics and Aeronautics, 1974: Chronology of Science, Technology, and Policy. (NASA SP-4019, 1977).

Astronautics and Aeronautics, 1975: Chronology of Science, Technology, and Policy. (NASA SP-4020, 1979).

Astronautics and Aeronautics, 1976: Chronology of Science, Technology, and Policy. (NASA SP-4021, 1984).

Astronautics and Aeronautics, 1977: Chronology of Science, Technology, and Policy. (NASA SP-4022, 1986).

Astronautics and Aeronautics, 1978: Chronology of Science, Technology, and Policy. (NASA SP-4023, 1986).

Astronautics and Aeronautics, 1979–1984: Chronology of Science, Technology, and Policy. (NASA SP-4024, 1988).

Astronautics and Aeronautics, 1985: Chronology of Science, Technology, and Policy. (NASA SP-4025, 1990).

Noordung, Hermann. *The Problem of Space Travel: The Rocket Motor.* Stuhlinger, Ernst, and J. D. Hunley, with Jennifer Garland. Editors. (NASA SP-4026, 1995).

Astronautics and Aeronautics, 1986–1990: A Chronology. (NASA SP-4027, 1997).

Astronautics and Aeronautics, 1990–1995: A Chronology. (NASA SP-2000-4028, 2000).

Orloff, Richard W. Compiler. *Apollo by the Numbers: A Statistical Reference.* (NASA SP-2000-4029, 2000).

Management Histories, NASA SP-4100

Rosholt, Robert L. *An Administrative History of NASA, 1958–1963.* (NASA SP-4101, 1966).

Levine, Arnold S. *Managing NASA in the Apollo Era.* (NASA SP-4102, 1982).

Roland, Alex. *Model Research: The National Advisory Committee for Aeronautics, 1915–1958.* (NASA SP-4103, 1985).

Fries, Sylvia D. *NASA Engineers and the Age of Apollo.* (NASA SP-4104, 1992).

Glennan, T. Keith. *The Birth of NASA: The Diary of T. Keith Glennan.* J. D. Hunley. Editor. (NASA SP-4105, 1993).

Seamans, Robert C., Jr. *Aiming at Targets: The Autobiography of Robert C. Seamans, Jr.* (NASA SP-4106, 1966).

Project Histories, NASA SP-4200

Swenson, Loyd S., Jr.; James M. Grimwood; and Charles C. Alexander. *This New Ocean: A History of Project Mercury.* (NASA SP-4201, 1966; *rep. ed.* 1998.)

Green, Constance M.; and Milton Lomask. *Vanguard: A History.* (NASA SP-4202, 1970; rep. ed. Smithsonian Institution Press, 1971).

Hacker, Barton C.; and James M. Grimwood. *On Shoulders of Titans: A History of Project Gemini.* (NASA SP-4203, 1977, rep. ed., 2002).

Benson, Charles D.; and William Barnaby Faherty. *Moonport: A History of Apollo Launch Facilities and Operations.* (NASA SP-4204, 1978).

Brooks, Courtney G.; James M. Grimwood; and Loyd S. Swenson, Jr. *Chariots for Apollo: A History of Manned Lunar Spacecraft.* (NASA SP-4205, 1979).

Bilstein, Roger E. *Stages to Saturn: A Technological History of the Apollo/Saturn Launch Vehicles.* (NASA SP-4206, 1980, rep. ed. 1997).

Compton, W. David; and Charles D. Benson. *Living and Working in Space: A History of Skylab.* (NASA SP-4208, 1983).

Ezell, Edward Clinton; and Linda Neuman Ezell. *The Partnership: A History of the Apollo-Soyuz Test Project.* (NASA SP-4209, 1978).

Hall, R. Cargill. *Lunar Impact: A History of Project Ranger.* (NASA SP-4210, 1977).

Newell, Homer E. *Beyond the Atmosphere: Early Years of Space Science.* (NASA SP-4211, 1980).

Ezell, Edward Clinton; and Linda Neuman Ezell. *On Mars: Exploration of the Red Planet, 1958–1978.* (NASA SP-4212, 1984).

Pitts, John A. *The Human Factor: Biomedicine in the Manned Space Program to 1980.* (NASA SP-4213, 1985).

Compton, W. David. *Where No Man Has Gone Before: A History of Apollo Lunar Exploration Missions.* (NASA SO-4214, 1989).

Naugle, John E. *First Among Equals: The Selection of NASA Space Science Experiments.* (NASA SP-4215, 1991).

Wallace, Lane E. *Airborne Trailblazer: Two Decades With NASA Langley's Boeing 737 Flying Laboratory.* (NASA SP-4216, 1994).

Butrica, Andrew J. Editor. *Beyond the Ionosphere: Fifty Years of Satellite Communication.* (NASA SP-4217, 1997).

Butrica, Andrew J. *To See the Unseen: A History of Planetary Radar Astronomy.* (NASA SP-4218, 1996).

Mack, Pamela E. Editor. *From Engineering Science to Big Science: The NACA and NASA Collier Trophy Research Project Winners.* (NASA SP-4219, 1998).

Reed, R. Dale, with Darlene Lister. *Wingless Flight: The Lifting Body Story.* (NASA SP-4220, 1997).

Heppenheimer, T. A. *The Space Shuttle Decision: NASA's Search for a Reusable Space Vehicle.* (NASA SP-4221, 1999).

Hunley, J. D. Editor. *Toward Mach 2: The Douglas D-558 Program.* (NASA SP-4222, 1999).

Swanson, Glen E. Editor. *"Before This Decade Is Out...": Personal Reflections on the Apollo Program.* (NASA SP-4223, 1999).

Tomayko, James E. *Computers Take Flight: A History of NASA's Pioneering Digital Fly-by-Wire Project.* (NASA SSP-2000-4224, 2000).

Morgan, Clay. *Shuttle-Mir: The U.S. and Russia Share History's Highest Stage.* (NASA SP-2001-4225, 2001).

Mudgway, Douglas J. *Uplink/Downlink: A History of the Deep Space Network.* (NASA SP-2002-4227, 2002).

Center Histories, NASA SP-4300

Rosenthal, Alfred. *Venture into Space: Early Years of Goddard Space Flight Center.* (NASA SP-4301, 1985).

Hartman, Edwin, P. *Adventures in Research: A History of Ames Research Center, 1940–1965.* (NASA SP-4302, 1970).

Hallion, Richard P. *On the Frontier: Flight Research at Dryden, 1946–1981.* (NASA SP-4303, 1984).

Muenger, Elizabeth A. *Searching the Horizon: A History of Ames Research Center, 1940–1976.* (NASA SP-4304, 1985).

Hansen, James R. *Spaceflight Revolution: NASA Langley Research Center From Sputnik to Apollo.* (NASA SP-4308, 1995).

Wallace, Lane E. *Flights of Discovery: 50 Years at the NASA Dryden Flight Research Center.* (NASA SP-4309, 1996).

Herring, Mack R. *Way Station to Space: A History of the John C. Stennis Space Center.* (NASA SP-4310, 1997).

Wallace, Harold D., Jr. *Wallops Station and the Creation of the American Space Program.* (NASA SP-4311, 1997).

Wallace, Lane E. *Dreams, Hopes, Realities: NASA's Goddard Space Flight Center, The First Forty Years.* (NASA SP-4312, 1999).

Dunar, Andrew J.; and Stephen P. Waring. *Power to Explore: A History of the Marshall Space Flight Center.* (NASA SP-4313, 1999).

Bugos, Glenn E. *Atmosphere of Freedom: Sixty Years at the NASA Ames Research Center Astronautics and Aeronautics, 1986–1990: A Chronology.* (NASA SP-2000-4314, 2000).

General Histories, NASA SP-4400

Corliss, William R. *NASA Sounding Rockets, 1958–1968: A Historical Summary.* (NASA SP-4401, 1971).

Well, Helen T.; Susan H. Whiteley; and Carrie Karegeannes. *Origins of NASA Names.* (NASA SP-4402, 1976).

Anderson, Frank W., Jr. *Orders of Magnitude: A History of NACA and NASA, 1915–1980.* (NASA SP-4403, 1981).

Sloop, John L. *Liquid Hydrogen as a Propulsion Fuel, 1945–1959.* (NASA SP-4404, 1978).

Roland, Alex A. *Spacefaring People: Perspectives on Early Spaceflight.* (NASA SP-4405, 1985).

Bilstein, Roger E. *Orders of Magnitude: A History of the NACA and NASA, 1915–1990.* (NASA SP-4406, 1989).

Logsdon, John M. Editor, with Linda J. Lear, Jannelle Warren-Findley, Ray A. Williamson, and Dwayne A. Day. *Exploring the Unknown: Selected Documents in the History of the U.S. Civil Space Program, Volume I, Organizing for Exploration.* (NASA SP-4407, 1995).

Logsdon, John M. Editor, with Dwayne A. Day and Roger D. Launius. *Exploring the Unknown: Selected Documents in the History of the U.S. Civil Space Program, Volume II, Relations With Other Organizations.* (NASA SP-4407, 1996).

Logsdon, John M. Editor, with Roger D. Launius, David H. Onkst, and Stephen E. Garber. *Exploring the Unknown: Selected Documents in the History of the U.S Civil Space Program, Volume III, Using Space.* (NASA SP-4407, 1998).

Logsdon, John M. General Editor, with Ray A. Williamson, Roger D. Launius, Russell J. Acker, Stephen J. Garber, and Jonathan L. Friedman. *Exploring the Unknown: Selected Documents in the History of the U.S. Civil Space Program, Volume IV, Accessing Space.* (NASA SP-4407, 1999).

Logsdon, John M. General Editor, with Amy Paige Snyder, Roger D. Launius, Stephen J. Garber, and Regan Anne Newport. *Exploring the Unknown: Selected Documents in the History of the U.S. Civil Space Program, Volume V, Exploring the Cosmos.* (NASA SP-2001-4407, 2001).

Siddiqi, Asif A. *Challenge to Apollo: The Soviet Union and the Space Race, 1945–1974.* (NASA SP-2000-4408, 2000).

Monographs in Aerospace History, NASA SP-4500

Maisel, Martin D.; Demo J. Giulianetti; and Daniel C. Dugan. *The History of the XV-15 Tilt Rotor Research Aircraft: From Concept to Flight.* (NASA SP-2000-4517, 2000).

Jenkins, Dennis R. *Hypersonics Before the Shuttle: A Concise History of the X-15 Research Airplane.* (NASA SP-2000-4518, 2000).

Chambers, Joseph R. *Partners in Freedom: Contributions of the Langley Research Center to U.S. Military Aircraft in the 1990s.* (NASA SP-2000-4519, 2000).

Waltman, Gene L. *Black Magic and Gremlins: Analog Flight Simulations at NASA's Flight Research Center.* (NASA SP-2000-4520, 2000).

Portree, David S. G. *Humans to Mars: Fifty Years of Mission Planning, 1950–2000.* (NASA SP-2001-4521, 2001).

Thompson, Milton O. with J. D. Hunley. *Flight Research: Problems Encountered and What They Should Teach Us.* (NASA SP-2000-4522, 2000).

Tucker, Tom. *The Eclipse Project.* (NASA SP-2000-4523, 2000).

Merlin, Peter W. *Mach 3+: NASA/USAF YF-12 Flight Research, 1969–1979.* (NASA SP-2002-4525, 2002).

ABOUT THE AUTHOR

Joseph R. Chambers is an aviation consultant who lives in Yorktown, Virginia. He retired from the NASA Langley Research Center in 1998 after a 36-year career as a researcher and manager of military and civil aeronautics research activities. He began his career as a specialist in flight dynamics as a member of the staff of the Langley 30- by 60-Foot (Full-Scale) Tunnel, where he conducted research on a variety of aerospace vehicles including V/STOL configurations, reentry vehicles, and fighter aircraft configurations. He later became a manager of research projects in the Langley Full-Scale Tunnel, the Langley 20-Foot Vertical Spin Tunnel, flight research at Langley, and piloted simulators. When he retired from NASA, he was manager of a group responsible for conducting systems analysis of the potential payoffs of advanced aircraft concepts and NASA research investments.

Mr. Chambers is the author of over 50 technical reports and publications, including NASA Special Publication SP-514 on the subject of airflow condensation patterns for aircraft, and NASA Special Publication SP-2000-4519 on contributions of the Langley Research Center to U.S. military aircraft of the 1990s. He has made presentations on research and development programs to audiences as diverse as the Von Karman Institute in Belgium and the annual Experimental Aircraft Association (EAA) Fly-In at Oshkosh, Wisconsin. He has served as a representative of the United States on international committees and has given lectures in Japan, China, Australia, the United Kingdom, Canada, Italy, France, Germany, and Sweden.

Mr. Chambers received several of NASA's highest awards, including the Exceptional Service Medal and the Outstanding Leadership Medal. He also received the Arthur Flemming Award in 1975 as one of the 10 Most Outstanding Civil Servants for his management of NASA stall/spin research for military and civil aircraft. He has a bachelor of science degree from the Georgia Institute of Technology (Georgia Tech), Atlanta, Georgia, and a master of science degree from the Virginia Polytechnic Institute and State University (Virginia Tech), Blacksburg, Virginia.